T0083713

PETTICOAT HEROES

PETTICOAT HEROES

Gender, Culture and Popular Protest in the Rebecca Riots

Rhian E. Jones

*The University of Wales Press acknowledges
the financial support of the Welsh Books Council.*

© Rhian E. Jones, 2015

All rights reserved. No part of this book may be reproduced in
any material form (including photocopying or storing it in any
medium by electronic means and whether or not transiently or
incidentally to some other use of this publication) without the
written permission of the copyright owner. Applications for the
copyright owner's written permission to reproduce any part of this
publication should be addressed to the University of Wales Press,
10 Columbus Walk, Brigantine Place, Cardiff CF10 4UP.

www.uwp.co.uk

British Library CIP Data
A catalogue record for this book is available from the
British Library.

ISBN 978-1-78316-788-3
eISBN 978-1-78316-789-0

The right of Rhian E. Jones to be identified as author of this work
has been asserted in accordance with sections 77 and 79 of the
Copyright, Designs and Patents Act 1988.

Typeset by Marie Doherty
Printed by CPI Antony Rowe, Chippenham, Wiltshire

To Mike Bowen, Frances Evans,
and all other heroes in petticoats

Contents

Acknowledgements

For their help and support in enabling me to produce this book, my thanks go to Professor Chris Williams at Cardiff University, Dr Kathryn Gleadle at Mansfield College, Oxford and Professor Penelope Corfield.

I

Introduction

The series of events known as the 'Rebecca riots' has made a more permanent and positive mark on history than many other nineteenth-century protests. In the generally gloomy annals of popular struggle and defeat, Rebeccaism is celebrated in Wales and beyond as a success story. It has been recorded as a 'freeing of the toll gates', a single-minded and respectable campaign against demonstrable injustice, carried out in a spirit of 'popularity and joke', 'frolic and good-humoured insubordination'.[1] The colourful and picaresque nature of events, their seizing of national press and parliamentary attention, and the iconic figure of 'Rebecca' herself, have secured them a significant place in Welsh history and folk tradition.[2] The riots have received cultural commemoration as the subject or background of novels, plays and even musical compositions.[3]

Rebeccaism is no exception to the rule that some of the best-remembered aspects of any protest movement will be those which made the deepest impression on the contemporary public imagination. The story of Rebecca as maintained in popular memory is that the imposition of toll charges for the use of Carmarthenshire roads generated mass outrage, which found its expression in moonlit attacks on toll gates by farmers on horseback in outlandish female dress. These 'riots' burst into view in 1839 and raged throughout the summer of 1843, only to melt away following government intervention that constitutionally demolished the hated turnpikes and their tolls. Official and popular references to the movement after 1844 present it as something surprising – highly uncharacteristic of the usually placid and lawful rural Welsh – and as an affair which, being motivated solely by problems with the imposition of turnpike tolls, was quickly laid to rest by the government of Robert Peel, whose Commission of Inquiry and subsequent amelioration of the system via the 1844 Turnpike Act effectively put an end to matters.[4]

Despite this story's vividness, and the familiarity it has gained through retelling, the impression of Rebeccaism as a single-issue campaign, straightforwardly addressed by central government, does not do the movement justice. Confusion and obscurity still surround significant aspects of Rebeccaism: its leaders and organisers – if there were any – are still largely unknown, and even the origin of its name remains the subject of debate. Rebeccaite activity addressed a range of popular grievances beyond the issue of toll gates, and did so using an equally broad range of symbolism, costume and ritual. Evidence given to the government's 1844 Commission of Inquiry makes it clear how many problems underpinned the movement – not least land ownership, poverty, social tension, the New Poor Law, and the payment of Church tithes – and unrest and disorder under the auspices of Rebecca persisted long after the Turnpike Act. Rebeccaite iconography continued to appear in protest up to and including the present century, becoming a general signifier of popular discontent in ways often far removed from its original function.

The term 'Rebecca riots' itself, although it has become their customary designation, gives a misleadingly limited impression of events and does not adequately express how varied and complex was the range of activities associated with Rebecca. In this book I will use the alternative term 'Rebeccaism', as did David J. V. Jones in his 1989 study, to convey the idea of a social movement which was more than simply 'riotous', broader than a single-issue campaign against toll gates, and loosely bound together by references to the name or image of 'Rebecca'. This movement encompassed not only attacks on toll gates but also protest against high rents, tithes, evictions, workhouses and the New Poor Law, in forms ranging from property damage to threatening letters and mass demonstrations. As such, Rebeccaism fits the historical and sociological definition of a 'social movement' as a 'sustained, intentional effort to foster or retard broad legal and social changes, primarily outside the normal institutional channels endorsed by authorities'.[5] Contemporary sources show that the term 'Rebeccaism', and its variants, were in fact in use at the time: the Radnorshire MP John Walsh wrote of his surprise at hearing a rumour that 'the Rebeccaites had broken out in Shropshire'; in Llanelli, William Chambers reported that the toll gates of his trust had been 'Rebeccaized'; while the High Sherriff of Glamorgan, Thomas Penrice, stated that discontent over toll gates in Swansea had made him 'afraid we shall have Rebeccaism there'.[6]

This brings us to a further fundamental question; why the name 'Rebecca'? Two main explanations exist for Rebecca's etymology, juxtaposing a high-minded biblical derivation with one more in keeping with the movement's comic and irreverent tendencies. The former explanation was given by *The Times* correspondent Thomas Campbell Foster in his June 1843 report on Rebeccaism, in which he claimed the name was derived from Genesis 24:60: 'And they blessed Rebekah, and said unto her, "Thou art our sister, be thou the mother of thousands of millions, and let thy seed possess the gates of those which hate them"'. The same claim had been made a few months earlier by the *Welshman* newspaper, which noted that the verse had been 'expatiated upon by many itinerant preachers' until 'the multitude doubtless believe they have a warrant for their lawless doings'.[7] Foster attributed this scriptural derivation to the strong religiosity of the Welsh and the 'fanaticism' which they channelled into opposing turnpikes. The *Swansea Journal* drew on Foster's claim when disapproving of the spread of Nonconformism in Wales, noting in July 1843:

This is a singular instance of the state of religious, or we should say, fanatical feeling in the Principality. It is curious to find the practice of dovetailing the language of Scripture to the purpose of Rebellion, so common with Cromwell's military saints, and the gloomy Scottish Covenantes, flourishing in full force in this quiet country, and in our enlightened times. This should be a strong incitement to the Church in Wales to increased exertion . . .[8]

At around the same time, an address by Edward Lloyd Davies, a landlord who had been threatened with a visit from Rebecca if his rents were not reduced, rebuked the Rebeccaites for their choice of allusion:

It is said that you have imposed upon many ignorant persons, by pretending to have Scripture authority for your acts. What an abuse of the Holy Scriptures! All learned divines are agreed, that the meaning of those words is ... that her posterity might be victorious over their enemies. Rebecca was really a woman, a good and pious woman, having the fear of God before her eyes...[9]

Foster's explanation has found varying degrees of sympathy with the movement's historians. Henry Tobit Evans's 1910 account makes the opposing claim, namely that Thomas Rees, the first man to play Rebecca at Efailwen in 1839, named himself after the similarly statuesque woman from whom his disguise was borrowed, who was known locally as 'Big Becca' or 'Great Rebecca of Llangolman'. The same origin was asserted in a letter to *The Times* in 1944 by a correspondent whose grandfather had been a Special Constable at the time of the riots. Both explanations are given equivalent weight by David Williams and David J. V. Jones, while Pat Molloy dismisses the 'Big Becca' origin story as apocryphal, arguing rather that a name imbued with 'the authority of the Scriptures and the chapel preachers' was required to make the movement 'a potent force'.[10] Little if any conclusive evidence has been advanced for either derivation and both seem equally compelling, not least for their illustration of the movement's multivalent and ambiguous nature.

Between early and later historians of Rebecca, other important differences of interpretation exist. Early works such as that of Tobit Evans tended to present the riots as anomalous, confined to the anti-toll gate activities of Carmarthenshire tenant farmers over the period 1839–44, and relatively peaceful before the intervention of outside agencies led them to degenerate into violence and criminality. Tobit Evans emphasised the exceptional nature of the 'riots' by likening them to 'an account of passionate Ireland ... rather than of quiet, peaceful Wales'.[11] David Williams's majestic and holistic study of events, published in 1955, achieved a greater understanding of the diverse discontents which motivated participants. However, he continued to view the activities of Rebeccaites as 'entirely an affair of small farmers', and followed his predecessors in disparaging the movement's latter phase as 'deviation' or 'degeneration' consequent on its corruption by a 'lunatic fringe' of violent extremists.[12] In 1988, David Howell outlined the movement in similar terms, depicting the discomfort felt by farmers at the increasing violence of Rebeccaite activity as a catalyst for their turning to more open, constitutional and 'respectable' forms of expressing their grievances.[13]

The brilliantly illuminating 1989 study by David J. V. Jones, *Rebecca's Children*, was the first to place events in a longer chronological perspective and to view the movement as having arisen naturally from the particular society and culture of contemporary south-west Wales. This helped to qualify the prevailing perception of events as something anomalous and extraordinary. Jones argued that Rebeccaism's tendency towards violence and petty crime could be more profitably explained by viewing it within the wider context of rural Wales, its social attitudes and extra-legal activities, rather than blaming it on the movement's 'corruption' by criminal or militant elements. He also observed that strands of the activity associated with Rebecca recurred up until the late nineteenth century, despite the conventional demarcation of 1839–44 which is reproduced in mentions of the movement as late as 2011.[14] In addition, by establishing Rebeccaism as 'larger than we thought and less respectable', Jones introduced the question of how its size, diversity, and ability to lend itself to the expression of abstract popular concerns, not only enabled it to spread beyond its initial sphere of influence but also produced internal tension, instability and fragmentation. Jones also noted the involvement in several disturbances of farm labourers, who were motivated variously by social ties with their employers and by shared resentment of the New Poor Law, tolls and tithes, as well as the assistance given to rioters by colliers in south-east Carmarthenshire in July 1843.[15] The movement's growing demographic complexity and collaborative nature further militates against a simplistic description of it as an affair of middle-class farmers or an atypical and limited protest aimed at a single specific target. Jones instead presents Rebeccaism as a geographically and chronologically varied movement, concerned broadly with the defence of traditional rights of rural communities and with popular opposition to injustice. From this perspective, Rebeccaism may be seen as forming part of the dislocation, conflict and resistance generated in eighteenth- and nineteenth-century Britain by the shift from a society regulated by paternalist obligations, the authority of popular custom, and what E. P. Thompson dubbed a pre-existing 'moral economy', to an economy, politics and society informed by industrial capitalism.

I am indebted to Rebecca's previous historians, especially Williams and Jones, for their accomplished mapping of the movement's scope and significance, but there are other avenues, of equal interest, which still await exploration. In particular, history has so far tended to gloss over gendered aspects of the events, and what insights they may have to offer on contemporary images of women and on contemporary ideas about women and men. The leading figures and the majority of participants in Rebeccaite activity were male, but women were also highly visible in the movement, not only as supporters but also symbolically in the images 'Rebecca' drew on for support and the kinds of women with whom 'she' was compared and contrasted. 'She' defended women against the strictures of the New Poor Law, and was presented in ways which showcased the spectrum of identities in which women could figure in Victorian society and culture. The idea of Rebeccaite protest-ers as 'men dressed as women' should be challenged and qualified, since the intricacies of Rebeccaite costume involved far more than the adoption of female disguise by male rioters. But the neglected dimension of what Rebeccaism revealed about contemporary women, both literal and figurative, deserves addressing too. Addi-tionally, the links between protest and popular culture, the use of Rebecca as an abstract character in press and political discourse, and the ways in which the events and the image of Rebecca have been integrated into popular memory and culture, all repay greater consideration than they have yet received. These concerns form the basis of my own revisiting of the movement. In the two and a half decades since Jones's study was published, advances have been made in social and cultural history, drawing on insights from the neighbouring fields of symbolic anthropology and discourse analysis, which can usefully be applied to the study of Rebecca-ism. This book's rethinking of Rebeccaism examines the movement with the view that its use of symbol, ritual and costume is vital in providing a fuller understanding of how these events were experi-enced both by participants and by those in wider popular culture and society. This interdisciplinary perspective builds on previous work on Rebecca, but hopes to supplement it by illuminating and analysing previously unexplored aspects of the movement's social and cultural impact.

The following chapter looks at the social, political and economic conditions which gave rise to Rebeccaism, and at the events of its best-known phase in 1839–44. Chapter 3 looks at the place of writing on Rebeccaism within broader historiographical trends. It then considers the attention given more recently within cul-tural history to the study of symbol and ritual content, which has demonstrated how techniques from social and cultural anthropol-ogy can decode otherwise incomprehensible past texts. Rebecca's intriguing oral-visual repertoire is one such text, which would have held meaning and coherence for participants despite how curious it may appear from a modern perspective. As James M. Jasper writes of modern and historical social movements, 'Humans always have multiple motivations, which is why we need a cultural perspective to make their actions intelligible'.[16]

Chapter 4 considers how the appeal and power of Rebeccaism stemmed from its basis in contemporary society and culture, with the symbolic and ritual frame of reference of Rebeccaite activity derived from that of local festival, popular custom and civic ritual. The movement drew on local tradition and custom while also responding to shifting political and economic circumstances, particularly those affecting the use and ownership of common land.

Chapter 5 looks in greater detail at the symbol and ritual used in Rebeccaite activity, including the widely noted adoption of feminine clothing by male protesters. While previous studies have interpreted this only as a method of disguise, or as an allusion to the social and community roles of women, Rebeccaite cross-dressing also reveals something of the contemporary experience and performance of masculine identity. In addition, considering cross-dressing in the context of what has until now been left unexplored – the equally theatrical use of masculine signifiers, and the presence within Rebeccaite costume of several binary oppositions – suggests that the contrast of feminine and masculine was intended to express a further binary, as part of a ritual intended to create a liminal space for participants to carry out extraordinary actions. The chapter then explores how Rebecca's identity became increasingly stylised, abstract and recognisable as it gained prominence in the public imagination. This familiarity allowed it to be adopted by individual males outside of protest activity, and enabled Rebecca and her actors to function as models of aspirational masculinity.

Chapter 6 looks at the relationship of Rebecca to contemporary images of women and changing ideas about female sexuality, and how these issues related to the operation of the New Poor Law introduced in 1834. The appearance of Rebecca herself can be shown to reflect, or actively to draw on, the various images of female power and agency which were available in south-west Welsh society and culture. Meanwhile, the attempts by Rebeccaites to oppose the bastardy clauses of the New Poor Law, in which they upheld the rights of unmarried mothers and illegitimate children, formed part of popular resistance to the centralising Victorian state's attempts at imposing social discipline upon pre-existing cultural attitudes that had granted women greater rights and agency.

Chapter 7 further analyses Rebecca's image as it appeared in the national press and in public and political discourse within Wales and beyond. Rebecca's use in protest as a symbolic representative of 'her' movement allowed her to take on a similarly symbolic identity in wider public discussion, but this identity was fluid and multivalent, and not limited to its specific use in protest. Rebecca's establishment as a popular cultural heroine (or anti-heroine) is shown in the variety of roles and narratives in which she could be cast, each with an associated constituency and set of moral standards and each reflective of particular contemporary attitudes. This treatment of Rebecca can be used to illustrate the complexities of gendered rhetoric in political satire and commentary, as well as demonstrating the range of feminine identities available in Victorian popular discourse.

Chapter 8's assessment of Rebeccaism's political and cultural aftermath considers which details of the movement lasted longest and most vividly in public consciousness, and the reasons behind this. An examination of how Rebeccaite grievances were presented and processed in the 1844 Commission of Inquiry reveals the systematic prioritising of toll gates over other factors. In subsequent references to Rebeccaism in popular and official rhetoric throughout the nineteenth century, this narrowed focus then allowed the government to present itself as having satisfactorily resolved the unrest through its legislative changes to the turnpike system. Conversely, this same focus enabled Rebeccaism to be presented 'from below', in press letters and editorials, as a successful popular struggle against injustice. The persistence of this particular impression of the movement may therefore be attributed to its ability to reinforce a narrative, either of innovative and beneficial government intervention or of a respectable and ultimately triumphant single-issue campaign. This retelling or co-option continued in debates on the inherent respectability or lawlessness of the Welsh character, in which mentions of the movement emphasised or downplayed its violent or criminal tendencies according to their argument.

Finally, in a brief Epilogue, I look at the instances of protest after 1844 which have adopted Rebecca's name or iconography, and at what similarities the movement may bear to twenty-first-century social and political struggle.

2

'Everything conspires to disorder': Politics and Society in Rebecca's Country

Society, politics and community at the time of Rebecca

In his exuberant account of Rebeccaism, Pat Molloy sums up the events as:

> a classic example of mass protest against a logjam of inequity which had been allowed to accumulate as a result of the tremendous industrial, economic and social changes of the early nineteenth century, to which the governing class had no coherent answer, and other circumstances peculiar to rural Wales [including] the remoteness of west Wales from all centres of influence and decision-making.[1]

What constituted these tremendous changes? In common with the rest of Britain, Wales experienced sustained population growth from the late 1700s well into the 1850s; the 1841 census return for Wales shows an increase of 78 per cent on the 1801 figures. In the south-west, the population growth of the 1840s owed more to rising birth rates and life expectancy than to inward migration. The consequent pressure on the rural Welsh economy led to large-scale depopulation and relocation to the mines and ironworks of the south-east, while the south-west remained sparsely populated and dependent on small-farming, with 80 per cent of its inhabitants living in communities of fewer than 1,500.[2]

By the 1830s the south-west's regional capital, Carmarthen, was the fourth largest town in Wales, an important market town and a centre of political and judicial administration. Its population of almost ten thousand was largely Welsh-speaking and two-thirds were employed in agriculture or trade. Elsewhere in the south-west, Llanelli, Pembroke and Aberystwyth housed between 5,000 and 7,000, while smaller but significant towns included Cardigan, Fishguard and Llandeilo. Most villages, townships and hamlets, however, held smaller populations of less than 500. The settlement pattern in the south-west consisted of small- to medium-sized market towns surrounded by scattered farmsteads and cottages. These dots were joined by footpaths, cart tracks and rudimentary roads which offered weak routes for transport and communication, with railway developments being largely confined to the industrialising south-east. Farmhouses were focal points of these networks, frequently forming a centre of social activity in the absence of a manor house or church. Despite this loose organisation, a magistrate commented during the course of Rebeccaism that the effect of the settlement pattern of south and west Wales was that 'everything conspires to disorder'.[3]

The social pyramid of Carmarthenshire, Cardiganshire and Pembrokeshire was capped by a handful of great landed dynasties. Just below them in status came several hundred landed families who also derived their wealth from the military, the Church, banking and legal professions. Below the landed gentry was an intermediate social group, mostly there to mediate between the gentry and the masses. They included estate managers, land agents, clergymen, traders, merchants, teachers, bailiffs and independent or large farmers who employed labourers. The remaining two-thirds of the south-west's population were employed mainly in agriculture and to a lesser extent in heavy industry and craft, and were in general dependent for continued employment and household maintenance on the gentry's resources and on their relationship with the gentry's brokers.[4]

Despite the increasing divergence of Welsh rural and urban populations in terms of settlement and lifestyle, both the economy and society of the south-west were more varied and diverse than is implied by the concept of a strict rural–urban divide. Gwyn A. Williams saw the three counties of Carmarthenshire, Cardiganshire and Pembrokeshire as a 'staging-post' between the rural south-west and the emerging industrial complex further east, while Jones identified Rebeccaism similarly as 'the child of old and new economic forces'.[5] A holistic picture of south Wales in the first half of the nineteenth century reveals the coexistence and co-dependence of agricultural and industrial economic systems, as well as several interlinked smaller trades. By the 1840s there were around two hundred coalmines in the south-west, providing precarious and low-waged employment for both men and women. Large iron-works at Carmarthen and Kidwelly were making a significant contribution to the south-west's economy, employing a tenth of the area's population in 1842 and generating a fifth of the area's wealth. It is, however, important not to exaggerate the extent of this: in 1841 the majority of people in the three counties were still employed in agriculture and domestic service, with Carmarthen-shire having the highest number engaged in agriculture in Wales. Occupational categories were non-exclusive, with the line between small farmers and labourers easily blurred. Census returns could not accommodate or reflect the complexities of rural employment, in which individuals typically rented a smallholding in addition to labouring on neighbouring farms, and village labourers could also keep pigs or sheep, and often spent the slack farming season work-ing in quarries or tramping the roads.[6]

In political terms, the absence of either an assertive middle class or an organised working class in the south-west had left the landed gentry's control over the area's twenty-six parliamentary constitu-encies 'virtually unchallenged from above or below'.[7] By the early nineteenth century, there were still few challenges to this electoral supremacy, and political control remained exercised through the massaging of electoral interests and the distribution of favours. In wider society, the influence of landlords and squires was mediated through religious and judicial institutions. The gentry's ownership of land made them materially dominant and they monopolised the local magistracy. However, this did not alleviate the need in local politics for personal popularity, vigorous campaigning and tacti-cal alliances. The unenfranchised majority was not excluded from political culture or campaigning; formal spaces were built into the electoral process in which the presence of the crowd was accepted and often encouraged, and the elite recognised a need to obtain the sanction of a whole community for their election. Political par-tisanship extended to all ages, classes and genders, who attended nomination meetings and hustings, wore partisan colours and con-sumed and distributed propaganda. Candidates and campaigners often circulated songs and squibs whose emphasis on key words and political in-jokes assumed a degree of knowingness in their audience as well as familiarity with local and national political drama – a squib against Church rates distributed in Carmarthen in 1854, for instance, lampooned 'many local characters'.[8]

11

In addition to their economic and political roles, individuals were involved in a wide range of civic, religious and recreational functions which increased their chances of social contact with those above and below them in the social hierarchy. The dependence of much of the country on a narrow agricultural base enabled the creation of intense and intimate social groupings and strong local and community allegiances, despite the high degree of economic stratification which existed.[9] As a Metropolitan policeman remarked on his first visit to south-west Wales, the populace 'know everybody, and see everything'.[10] This social integration could be reinforced by popular custom, with mass gatherings and house-visiting both facilitating and institutionalising conviviality. An early nineteenth-century Welsh custom was the 'bidding wedding', which allowed a couple without a dowry to hire a 'bidder' to announce the marriage and invite the local community along, each of whom would contribute a small sum to cover the cost of the ceremony. At Llansadwrn in 1846 a couple themselves invited neighbours to a bidding at their house, at which 'whatever donation you may be pleased to bestow on us then, will be thankfully received, and cheerfully repaid, whenever called for on a similar occasion'.[11] Guests could also participate in the construction of a dwelling on waste land, known as a *tŷ unnos* ('one-night house'), where the couple were then entitled to settle. As we shall see, the high degree of collective participation and reciprocity which characterised such customs would also have an impact on Rebeccaite activity.

Social division and discontent at the time of Rebecca

Of the divisions and grounds for resentment between small farmers and labourers and those with landed wealth, the most obvious and pressing may have been those based on income and financial security, but other long-term causes of social friction were also present. Unrest in late eighteenth-century Wales over food prices, enclosure and militia conscription had still not fundamentally challenged the gentry's oligarchic control.[12] At the time of Rebecca, however, this was changing. For the British landed elite in general, the impact of the French Revolution had changed their attitude towards the poor of their communities from one of active collaborative paternalism to one of paranoid and repressive withdrawal.

In Wales, this rescinding of the gentry's former paternalist duties, which had included local charity, leadership of societies for agricultural improvement, stewardship of popular entertainments and sponsorship of Eisteddfods, eroded the community respect they had formerly been able to rely on. As the country became incorporated into an expanding capitalist system, its ruling class became increasingly integrated into the world of the English aristocracy. A number of landlords withdrew from their local estates to spend time in London, taking little direct interest in the management of land except in terms of the income it provided, and leaving their properties in the hands of farm agents and estate managers, who generally were not Welsh either by birth or culture. The breakdown of deference was further encouraged by this physical distancing, and exacerbated by the gentry's increasing drift towards Anglicanism and the English language, which distanced them culturally from the overwhelmingly Nonconformist and Welsh-speaking farmers and labourers. The gentry's paternalistic image and function was further damaged by the introduction of the New Poor Law, which lessened their ability to engage with and intervene in the lives of those affected by its changes. The 1834 Poor Law Amendment Act was widely seen as confirmation that large farmers, landlords and clergymen placed their economic interests ahead of those of the community. Boards of Poor Law guardians were dominated by farmers who used them 'to keep wages low and to remove the idle and desperate from the parish'. Witnesses to the 1844 Commission of Inquiry specified their dislike of the infringement of local autonomy involved in the removal of the poor from the immediate responsibility of those that knew them.[13]

In the soil from which Rebeccaism sprang, resentment of the New Poor Law merged with the more pressing concerns of low prices for farm produce, unemployment, wage cuts and the apparent lack of sympathy or interest from local authorities in these problems. The *Times* reporter Thomas Campbell Foster, and other contemporary investigators and commentators, attributed the discontent underlying Rebeccaism in part to the indifference or ignorance expressed by those in power to the growing social and economic problems besetting south Wales.[14] Foster urged that the gentry forsake their 'sulky exclusiveness and come forward and meet the people', while the writer of an angry letter to *The Times* in April 1844 blamed Rebeccaism squarely on 'the supercilious insolence of the squirearchy' and deplored 'the state of society in our rural districts':

> Could a Kentish yeoman, or a Yorkshire farmer, take his stand in a Welch town during an assize week, and see a Welch squire issue from his inn, followed by a tenant or two, he would blush with indignation. The 'master', as he is still slavishly designated, striding along, snuffing and snorting, ready to burst with self-importance, and the poor serfs, hats in hand, bowing and crouching at every step![15]

As an explanation for social discord, the concept of a rigidly divided society and its unfortunate results takes insufficient account of the range of occupations and limited social mobility that did exist in south-west Wales. However, comments such as the above are instructive in terms of contemporary social perceptions. The cultural and often physical withdrawal by the gentry, with its consequent removal of community leadership and paternalist ties, left a vacuum in which popular discontent and resentment was easily generated. The resultant breakdown in the social deference which had previously characterised Welsh society made possible the questioning and reconstituting of authority on alternative bases, in ways which were utilised in Rebeccaism.

The 'unmistakeable collapse' of the gentry's standing in early 1840s south-west Wales was not only due to differences of language and religion, but also to the unwillingness to lower rents after the crash of 1842–3.[16] Antipathy to high rents and tithe payments was evident in statements to the 1844 Commission of Inquiry and in the observations of contemporaries such as Thomas Cooke, manager of the Carmarthenshire estate of Edward Adams at Middleton Hall. In August 1843, Cooke wrote:

> the curved horns are sounding in every direction, announcing a meeting somewhere for the committal of some outrage or other. [Rebeccaites] are not satisfied now with tollgates, but they hold large meetings frequently in the daytime, and demand that rents shall be lowered at least a third – the tithes they say shall be lowered 50 per cent.[17]

No less apparent was the local population's hostility to and lack of confidence in an indifferent and corrupt judicial system in which prohibitively high fees were charged by magistrates' clerks.

The mid-nineteenth century in Wales as a whole saw a rise in complaints levelled at the personal behaviour of landlords and magistrates, and at the MPs representing south-west Wales, who throughout the 1840s were notorious for their lack of attendance at or interest in parliamentary debate. These issues had received political expression throughout the second quarter of the nineteenth century as, in the words of Gwyn A. Williams, 'a populist nation began to shape itself behind a linguistic and religious line that was also a class line'.[18] Between the first and third Reform Acts, Welsh politics were dominated by the conflict between an Anglican and Anglicised landed aristocracy and a middle-class-led popular radical movement based around the agenda-setting issues of Dissent and the problems of the countryside, including relations with landlords and payment of Church rates. A Carmarthen writer against Church rates noted: 'As the squirearchy generally attended the Church, it was considered by many that have false notions of respectability that the Church was superior to Dissent in that respect'. The writer went on to condemn Dissenting 'turn-coats' who 'prided themselves upon being bundled together with the aristocracy, and awkwardly aped their manners', as well as the appointment of English officials who were 'exultingly ignorant of the Welsh language'.[19] The widespread antipathy to high rates, rents and tithes, as well as growing awareness of linguistic and religious divisions, provided labourers, tenant farmers and the emergent professional and commercial classes with a common enemy in the form of landowners, clerics and large farmers. As we shall see, Rebecca frequently intervened in disputes between landlords and tenants, by calling for lower rents or opposing evictions and the private enclosure of common land.

Discontent over these social and economic problems, and the related perception of a social and cultural divide between an Anglicised gentry and the rest, was channelled throughout the 1830s and 1840s into newspaper columns, pamphlets and broadsides. The early nineteenth century saw the emergence of a significant Welsh weekly press: the *Cambrian* appeared at Swansea from 1804 and the *Carmarthen Journal* from 1810, with the Reformist *Welshman* founded at Carmarthen in 1832.[20] From 1835 the anti-slavery and pro-Reform *Y Diwygiwr* ('The Reformer') tackled the political role of landowners and tenant–labourer relations alongside issues of Church and state. Newspapers played an important role in creating and sustaining political networks and in reinforcing identities which, though most prominently displayed during election campaigns, were a constant part of Welsh social life.[21] These papers carried reports, letters, editorials and lampoons on Rebecca throughout the period of her activity which, in addition to *The Times*'s detailed reports, gained the movement greater attention and firmly established Rebeccaism in public consciousness within Wales and beyond.

Rebecca's demands can be seen as linked to the struggle for political reform, which was supported by the lower and middle classes but opposed by the gentry, and, more immediately, as appealing to the paternalistic ties of the old rural economy. Can the movement be more definitively categorised as an exponent of what E. P. Thompson described as the 'moral economy'? Thompson claimed that participants in eighteenth-century crowd actions, particularly food riots, saw themselves as acting in defence of a traditional 'moral economy' against a disruptive and expropriating market economy. His thesis has been comprehensively tested and extended in subsequent studies of protest. Despite Thompson's own stated reluctance to take the concept beyond the arena of food riots, several historians have identified a 'moral economy' in the English countryside which was gradually and painfully eroded over the eighteenth and nineteenth centuries as agrarian capitalism, urbanisation and proletarianisation of rural workers accelerated. This nebulous but strongly felt set of customary entitlements has been seen as including the right to common land, the right to obtain food or grain at a 'just' price, and the right to poor relief.[22]

Revisiting the concept in *Customs in Common*, Thompson stated that a looser definition of 'moral economy' can be applied to early industrial communities in which:

> many 'economic' relations are regulated according to non-monetary norms. They exist as a tissue of customs and usages until they are threatened by monetary rationalisations and are made self-consciously as a moral economy . . . summoned into being in resistance to the economy of the free market. The rationalisations and 'modernisations' of the capitalist market offended against community norms and continually called into being a moral antagonist.[23]

This definition resonates more strongly with the conditions that generated Rebecca, in which protesters appear to have attempted

Thompson's idea of 'a selective reconstruction of paternalist legislation' – perhaps even in the knowledge that the basis for such
a reconstruction, in light of the cultural and material withdrawal
of the gentry, was becoming increasingly implausible. Randall and
Charlesworth note that, for food rioters in particular, 'the role
of the authorities was a crucial one . . . The moral economy was
the obverse of paternalism and the crowd was able to challenge
their rulers to fulfil the role they had assigned for themselves.'[24]
The response to Rebecca by much of the landed interest of south-
west Wales, far from being a return to paternalist duty, was to
call upon central government for repressive military aid against a
discontented populace, including the stationing of a regular yeo-
manry in the areas affected. Some, notably the Newcastle Emlyn
squire Edward Crompton Lloyd Hall, heir to the Cilgwn estate,
responded by publicly engaging with locals at meetings, or by public addresses appealing to reason and urging the lawful pursuit
of redress. Others threatened to remove themselves to England,
becoming absentee landlords or magistrates, thus further reducing local employment and rendering Wales 'like Ireland'.[25] The
gentry's abandonment of their duties at the time of Rebecca, and
growing awareness of the conflicting economic interests between
estate owners and large farmers and the rural masses, may have
engendered a situation where protesters, rather than calling on
the gentry to adhere to paternalism or pre-existing custom, were
instead compelled to claim common-law precedents themselves by
directly and forcibly demanding free access to roads or insisting on
former criteria for entitlement to poor relief.

South Welsh protest in the early nineteenth century, then, was
generated by the combined effects of population growth and rapid
industrial expansion upon an oligarchic machinery of government
that was both unable and disinclined to adapt at an equivalent
rate. Rebeccaism took place against this backdrop of demographic,
economic and political pressures on outdated and crumbling
administrative institutions, and the fracturing of deference towards
those at the top of society. These conditions had already produced manifold social, economic and industrial protests across
south Wales, generating a tradition of popular agitation in which
Rebecca would become one of several intertwined strands. In 1795
the town of Haverfordwest had seen a mass riot over food prices
in which the local labouring population, ranged against fifty of the

Carmarthenshire Militia, declared 'they would have fresh butter as well as the gentry, and would live as well as the gentry'.[26] In 1816 a strike over cuts to wages paralysed much of the south-eastern coalfield, while in the same year Aberystwyth was convulsed by anti-enclosure riots. Two years later, widespread disturbances took place across Wales aimed at preventing the export of food and grain from deprived areas. The Scotch Cattle's drives for industrial organisation in the mines and ironworks of south-east Wales stretched throughout the 1820s and 1830s. In 1831 Merthyr Tydfil, one of industrialisation's iconic forcing-houses, saw a sustained uprising by industrial workers over unemployment, low pay, debt and distraint of property, which involved, reputedly for the first time in European protest, the raising of a red flag. After Hugh Williams's founding of the country's first Chartist branch at Carmarthen in 1837, the spread of Chartism in Wales culminated in the ill-fated 1839 march on Newport.[27]

Systems of maintaining order in the face of such unrest had been under strain before the advent of Rebeccaism. The eastern coalfield and Carmarthen, in particular, were notoriously underpoliced and turbulent, with outside assistance needed in the latter location to deal with a wave of pro-Reform demonstrations in 1831–2. With no national police force established until 1856, informal lawkeeping was largely in the hands of landlords and employers, as 'social prosecution' through the loss of one's home or employment could be as effective as legal prosecution. Further down the social scale, and in social rather than economic or political matters, individuals could be subject to verbal and physical intimidation and forms of ritual community sanction. These included regional variants of charivari or 'rough music' – the customary enforcing of community morality or other standards through public noisemaking, parading and use of symbol and ritual.[28] A superficial comparison of the nineteenth-century Welsh countryside with the chaotic lawlessness of the new urban populations further east may encourage us to think of the former as placid and innocent. In places, however, the countryside was equally restless, the location of both spectacular popular protest and the varied types of low-level crime – poaching, arson, sheep-rustling, livestock-maiming, attacks on bailiffs and constables, and the looting of shipwrecked vessels – which formed part of the fabric of rural Welsh society and which naturally found an additional outlet through Rebeccaism.[29]

Rebeccaism 1839–44: what happened and when?

For those who took part in the events that became known as the Rebecca riots, the turnpike trusts and the tolls on road travel they imposed were only one among several pressing social and economic grievances. Toll gates were singled out as suitable targets for assault since they were highly visible objects, less easily defended and more easily attacked than other symbols of discontent such as workhouses or landed estates, or indeed the intangible vagaries of the rural economy itself. In 1839–41 in south-west Wales, a succession of wet seasons and unproductive harvests, combined with a fall in the price of cattle and butter to below the national average, had done much to reduce the little capital which tenant farmers possessed. Faced with this sharp drop in income, farmers found no relief in the expenditure required of them in the form of rents, tithes, poor rates and county rates, all of which either remained constant or increased over the period.[30] Thomas Frankland Lewis, a Radnorshire landowner and MP who would later chair the Commission of Inquiry into Rebeccaism's causes, noted in 1843:

> This country is in an unsatisfactory state – the farms are generally small, the tenants poor – some of them have leases for lives, contracted in times of high prices – landlords hold fast by the contract and many must be ruined . . . they who suffer complain and struggle.[31]

In the same year John Walsh, MP for Sudbury and Radnorshire, recorded in his dealings with farmers and shopkeepers in his constituency that 'Money Money Money is never out of the minds of these people . . . the farmers are all ruined, totally apathetic and reckless'.[32] A contemporary editorial in the *Welshman* described in greater detail the growing sense of economic crisis occasioned by the price collapse of 1842–3 and the persistence of high rents:

> Distress and ruin are progressing with giant strides all over the country. The manufacturers are stopping work because they cannot sell their goods; and their workmen are thrown upon the parishes and cease to buy the food, clothing and provisions which the farmers have to sell. This produces distress among the farmers, besides a heavy increase in their poor rates; and then as the farmers find they cannot dispose of their cattle and their corn, they will by degrees cease to produce them;

up will go the prices to those few of the public still able to buy, and then will come in a flood of corn and cattle from foreign countries which will . . . put the finishing stroke to [the farmer's] misery, unless his land-lord will give up his rents – a thing not very likely to happen.[33]

These problems were exacerbated when a group of English toll-renters took over the road-maintenance trusts of the region and, in exchange for paying higher rents for the toll gates, made their collection of tolls far more exacting and pernicious, as well as raising the number and incidence of gates. The government's detailed inquiry in 1844 into the operations of the trusts found no evidence of systematic mismanagement, but did uphold several popular objections to them, including excessive charges and the situating of several gates belonging to adjacent trusts on the same road or on county borders: Carmarthen, for instance, was ringed by the toll gates of five trusts whose boundaries met there. The Whitland Trust was criticised for 'placing gates and bars on roads which they themselves did not repair, but the parishes had to keep in proper condition for travel'.[34] Particularly despised was the increased number of 'side-bar' gates, placed strategically on by-roads to catch any travellers trying to evade charges by bypassing the main roads. Tolls placed on the movement of lime, which was commonly used as fertiliser or to counteract acidity in soil, drastically increased the unavoidable costs incurred by farmers who purchased lime at Cardiff docks and then carted it back to their rural parishes.

The first instance of protest associated with Rebecca was recorded on 13 May 1839, when a toll gate at Efailwen on the Pembrokeshire–Carmarthenshire border was demolished and its tollhouse set on fire. This incident followed the posting of hand-bills 'on many public doors' at Efailwen, calling for a public meeting 'to take into consideration the propriety of the toll gate'. At the meeting's conclusion, a crowd of around four hundred, led by men, 'some dressed in female garments, and others with black-ened faces', made their way to the toll gate 'huzza-ing for free laws, and free travelling to coal-pits and lime-kilns'. The local historian Alcwyn C. Evans recorded that the crowd then:

drove the Specials from their stations, and pursued them over the adjoining fields. Having done so they returned to the gate, and in the course of three hours, the house was torn down to within a yard to the ground, the gate was shattered to pieces with sledgehammers, and the gate-posts were sawn off and carried away.[35]

Over the next few weeks the Efailwen gate was re-erected and destroyed twice, with each occasion displaying much of the symbol and ritual that would come to characterise the movement. The third attack, on 17 July, saw the first recorded appearance of the 'distinguished' leadership figure of Rebecca, who was observed at the head of 'a large body of men . . . of whom a number were dressed in women's clothes' and with their faces blackened.[36] Meanwhile, at St Clears on 15 June, a second toll gate had been targeted by a crowd of men who fired off their guns before dismantling the gate. Despite the presence of troops and magistrates at the scene of destroyed toll gates, no admissions of responsibility were made or convictions achieved for any of the incidents, and on 23 July a meeting of local trustees, gentry and magistrates advised the trust in question not to re-erect the Efailwen gate.

After a period of quiet, Rebecca re-emerged in the winter of 1842, with farmers facing a slump in corn prices but again receiving no relief in the costs incurred by rents, tithes, county rates, poor rates and turnpike tolls. Throughout November and December a spate of attacks took place on newly erected toll gates in Carmarthenshire, provoking the authorities behind the trusts to issue statements defending their operations. Disturbances continued in the spring of 1843. Large public meetings were held at night, in secluded spots on the Carmarthenshire hillside and moorland, at which multiple grievances were raised by attendees. Local officials, including Edward Crompton Lloyd Hall of Newcastle Emlyn and the Carmarthenshire MP George Rice Trevor, were moved to discuss the events publicly and counsel their constituents against taking part in them.[37]

On 19 June 1843, a mass procession took place in Carmarthen. The intention was that participants would parade through the town and arrive at Carmarthen Guildhall, where they would present popular grievances to local magistrates. These social and economic criticisms, as contemporary reports noted, were far-reaching and not confined to toll gates:

They then read a list of their complaints and of the changes they desired, which included, not only the removal of all the turnpike gates

21

in the country, but also the abolition of all tithe and rent charge in lieu of tithes, the alteration of the present poor law, towards which they expressed the most bitter hostility, abolition of church rates, and an equitable adjustment of their landlord's rents. These with other alleged grievances, six or seven in number, they stated their determination to get remedied.[38]

The crowd that converged on Carmarthen on the morning of 19 June, several thousand strong and containing both men and women, had been summoned by notices fixed on church and chapel doors and by word of mouth. Their procession through Carmarthen's streets, closed for business and thronged with supporters, was headed by a hired band playing 'popular airs', followed by 'the rabble of the town'. This section was followed by a marcher carrying the placard 'Justice and lovers of justice are we all', then by 'Rebecca' on a dark bay horse, on this occasion 'ornamented with a profusion of artificial ringlets'. Around three hundred farmers on horseback brought up the rear. Some reports alleged the presence of Chartists in the crowd, and of 'inflammatory placards'. Alcwyn C. Evans's detailed account reflected:

> although to some, there might have been something whimsical to excite the laughter of the thoughtless, yet there was also in the visible spirit of defiance, and determination to resist their unlawfully being taxed for passage over roads which they themselves repaired, much that was conducive to inspire alarm, and to force the mind to enquire what will the ultimate issue be, of all Rebecca's decided resistance.

As the demonstration passed Carmarthen workhouse, a proportion of the march was diverted into its attempted ransack and demolition. The crowd invaded the front yard and a few hundred stormed the building, occupying the dining-hall and turning out the inmates while workhouse staff and local dignitaries remonstrated with them. The arrival of a troop of the 4th Dragoon Guards and reading of the Riot Act saw the crowd disperse, with some rioters, hemmed in by the military, risking injury by escaping over the workhouse walls. There was little bloodshed but much potential for it – the *Welshman* noted drily that the military 'behaved with great coolness, and used the flat of their swords only'. Those arrested at the scene included 'several respectable farmers' and members of the band, which had continued playing in the work-house yard throughout proceedings.[39]

The importance of the Carmarthen riot as a turning-point for the movement lay in its capturing of national press – and therefore public – attention. There were now national reports and editorials written on Rebeccaism, rather than the previous syndicating of local reports from the Welsh papers. The dramatic nature of events led *The Times* to dispatch Thomas Campbell Foster to the area as a special correspondent, where his regular reports on 'The State of South Wales' did much to raise Rebecca's national profile. On the whole sympathetic, Foster's reports attributed the riots to 'distress', which he defined as long-term poverty among farmers, exacerbated not only by the immediate imposition of turnpike tolls, but also by rents, tithes and the New Poor Law. He emphasised the role of 'error or neglect' by central government in bringing about the circumstances leading to unrest through its 'centralizing, theorizing' tendencies and lack of consideration for local circumstances.[40] The workhouse riot also exacerbated the fears of the landed interest, since it marked a switch in the focus of attacks from toll gates to state property. The *Quarterly Review* considered it the start of 'a new stage in the movement' after which 'Becca's broad name covered the designs of every desperado who had an end to gain or an enmity to gratify'.[41] The *Swansea Journal* compared the incident with 'parallel cases' from history including 'the Jacquerie of France, the Peasants' War in Germany, the multitudinous risings of the Commons of England under Norman and Plantagenet kings'.[42]

Throughout July and August 1843 Rebeccaism took on a prominence and volatility which David Williams termed 'midsummer madness', in which the disturbances grew more diverse in terms of geography, demographics, tactics and targets. The *Quarterly Review* recorded that 'Gate after gate was swept down ... and almost every other day's newspapers recorded some new fact of demolition'.[43] In July, attacks on toll gates in Pontarddulais and Llangyfelach marked Rebecca's first arrival in Glamorganshire.[44] Threatening letters, damage to property, arson and physical assaults were directed at landowners, bailiffs, estate managers, tithe agents, Anglican clergymen and local civic and judicial officials. An editorial in the *Welshman* described both the incendiary state of affairs and its roots in the failures and neglect of existing law:

'Rebecca' and her daughters are riding rampant over us, and do not confine themselves to uprooting turnpike gates and destroying toll-houses but have in Cardiganshire, we are informed, already begun to resist the execution of writs of levy for a debt. Threatening letters have been sent to more than one magistrate . . . No rewards that may be offered will draw forth the smallest evidence against them . . . added to which it cannot be disguised that the primary efforts of 'Rebecca' were directed against certain public grievances which the state of the law permitted to be carried into effect, and which the public felt could only be removed by the lawless proceedings adopted.[45]

Despite an increased military presence in the area under the distinguished Col. James Love, unrest continued throughout August and September, with 'Rebecca' urging farmers to collectively petition landlords for rent reductions, as well as the first reports of the 'black footman' incidents in which Rebeccaites demanded support and recompense for unmarried mothers. Significantly, disturbances had now spread to the semi-industrialised south-east of Carmarthenshire, where farmers attacking toll gates were assisted not only by their farm labourers but also by local mineworkers, who were themselves experiencing falling wages and unemployment.[46] This expression of solidarity by industrial workers and 'peasants' with the objectives of tenant farmers was followed by autonomous meetings among labourers themselves to articulate their own grievances. Thomas Campbell Foster reported:

[The labourers] are holding meetings every night on the hills in [Carmarthenshire] and Cardiganshire. They complain that the farmers pay them ill and treat them badly . . . They say to the farmers 'We have heard your grievances and helped you to get them redressed, and now we will tell you ours'.[47]

Rebecca's historians have interpreted this development as a watershed in the movement's subsequent trajectory. Unrest continued to spread beyond south-west Wales throughout late summer and autumn, with several disturbances in Radnorshire and Montgomeryshire carried out with 'all the pomp and paraphernalia of Rebeccaism', as well as the first attack on a toll gate in Brecon on 12 October. By December, there were reports from as far away as Anglesey of Rebeccaite crowds assaulting bailiffs and rescuing distrained property.[48] However, Foster's contemporary reports had by this point observed a trend amongst the farmers of Carmarthenshire away from nocturnal violence and towards public meetings in daylight where attendees openly discussed grievances and drew up petitions.[49] This shift may have reflected the alarm expressed by farmers at the increasingly 'strident tone' of their labourers, as well as the caution induced among them by the increased presence of troops. The emphasis on what the local MP John Walsh recorded as 'meetings and complaints, instead of outrages' may also have been a reaction to the increasing violence of attacks on toll gates such as those at Pontarddulais and Hendy in September 1843. In the former incident a battle took place between Rebeccaites and the military, with shots exchanged and seven arrests made, while the destruction of Hendy toll house saw its female tollkeeper, Sarah Williams, shot and killed.[50]

The majority of historians argue that Rebeccaism now entered a disreputable stage characterised by the excessive violence and criminality of a 'lunatic fringe', typified by the activities of Shoni Sguborfawr and Dai Cantwr. Arriving in Rebecca's country from the industrial south-east, this nefarious pair and their associates spent late 1843 engaged in extortion, press-ganging, arson and vandalism, as well as joining in Rebeccaite attacks on toll gates and property, for which they were eventually tried and transported in December. David Howell, noting that incidents after the autumn of 1843 decreased in frequency but increased in violence, asserts that such activities 'turned respectable farmers of that area against Rebecca' and saw them turn instead to public meetings and petitioning, concluding that 'by the end of [September] the farmers themselves had brought Rebecca to a halt'.[51] Late in 1843, a Swansea magistrate recorded the thoughts of 'a very advanced radical' with whom Rebeccaism was nonetheless losing favour due to its growing violence and extremism:

> I begin to fancy that the Rebeccas are going a little too far. – at first I thought they had some real grievances to complain of and sympathized with them, but now I find that they are levying black mail – and a bad set of fellows are joining their ranks – men coming from a distance in the hope of disturbance and plunder. They are going too far, and talking about division of property – and as I have a shop full of goods I don't approve of that.[52]

However, David J. V. Jones provides a reminder that these militantly egalitarian and unsavoury criminal elements had in fact been present from the earliest days of Rebeccaite activity, and argues that Sguborfawr's opportunist brand of Rebeccaite protection racket did not 'as several writers state, introduce these things into the movement; rather they brought them to a fine art'.[53] What is certain is that by early 1844 the movement's anonymity and immunity from prosecution were beginning to break down, with several participants arrested and transported. The Commission of Inquiry charged with examining the circumstances behind the riots, having spent the previous autumn and winter touring south Wales and compiling copious evidence, reported its findings in March 1844. Its conclusions formed the basis for subsequent legislative changes to road administration and seemed to mark the end of Rebeccaism in its 'classic' phase.

Rebecca's partners in protest and resistance

While the above narrative summarises the best-known stage of Rebeccaism, it remains reliant on a narrow definition of the movement as confined to Carmarthenshire and to the custodianship of tenant farmers. Tobit Evans and Williams take 1843–4 to be the end of Rebeccaism proper, as defined as the 'respectable' social and economic protest of tenant farmers. They view the escalating violence and criminal activity among more diverse occupational groups, which gained the ascendant from the autumn of 1843, as undeserving of the label of Rebeccaism.[54] What may be termed the classic stage of Rebeccaism in Carmarthenshire and environs had indeed begun to dissipate by the time the Commissioners of Inquiry arrived, allowing the government to present its report and subsequent legislation as having resolved the matter. However, outbreaks of rioting and isolated attacks continued well into 1844 in both Carmarthenshire and Cardiganshire, and, as statements to the Commission of Inquiry itself show, threatening letters continued to be received in the same period.[55] Rebeccaism is more plausibly and less restrictively viewed as divided into phases, defined by location and targets as well as by chronology, and with the capacity to spread beyond its area of origin and to transcend its initial remit.

While the friction produced by population growth, industrial expansion and the consequent dislocation of older social and governmental institutions was not exclusive to south Wales, south Welsh protest movements in the early nineteenth century were distinguished by these shared background factors. It is unsurprising that separate strands of protest also produced or encouraged specific tendencies in each other, with their similarities exacerbated by the migratory movement of many of their participants. The reliance of pre-industrial and early industrial Welsh protest on a commonly acknowledged oral-visual repertoire meant that the symbolism, vernacular or techniques of particular movements could outlast or transcend their originating movements, becoming blended into a more general idiom of threat, subversion or opposition. Jones argues that the violence endemic to Scotch Cattle operations, for instance, fed naturally into Welsh Chartism's inclination towards physical force – particularly since those involved in both activities shared a background in the harsh and brutal conditions of the coalfield which they, of necessity, reflected in their tactics and attitudes.[56] Workers of rural origin who returned from the coalfield to their home parishes in the depression of 1843, at least some of whom would go on to participate in Rebeccaism, would have been subject to these same influences. In September 1843 Charles Napier, Chief Constable of Glamorgan, reported a turnout by miners in Maesteg which had apparently been stimulated by both 'threats of Scotch Cattle and visits from Rebecca'.[57] Later that autumn, the jury that convicted several Rebeccaites of rioting at Pontarddulais contained men from the south-east iron town of Merthyr. These jury members subsequently found themselves named in anonymous letters posted at a local ironworks threatening to 'scotch' them for their verdict.[58] Both the technique and the language of intimidation here are those of the Scotch Cattle, and are less an anachronism or anomaly than an example of the mutual informing of movements which occurred within a relatively small area and a short space of time, and with similar preoccupations. The small and interconnected nature of south Wales as an arena of protest meant that Rebecca was both a distinctive strand among several intertwined popular movements sharing values, background and a vocabulary based on symbol and ritual, and a broad and multivalent platform on which the same vocabulary could be used to engage with a variety of social and economic issues.

Like the movement's use of symbolism in general, the presence of a symbolic leadership figure was not original or unique
to Rebeccaism. While Rebecca's most obvious and frequently
cited counterparts were Ned Ludd, Captain Swing and, elsewhere
in Wales, the Scotch Cattle's *Tarw Scotch* or Scotch Bull, similar
figures were recorded in social and industrial protest throughout
Britain from as early as the fourteenth century.[59] The tradition
of 'pseudofeminine' leaders in particular was pondered by A.W.
Smith, who counted various Lady Ludds or 'General Ludd's wives',
Lady Skimmington and the Irish Molly Maguires among their
number.[60] Norman Simms, developing Smith's ideas, saw such figures as characteristic of 'pre-political, essentially rural communal
groups', whose protest required the assertion of archaic popular
justice through symbolic agency.[61] As D. C. G. Allan wrote of an
earlier cross-dressed leader of anti-enclosure protest, Lady Skimmington, Rebecca belonged in the pantheon of 'the quasi-comic
and quasi-religious leader – combinations, as it were, of saviours
and lords of misrule'.[62] As the movement progressed, the character
of 'Rebecca' became an increasingly stylised and abstract figure.
This enabled her image and name to transcend their original
objectives and to function as multivalent symbols expressing the
pursuit of popular concepts of justice, the defence of established
rights and the legitimisation of activities – including poaching,
arson and the writing of threatening letters – which were otherwise
being placed beyond the pale of constitutional law.

The evolution of Rebeccaism illustrates that specific modes of
protest did not originate with or remain the property of specific
movements or demographics, but were utilised, adapted and channelled as the occasion demanded. The attacks on toll gates which
made Rebecca notorious in rural south-west Wales also took place
across the industrial south-east in the autumn of 1843, including
at Cardiff, Llantrisant and Pontypridd. At the same time, poachers on the Wye in Radnorshire, and anti-bailiff protesters in places
as diametrically apart as Anglesey and Pontypool, were also being
accused of 'playing Rebecca'.[63] There was no evidence and little
suggestion that such instances of unrest had direct links with each
other, or that they resulted from external agitation by marauding
Rebeccaites from the south-west. Indeed, Thomas Frankland Lewis
scoffed at the suggestion that repression of Rebeccaism in its initial
locations had caused its participants to make trouble elsewhere,

responding that 'not a soul in Carmarthenshire cares a farthing or knows anything about Radnorshire'.[64] Rather, the spread of Rebeccaism reflected the range of commonly perceived oppressions and injustices across much of Wales, as well as the interlinked nature of much contemporary protest and the shared awareness of its techniques, which enabled them to be spontaneously deployed in disparate local actions. Similar evolution and spread of a particular set of iconography can be seen even today – for instance, in the use of the stylized Guy Fawkes mask worn by members of Anonymous, Occupy and the autonomous anti-austerity movements now gathering pace in several countries.

Rebecca and the Historians

Aspects of historical writing on Rebeccaism mirror broader developments and debates on the history of Wales. Both reflect a certain concern with stressing the distinctive nature of Welsh development and with representing 'authentic' Welsh experience. In addition, studies of Rebeccaism underline the comparative absence of gender as a category of analysis and the lack of postmodernist influence in Welsh historiography. Filling in these gaps can best be done through analysing the costume, symbol and ritual contained in the Rebecca movement, and recent cultural histories which utilise the techniques of anthropology and literary theory demonstrate effective ways of doing so.

Wales and Rebeccaism in twentieth-century historiography

Early attempts at a comprehensive survey of Welsh historical development, such as that with which Owen Morgan Edwards launched the journal *Wales* in 1880, examined the determining influence of the environment upon Welsh history. They drew on the prevailing trend in nineteenth-century thought which Neil Evans has termed 'geographic determinism'. Edwards presented the Welsh landscape both as a source of continuity throughout successive waves of migration and as a means of preserving what he regarded as essentially Welsh characteristics – including internal divisions and isolationism.[1] The progress of Welsh history from the medieval to the modern period was consequently depicted as a slow encroachment of external influences into the Welsh heartland, with a resultant loss of those characteristics deemed integral to Welsh culture. This view was influential on historians writing in the early twentieth century, whose work defined the Welsh primarily in terms of their relationship with the land. Emrys Bowen presented Welsh history as turning on a contrast between rural areas in which established and 'authentically' Welsh traditions and cultures were preserved, and modernising industrial areas where the same traditions were subsumed or undermined.[2] Despite criticising 'geographic determinism', Bowen nevertheless distinguished between a mountainous heartland of 'inner Wales' and outer border or lowland areas considered more open to external influences. From this perspective, Welsh history appeared as a gradual retreat of the older culture, a process culminating in the inexorable spread of industrialisation with the old culture corrupted or destroyed apart from remnants in mountainous redoubts.

This trope is present in the work on Rebeccaism of both Williams and Tobit Evans. Their accounts depict Welsh rural radicalism, preserved in the countryside and based around pre-industrial values and traditions, as opposed to the modernising forces of industrialisation and urbanisation. The later phase of Rebecca is characterised as 'deviation' or 'degeneration' by virtue of its corruption by industrial south Wales, represented by the 'rogues' or 'lunatic fringe' of Sguborfawr and Cantwr. David J. V. Jones identifies in such accounts the influence of 'indoctrination theory': a wish to lend 'respectability' to Rebecca in order to situate it within a progressive teleological account of Welsh history. Earlier accounts, he argued, attempt to treat attacks on toll gates as qualitatively different from the generalised and less respectable Rebeccaism of later years which operated under the auspices of Rebecca as a figurehead for general community revolt.[3] This approach presented an artificial divide between 'respectable' and 'pre-political' rural Welsh, engaged in the essentially conservative defence of established rights, and the unwarranted intrusion of south-east militants influenced by imported ideas of Chartism or Reform. Conversely, Rebeccaites were frequently dismissed by contemporary militants as 'middle-class farmers', their protest seen as principally reactionary and of little importance to the progress of industrial organisation.[4] As Sharon Howard has argued, this approach left rural 'reactionary radicals' of the type prevalent in Rebecca in a historiographical blind spot, and does not withstand the challenge of evidence uncovered by subsequent research.[5] Jones uses Rebecca's sanctioning of attacks through the sending of anonymous letters and symbolic appearances during disturbances to point out continuities between attacks on toll gates and other economic and social protest carried out under 'her' authority. He suggests that little useful distinction can be drawn between the various actions involving Rebecca, all of which display, in his view, a preoccupation with upholding 'the people's law' and opposing injustices of which the imposition of tolls was one among many.[6]

Gwyn A. Williams attributes the historiographical tendency to marginalise or dismiss Rebeccaism's less respectable forms to the wish to reinforce a historical perspective, informed by Nonconformity, which views early nineteenth-century Wales as a country in placid 'political apathy', its people essentially quiescent, loyal to national institutions, and 'stirred only by poverty and outsiders'. In the aftermath of the Rebecca riots, Liberal Welsh commentators like Henry Richard and Thomas Philipps denied that the events held any politically radical dimension, or that they indicated any disloyalty to English institutions.[7] The reluctance to recognise any significant political dimension to Rebecca beyond the immediate desire for self-preservation and defence of established values hampered initial attempts fully to understand the movement. This situation altered with the emergence after 1950 of new historiographical approaches, pioneered by Marxist historians including E. P. Thompson, Eric Hobsbawm and George Rudé, which affirmed the agency of those excluded from social elites and which, more significantly, regarded industrialisation as a globally significant transforming process rather than a disastrous termination.[8] These approaches were instrumental in the founding of *Welsh History Review* in 1960 and the journal *Llafur* in 1971, and in the accompanying focus on oral tradition as a method of historical recording.[9] This new perspective provided the basis for a reassessment of the organising principles of Welsh history. Glanmor Williams's work on nineteenth-century Wales, which criticised the geographical basis of earlier work, posited industrialisation not as the destructive climax of a negative trend in Welsh history, but as a critical turning-point dividing pre-modern from modern Wales.[10]

By the 1970s, a majority of historians had taken up Williams's view that the connecting thread of Welsh history was social development rather than the decline of authentic Welsh culture. Previous geographical determinist models were implicitly or overtly rejected as 'enfeebled allegory'.[11] This newer understanding of Welsh historical development allowed greater scope for the study of economic, social and cultural changes and their links with protest. Theories such as Hobsbawm's on 'primitive rebels', which broadened the definition of political activity to encompass previously neglected small-scale and peripheral action including food riots and banditry, also enabled historians to study social and political movements outside the pale of industrial organisation.[12] This provided a useful corrective to the tendency to marshal labour history into a respectable teleology of union lodge-forming, marching and petitioning, with workers earning concessions by proving their ability to fit within the sober, constitutional pale. While one can indeed make out this progressive general narrative in the development of Welsh labour organisation, it is also true that far messier, more recalcitrant and less modern forms of protest persisted across Wales throughout the nineteenth century, including the multitudinous mass resistance of Rebeccaism, whose organisational basis was more than strictly occupational.

In his study of the 'frontier years' of the Welsh working class, Gwyn A. Williams drew on the concept of industrialisation as a basis for the understanding of subsequent society and culture, casting the Welsh as historical actors with agency rather than as passive observers of change.[13] His survey of the society and culture, including protest, of nineteenth-century Wales identified the coexistence of a plurality of modes of production. This view contradicted previous assumptions of economic backwardness and presented the Welsh as sophisticated political actors rather than primitive rebels, but it also stressed the economic as well as environmental basis of changes in Welsh culture and society. The majority of later works on Rebeccaism similarly display some degree of synthesis of preceding historiographical approaches, in which the environment, and the contrast and clash of urban and rural, remain significant but not exclusive factors in explaining Rebeccaism as the response of a traditional rural culture to external modernising forces of industry, urbanisation and political economy. Howell, accounting for the relative lack of collective organisation among labourers in nineteenth-century Monmouthshire and Glamorgan, offers the explanation that the mode of living 'in scattered farmhouses over most of the principality . . . prevented easy combination of effort'.[14] Jones presents the history of Wales from the eighteenth century in terms of the removal from the land of a people 'rural by work and by instinct', while also recognising the greater prevalence of crime and disorder in the affected areas than is usually admitted, and the social divisions, often exacerbated by language and religion, which were present between landlords and their tenant farmers and labourers.[15]

Welsh history and the theoretical turn

The concern of much previous Welsh labour history with relations between classes and the totalising concept of working-class community has often entailed a reluctance to address inter-class tensions, conflict or disparities of experience. Research on nineteenth-century Welsh social and cultural life frequently based its study of popular culture and national identity on groups of industrial workers and forms of associational life including choral singing and the Welsh Rugby Union, in addition to more established associational and organisational groups like trade unions. Much of this otherwise valuable work assumed that these experiences of urban industrial popular culture represented the 'authentic' Welsh experience, in contrast to the romantic idealism of earlier work which focused on rural Wales as a reserve of traditional values. The historical narratives thus created tended to prioritise the particular cultural and social experience of the male and indigenous Welsh working class, to the exclusion of others.[16] More recent historiography, responding to and influenced by the economic, social and cultural disjuncture of the 1980s, has focused on breaking down established tropes of class and community solidarity, seeking to establish a more complex reality with room for a variety of social identities including those based on gender or ethnicity.[17]

The development of women's history has been instrumental in attempts to widen the focus of established narratives. Joan Scott, one of several feminist historians to criticise E. P. Thompson's lack of attention to women's experience in *The Making of the English Working Class*, argued that this lack could not be remedied without problematising class as a historical category, attending to how class and gender are constructed together and linked 'as representation, as identity, as social and political practice'. She also argued that women could not be incorporated into existing histories by being 'awkwardly included as special examples of the general (male) experience, or [by being] treated entirely separately'.[18] In 1986, writer and historian Deirdre Beddoe sharply observed that

'Welsh history, like English history, has been about chaps'.[19] Since that point, Angela John in *Our Mothers' Land* has suggested an alternative chronology for Welsh history based on events relevant to the lives of women, supplementing the Reform Act with such incidents as the 1842 legislative ban on women working below ground in the mining industry. The studies collected in *Our Mothers' Land* have shed valuable light on the formerly marginal histories of women in nineteenth-century Wales, as Beddoe's 2001 anthology *Out of the Shadows* has done for the twentieth century. Both John and Rosemary A. N. Jones have focused on the types of Welsh community ritual acknowledged to have preceded and inspired Rebecca, notably the form of charivari known as *ceffyl pren* and its enabling of female authority and agency.[20] John argues that the strong female presence within Rebeccaism, as well as in the *ceffyl pren*, allowed women to breach boundaries between the public and private sphere and to negotiate some limited regulation of their community. Jones draws a parallel between the need to recognise the continuity of these earlier forms of political action and the recognition of the importance and presence of women in pre-industrial communities which such forms often enabled.[21]

However, these attempts to integrate examples of women as political actors can have limited influence on a historiography whose narratives remain rooted in the conceptions and chronologies of traditional labour history. As a category of analysis in the history of Wales, gender has tended to function as a means of understanding women's experience alone, rather than as a relational concept.[22] David Smith, introducing a collection of essays on nineteenth-century Wales, recognises that women 'have been almost forgotten in our written history', but makes no moves to address this absence, on the grounds that 'no single essay in this book could have been anything other than tokenism'. He argues that women 'will require a separate history before they can figure in our male-dominated historiography with integrity, and therefore integrally'.[23] Thus the less than helpful idea of separate male and female histories marches on, avoiding opportunities for an integrated view of how Welsh society developed around the sexual division of labour and construction of gender identities.

Paul O'Leary attributes the failure to integrate gender to a distaste for overt theory among Welsh historians, stemming partly from a concern with allowing those outside academia ownership of their own history and a consequent reluctance to alienate a wider audience through use of obscurantist theoretical language.[24] It is debatable how far the idea of theory-phobia among Welsh historians holds true: Glanmor Williams, in common with his 1960s contemporaries, placed great theoretical emphasis on the industrial revolution as social, cultural and economic transformation, bringing in Marxist theory to 'fructify' economic and social history and to break down the artificiality of older political history.[25] O'Leary's argument holds more weight when he points out that there has been little movement beyond the fundamental approach of social history to embrace cultural history or postmodernism. This becomes particularly significant in explaining the limited incorporation of gender into the traditionally male-centred concerns of labour history, including those dealing with Rebeccaism. Joan W. Scott identifies an attention to theory, in particular consideration of how reality is constituted by language, as a means of integrating gender into history. The relative imperviousness of Welsh historians to the linguistic turn may therefore be a factor in the failure to assimilate gender fully into general narratives of the development of Welsh society.

Within Rebeccaism, the aspect most amenable to a gendered analysis is the movement's use of ritual and symbol, especially its extensive use of feminine signifiers. Malcolm Thomis and Jennifer Grimmett, in their survey of women in nineteenth-century protest, note that the incidence of male cross-dressing is at its highest in Welsh protest, but also that there have been few explorations of first causes.[26] Rebeccaite ritual cross-dressing, although invariably mentioned as an integral part of the movement, has received little sustained analysis beyond its implicit resemblance to the *ceffyl pren* and the speculation that it functioned as a method of disguise or as deference to the domestic jurisdiction of women. Graham Seal's examination of traditional ritual and symbol in agrarian protest is typical in its minimalist references to the use of cross-dressing, which, while recognising that the device's usefulness as disguise was 'an incidental advantage rather than an explanation of motive', offer no greater attempt to arrive at that explanation.[27]

Outside the study of protest, more historiographical attention has been given to the phenomenon of female cross-dressing, whether for the purpose of gaining entry to an otherwise inaccessible lifestyle or career, or in theatrical or literary contexts, than to its male equivalent. Most work on the latter falls into sociological fields, such as its role in the development of eighteenth-century homosexual subcultures, rather than its use in protest.[28] Not only could the neglected subject of male cross-dressing in protest illuminate the experience of male protesters, but also, as Shoemaker and Vincent discern in the study of cross-dressed pseudo-feminine characters, considering the use of symbols or visual signifiers can reveal 'the presence, rather than the assumed absence, of the feminine in political activity'.[29] Attention to the capacity of women for social and community influence and their cultural presentations, as covered in the following chapters, can also help to supplement accounts of the political position and agency of women in early nineteenth-century Wales. The under-researched themes of gender and the use of symbol and ritual, therefore, appear a promising area of study for a deeper understanding of nineteenth-century protest and its social basis, in Rebeccaism and beyond.

Decoding the use in protest of symbol and ritual

The following chapters consider ritual and symbol in Rebeccaite activity and what their use may have signified for participants. Previous study of these aspects has been hindered by the difficulty of discerning a coherent or logical basis to the use of symbol and ritual in protest, and a related lack of analytical techniques through which to explore it. Symbol and ritual have also been of largely incidental concern to labour historians, most of whom have understandably prioritised the structural and ideological issues involved in the pursuance of political objectives and the degree of success in accomplishing them. The theatrical and performative aspects of Rebeccaism have therefore been noted without attracting further analysis. In the period since Rebeccaism last received detailed attention, however, advances in social and cultural history have rendered these obstacles less insurmountable.

The perception of how politics and society interacted in eighteenth- and nineteenth-century Britain has undergone a significant shift, from the concentration by Liberal and Conservative historians on elite and institutional high politics towards recognition of the unofficial exercise of political influence, engagement and activity outside the formal structures of power. Frank O'Gorman in particular has reinterpreted the eighteenth-century electorate as 'independent agents with power of judgement and conscience'. Focusing on how votes were sought and won during contested elections, he argues that the corruption, deference and patronage identified by Namier as endemic to the British electoral system before 1832 did not preclude the existence of an active and independent electorate within a vibrant participatory and popular electoral culture.[30] The relevance of this work to the study of movements like Rebecca lies in its identification of a context of electoral and street politics in which influence could be exercised and allegiance conveyed through a theatrical and ritualised display of symbols. Since the 1990s, a succession of studies of public protest have focused on its use of symbol, ritual, space and narrative, as a way of supplementing, challenging or qualifying its instrumental aspects and socio-political impact.[31]

In her study of more recent protest movements, Pollyanna Ruiz argues that 'traditionally organised demonstrations are remarkably text-based', with 'political ends ... articulated via banners, placards and flyers which spell out the protesters' demands'.[32] This is a somewhat limited perspective on nineteenth-century protest, which ignores the degree to which a symbolic oral-visual repertoire persisted as a way of transmitting information and demands both to those within and those beyond the plebeian public sphere. Rituals of electoral contestation in the eighteenth and nineteenth centuries allowed voters and non-voters to express support through the wearing of party regalia and colours and the ceremonial exhibition of banners and effigies. Work by Nicolas Rogers, James Vernon and James Epstein has demonstrated the importance of symbol and ceremony as a means of establishing political allegiance and identity.[33] Rogers links this aspect of popular political culture to the conflicts over occupation of public space which characterised eighteenth- and early nineteenth-century Britain, arguing that the use of effigies, colours, illuminations and other components of political festival were instrumental in how radicals and loyalists 'marshalled popular support in the public domain'. He also identifies the visual display of symbols as a mass collective form of political expression, in contrast to the shift towards individual, privatised acts of protest such as graffiti or anonymous letters which developed throughout the 1790s as the state allied with popular loyalism to restrict radical opportunities for occupying political space. Oral-visual political expression did indeed decline over the nineteenth century, in line with the development of print culture, in favour of political mobilisation and communication via newspapers, pamphlets and speeches, but its endurance in pre-industrial and early industrial protest should not be underestimated.

While oral-visual symbols were a logical method of communication in a primarily non-literate society, they also obtained their effectiveness through their capacity for mass communication and the immediate expression of ideas. This effectiveness depended on the existence of a symbolic frame of reference which was recognised within a given community. E. P. Thompson situates this type of popular expression, extending to local municipal and community ritual as well as national political occasions, within a plebeian–patrician dichotomy which he sees as determining the operation of eighteenth-century popular civic and festive culture. He argues that the ceremonial displays through which elites established their political and municipal hegemony were accompanied by a form of plebeian 'counter-theatre' in which the ordinary and unfranchised could draw on and subvert the ritual forms and symbols used by their 'betters', in order to express an independent opinion or to legitimise their own actions.[34] This assertion is qualified by Rogers, who, despite acknowledging the theory's importance in underscoring plebeian agency, sees crowd actions as more mediated than allowed for by Thompson's suggested polarity. His study of the use of symbolic display by both loyalists and radicals in 1790s England concludes that the plebeian class did not always act uniformly to create a 'counter-theatrical' parody of official culture, but could be drawn into factional politics, mobilised by the superior resources of the propertied classes in the ways described by O'Gorman.[35]

While the above developments have elevated the symbol and ritual of popular culture and political discourse to the level of a serious subject of study, the integration of insights gained from anthropological studies have enabled attempts to decode the vocabulary of ostensibly obscure historical practices, from charivari to sectarian massacres.[36] The value to historians of interdisciplinary techniques, especially those of cultural and symbolic anthropology, was most comprehensively asserted by historians of the Annales school. The subsequent use by social and cultural historians of these techniques suggests that a similar application would help illustrate the rationale behind Rebeccaite use of costume, signifiers and ritual behaviour.[37] Traditionally, symbolic anthropology has focused on social groupings, including those involved in religion, cosmology and ritual activity, and on expressive customs such as mythology and the performing arts. Its integration into historical study has witnessed a shift in emphasis towards collective behaviour in contexts of cultural significance. Symbolic anthropology places a premium on the study of symbol and ritual as enabling the expression of cultural values reflecting a coherent pattern of thought and behaviour which may form the basis of a cohesive social structure. The leading exponent of this approach, Clifford Geertz, clarified the object of cultural study as the close reading – 'thick description' – of publicly available symbols, practices and behaviours in order to disclose through them the 'semiotic structure' of wider culture and society. In Geertz's 'text analogy', culture is likened to a text or language which must be studied as something in itself rather than as a transparent representation of economic or social trends. Geertz's understanding of symbol and ritual is broad and inclusive, eliding the divide between high and popular culture and encompassing folk customs and the everyday actions of individuals. As 'texts', these can then be read and interpreted in order to explicate the meanings which organise the popular culture and belief systems of other societies.[38]

The emphasis on analysing collective behaviour and particular 'texts' for what they reveal of a society's deeper cultural patterns has reduced the reliance of historians on 'hard' data of birth, death, marriage and material life, facilitating the study of periods of the past for which such hard data are sparse or uneven. Perhaps the greatest advantage of the symbolic approach lies in the analytical strength of thick description, which, in its orientation towards the perspective of participants, is essential in order to explain movements or events previously dismissed as marginal or incomprehensible. Natalie Zemon Davis and E. P. Thompson have both drawn on the work of a range of anthropologists to examine the role of ritual in social and political life, whether established calendrical festivals or community rituals, or more extraordinary and spontaneous events such as food riots.[39] Davis, Thompson and Robert Darnton have developed readings of popular protest or disorder which divulge the agency and intentions of participants, even when these have received only symbolic expression in the historical record. Thus Thompson asserted the existence of a paternalist 'moral economy' which animated eighteenth-century crowds, based on a reading of their use of symbol and ritual during food and price riots, and Darnton explained the ritualised murder of cats by apprentices in eighteenth-century Paris by relating it to themes in contemporary culture through which workers 'made their experience meaningful'.[40] Both concepts go some way towards illuminating otherwise baffling aspects of the Rebecca movement.

Oral-visual communication has often been ignored by historians of protest in favour of written communication in the form of newspaper articles and editorials, pamphlets and minute-books.[41] James Epstein, conversely, 'embraces an expanded notion of the repertoire of symbolic practices that constitute political culture, or language' and emphasises 'the indeterminate meanings associated with signs' including visual symbols such as clothing.[42] Paul Pickering's contribution to the study of Chartism argues similarly that language is 'a social action performed in a variety of contexts', and that an exclusive focus on written or spoken communication 'confines Chartist ideology to the statements of a relatively small number of literate and articulate leaders, leaving the rank and file as a receptively silent majority'.[43] This is especially salient when considering movements like Rebeccaism which revolved around the collective action of participants, and in which the identity of any single leader was not only obscured and downplayed in importance, but was also secondary to the authority which any individual could gain by performing the identity of 'Rebecca'.

Rebeccaism's richness in visual signifiers makes it a suitable subject for study both on its own terms and within the myriad symbols and rituals of contemporary plebeian life. By distinguishing the movement's performative, ritual and symbolic elements, analysing them, tracing their antecedents and situating them within their contemporary social and cultural context, we can gain insights into the bases on which social and cultural interaction was predicated, as has been done to great effect in other contexts by Mervyn James, Richard Suggett and Paul O'Leary.[44] Much of our knowledge of Rebecca comes from press or court reports, in which the retelling of events is itself performative. As Tobit Evans notes, commentators 'drew largely on the imagination when describing ... the dreaded lady'.[45] This type of material draws attention to the movement's intrinsically theatrical nature and its reliance on oral-visual signifiers, but it can also be analysed on its own terms for what it discloses of contemporary views of gender and the available range of abstract identities to which the figure of Rebecca could be related. Chapter 7's discussion of the use of Rebecca's image in press and popular consciousness will show that the act of recording and inscribing incidents of Rebeccaism was not merely a window on events but very often a 'performance' in itself, which could engage with, reinforce or challenge other contemporary images and narratives in popular discourse.

Such an approach is of course not without limitations and qualifications. Tosh and Darnton point out that, whereas anthropologists have direct access to their area of study, historians are of necessity using intermediary texts which require a preliminary process of reading before the actions they describe can be reconstituted in a way which may allow access to the perspectives of participants. More specific criticisms have been made of the elevating of symbol and ritual into a primarily aesthetic consideration into which issues of historical change, politics and social conflict are collapsed. Elucidating the possible meanings of symbol and ritual thereby becomes an end in itself, leading the historian to focus on the 'text' itself rather than on the process of contextualising.[46] Taking symbolic representation as the primary subject of study need not entail disparaging all other aspects. Geertz himself advocates that cultural analysis should connect theoretical formulations closely with descriptive interpretations by keeping symbolic forms as closely tied as possible to concrete political and economic realities.[47]

Life in 1840s Carmarthenshire cannot be conceived of simply as a symbol-laden text or drama: several aspects of the use of costume and symbol by Rebeccaites directly reflect both the conditions of their production and the targets of their antagonism. The form in which action was taken by Rebeccaites was directly linked to surrounding issues including the altered economic situation occasioned by the New Poor Law, and to changes in land ownership and use. In wider Rebeccaite activity, as explored in Chapters 5, 6 and 7, the feminine signifiers used by participants, and the ways in which Rebecca's public image took shape, utilised what female archetypes were available in contemporary society, culture and politics. In interpreting these activities, I give equal weight to the use of symbol and ritual and to the changing material realities to which such activity was a response. Text and context are both essential since each illuminates the other.

'Pomp and paraphernalia':
Custom, Festival, Ritual and Rebeccaism

This chapter takes as its starting-point David J. V. Jones's argument that Rebeccaism's violence, disorder and petty criminality were a natural consequence of the prevalence of these qualities in the social conditions from which Rebeccaism arose.[1] Other characteristics of the movement also reflected the social and cultural life of participants. The following outline of the conditions in which Rebeccaism developed will demonstrate that the movement's motivation, form and content were deeply rooted in the social life, ritual calendar and popular culture of early nineteenth-century southwest Wales. Rebeccaite protest gave itself legitimacy and coherency by referencing the ritual and symbol of local festivals, ceremonies and popular customs. This chapter compares Rebeccaite activity with other contemporary popular rituals in order to highlight the frames of reference and rationales which they shared. I then consider how Rebeccaite resistance to toll gates was informed by the clash of established attitudes surrounding land use with newer legislative changes. As with the way protesters responded to changes imposed by the New Poor Law (for which see Chapter 6), this establishes Rebeccaism as an active response to social and political change rather than simply a product of popular custom.

Traditions of popular ritual and collective regulation

Studies of eighteenth-century England and Wales have proposed the existence of a popular or 'plebeian' culture consisting of structured attitudes and practices through which ordinary people experienced, articulated and responded to their circumstances. Barry Reay draws on contemporary accounts to argue for a pre-industrial society in which 'customary rites were integrated into the rhythms and patterns of work, leisure, religion and community'.[2] E. P. Thompson identifies the particular equilibrium of eighteenth- and early nineteenth-century social relations as the factor which lent popular symbolic discourse its significance. In a society where the gentry asserted their hegemony through a studied theatrical style involving pageants, processions and the display of emblems and favours, it was natural for the 'plebs' accordingly to assert their own presence and values through a collective 'counter-theatre' of symbolism and drama. Thompson sees community ritual and festival as a conscious and mocking counterpart to the official ceremonials of Church, state and law.[3] The incidents known as 'Rebecca and her black footman', discussed in full in Chapter 6, may provide an instance of what Thompson identifies as deliberate allusions to or mockery of bountiful 'public exhibitions of justice or of charity'. The bailiffs assaulted at Pound farm early in 1844 were made to kneel while 'Rebecca' held out a bible and administered a mock oath which bound them not to return.[4] Such examples demonstrate the degree to which the use of ritual was entrenched in the society which produced Rebecca, and the ease with which its 'official' forms could be appropriated and subverted. The function of this appropriation was not merely mocking or subversive, but also lent Rebeccaite activity a veneer of legitimacy and authority by establishing it within a familiar context. That these counter-theatrical elements were fundamental to Rebeccaism is demonstrated by the degree to which the movement mirrored the ritual form and symbolic content of ceremony, festival and community ritual.

Contemporary sources attest to the incidence and importance of civic ritual in Rebecca's country. In June 1843, following panicked reporting of the mass demonstration at Carmarthen, the *Welshman* sought to reassure its readers with a tongue-in-cheek but indicative survey of the ritual and ceremony present in everyday Welsh life:

[Although assemblies of over a hundred may appear alarming to English readers] in Wales it is quite different. We have processions every week. We never bury our dead without a procession; we never marry without a procession; we are all Ivorites, Odd Fellows, and Rechabites as well as Rebeccaites parade the country eternally – come rain or shine, we Odd

Fellows must have our procession. We dress ourselves . . . in coats made for any body, with ribbons of all hues and colours, and we walk each with an umbrella either under his arm or above his head, according as the weather is fair or foul. From our Club-house to church, men continue to exhibit themselves to gazing hundreds, until they are tired at looking and we at walking. Then we dine, speechify and sing. In short, a procession is the only public amusement we have.[5]

This 'public amusement' permeated social, political and cultural life at all levels of society. A wealth of symbolism was included in the elaborate funerals of the gentry, which could involve huge processions with heraldic emblems and mourners in symbolic dress.[6] Electoral culture was also highly ritualised, with crowds at hustings often employing symbolism to convey their feelings, including the display of loaves to express support for repeal of protective duty on corn and wooden screws carried on poles to indicate the oppressive or coercive nature of landlord/tenant relations.[7] The extent and availability of this symbolic vocabulary would have made it a natural resource for the mass popular expression of support or opposition.

Acknowledging the familiarity of ritual and 'counter-theatre' contributes to our understanding of the comparable elements of Rebeccaite activity. In November 1843, gates around Lampeter were demolished following a march round the town by several hundred costumed Rebeccaites, who walked four abreast 'in a slow and measured pace . . . in perfect order' and fired off muskets as they went.[8] Gates at Porthyrhyd and Pontyberem were destroyed in July after a procession by Rebeccaites 'walking two abreast, three being in advance and three in the rear', and at Narberth the destruction of gates was followed by a march round the town.[9] The mass march to Carmarthen Guildhall in June 1843 was structured akin to many processions by the Dissenting and friendly societies which flourished in early nineteenth-century Wales.[10] Assembling at noon, the marchers took an elaborate path round Carmarthen in a socially hierarchical procession with 'respectable farmers' on horseback and 'the rabble of the town' on foot, complete with flags, banners and placards and preceded by a band playing 'popular airs of the day'. Three processions recorded in the same week as the march took similar forms to it, with a Swansea branch of the 'true Ivorites' walking 'in full dress with their splendid regalia, and preceded by an excellent brass band'; the Druids of Tivy Lodge assembling at noon before processing to church 'preceded by the Bronwydd band, and accompanied by the population of the neighbourhood'; and an Oddfellows procession in Gower 'starting around noon and proceeding through the neighbourhood followed by a ceremonial dinner'.[11] Cuttings preserved by Thomas Brigstocke contain several notices of processions following this formula, with separate sections of marchers on foot and horseback and strategically placed banners.[12]

However, the Carmarthen march's superficial ascription to the structures of patrician society was offset by the prominence of an elaborately dressed Rebecca, crowned with 'a profusion of artificial ringlets', and marchers bearing brooms with which 'to sweep the foundations of the tollhouses and the workhouse', a symbolic anticipation of their complete destruction.[13] These subversive additions allowed Rebeccaites to occupy public and civic space through counter-theatrical ritual. Paul O'Leary has analysed urban processions as a means of performing and reconciling different and potentially divisive social identities, and of individuals visibly 'becoming the public'. In early nineteenth-century Wales, the physical environment in which these performances took place was dynamic and changing, partly as a result of economic expansion and population growth.[14] It is possible to view the Carmarthen march in this context as partly a clash between disputed versions of 'the public', which witnessed the intrusion of 'the rabble of the town' into the attempted expression of an exclusionary 'respectable' civic identity by other marchers. The incident also witnessed the riotous eruption of anti-workhouse sentiment among all sections of the march, resulting in unpredictable actions which spilled beyond the containing and disciplining framework that the processional form attempted to impose.

Ritual, symbol, and occupation in popular culture and popular protest

Ritualised form and symbolic content were present to some degree in all forms of Rebeccaite activity, from chasing off bailiffs to returning illegitimate children, but they are particularly apparent in dealings with toll gates. Aside from the march or gathering which preceded attacks, the formulaic nature of dismantling toll gates themselves is evident from an examination of court and press reports. Crowds numbering from a few dozen to several hundred would gather at a meeting point, usually on wasteland or mountainside, before proceeding to a designated toll gate. The toll collector was warned either to remain indoors or, if the toll house was also to be demolished, to remove himself and his family and possessions. The gate was then dismantled or 'pulled down' with saws, axes or other bladed implements amid a cacophony of gunshots, shouts and horn-blowing. That firearms could have played a part in the ritual aspect of attacks, besides their inclusion in 'rough music', is suggested by the firing of shotguns during marriage ceremonies in the rural districts of south-west Wales, which folklorists and historians have attributed to attempts to gain supernatural protection by warding off evil spirits that might be at hand.[15] Following the dismantling, the gate or toll house's remnants were frequently carried off by the crowd and cast into a nearby body of water.[16] Like charivari and other forms of community ritual, the removal of toll gates was collaborative and self-regulating, with a designated onset and a quantifiable measure of destruction, after which matters were understood to be concluded and the crowd departed. The consistent nature of this pattern in itself challenges the idea of Rebeccaism as a series of uncontrolled bursts of random violence, indicating rather that participants operated within recognised boundaries, derived from established custom, by which all were expected to abide.[17]

The ability of Rebeccaite protest to adapt the techniques of traditional popular culture to the new demands of changing material circumstances is demonstrated by the links between the symbolic and ritual repertoire used by protesters and that of contemporary festival. Significant dates on the rural Welsh calendar included the coming of spring and winter, Christmas, New Year, St Valentine's Day, May Eve, Easter and Whit Monday – the last two of which were marked by noisy public and collective perambulations of town and parish boundaries. Such times were licensed for the telling of uncomfortable truths, usually relating to the sexual, marital or domestic conduct of peers, or the public and collective correction of breaches of community morality.[18] Historians of popular culture have further studied the ways in which festive occasions encouraged the temporary loosening of order and the overturning, questioning or mockery of authority and hierarchy.[19] The forms of guising or symbolism utilised in such action included effigies, animal masks or hides, cross-dressing and role-playing. Trefor Owen's study of the mental world of the Welsh peasantry notes that this use of symbolism legitimated censorious or mocking behaviour by marking it as part of a festive occasion.[20] The display during protest of symbols associated with festival or the carnivalesque would have acted similarly to give visible sanction to the activity. The reproduction or adaptation of festive and ritual vocabulary within aspects of Rebeccaism would have lent the movement popular legitimacy through familiarity in the eyes of both participants and observers.

Most prominent among Rebecca's borrowings from the popular cultural frame of reference are the horse motif and the use of cross-dressing and disguise. Participants on horseback are recorded in Rebeccaite activity throughout 1843 and 1844.[21] In March 1844 during the trial of two suspected Rebeccaites for riot at Prendergast toll gate, the typical rioter was described as 'the man on horseback, with a beard'.[22] The false beards and wigs worn in protest are also mentioned as being made of horsehair, occasionally specified as a mane or tail.[23] Horses are significant as an identifying component of Rebecca herself, who frequently appeared on a white horse.[24] While the use of horses and horsehair by protesters was almost certainly primarily one of necessity or convenience, it may also have had secondary associations relating to horse-riding's connotations of respectability and its inclusion in contemporary civic ritual and popular custom. At the time of Rebecca a 'horse wedding' or 'riding wedding' constituted a symbol of status, with horses often borrowed for the occasion from wealthier neighbours by those too poor to own them.[25] The association of horses with status and respectability saw them used within ritual and ceremony to signify hierarchical differentiation, as in the march to Carmarthen in which farmers rode on horses distinct from the 'rabble of the town'. This could also inform their symbolic use in protest: in September 1843 eighty Rebeccaites, arriving on horseback, turned bailiffs out of the house of the mayor of Kidwelly. Having made them kneel and swear not to execute another distraint warrant, the mock ceremony continued with Rebecca urging them to mount 'a dog-horse destined for the kennel or perhaps a pound' on which, symbolically disgraced, they were forced to exit the scene.[26] Finally, Edward Crompton Lloyd Hall, appealing to local supporters of Rebecca for calm in the 'mad' summer of 1843, attempted to present his own paternalistic authority to intervene in the operations of the turnpike trusts by using the metaphor of horse-breaking:

> Or do you think I am ignorant of the means of screwing it out from the Trustees, let them be as reluctant as they will? They have not been accustomed to being brought authoritatively to account. Like young colts not broken, they must be treated at first both gently and firmly. Do you think any firmness is wanting in me? Why then will you do anything that will prevent my getting the bridle into their mouth?[27]

As Rebeccaism progressed throughout the summer of 1843, horses became prominent in the actual and symbolic occupation of public space, as the incessant and often fruitless movement of mounted troops around the countryside was interwoven with protesters' attacks and triumphal processions. The clash between Rebeccaites and mounted dragoons at Carmarthen workhouse saw several of the former abandon their horses – the *Welshman* reported that in the conflict's aftermath unclaimed mounts were 'as plentiful as blackberries' in the fields around Carmarthen.[28] The contestation of the public arena through Rebeccaite massing and military occupation reflected both civic ceremony and popular culture. Studies of Welsh wedding customs record examples of the ritual demanding and refusal of entry to a bride-to-be's house by opposing groups of guests on horseback, often expressed in an oration between the two, with the bride and groom parties then racing to and from church while battling for custody of the bride.[29] This example of the importance of horses in popular custom also demonstrates how ritualised occupation of public space and land was entwined with the structure of contemporary social life.

Rebeccaite activity also borrowed from popular festival the custom of covering, marking or disguising participants' faces with blacking, veils, animal hides, sprigs of fern, berry juice and other flora and fauna, as well as the expression of inversion or polarity through blackened faces contrasting with white hats and gowns, jackets turned inside out, and ritual cross-dressing.[30] The custom of *Mari Lwyd* ('Grey Mare' or 'Grey Mary'), a legitimised form of levying for money and food which took place on Twelfth Night, included the horse motif alongside a host of other symbol, ritual and guising. *Mari Lwyd* involved a real or makeshift horse's skull carried from house to house by a man draped in a sheet, accompanied by a party including musicians and members cross-dressed or decorated with ribbons or sashes. Again, the demanding and refusal of entry was ritually emphasised, with entry to a house obtained and hospitality provided only after the party had knocked, sung or recited.[31] Owen records that 'Punch and Judy' were listed as members of the *Mari Lwyd* party, both of whom had blackened faces with 'Judy' often portrayed by a cross-dressed male. Whitsun morris dancing in Glamorgan also included cross-dressed male participants, and the winter practice of wassailing, involving the carrying and display of a ritual object from house to house, often featured cross-dressed or masked participants each with a specific title.[32]

There appear to be definite links between the *Mari Lwyd* ceremony and that of the *ceffyl pren* ('wooden horse'). A regionalised form of charivari or 'rough music', based around a public procession involving a hobby horse, the *ceffyl pren* was used to enforce community norms through the exposure and ridicule of those in breach of them. Although by the 1870s the custom was reported as 'fallen into desuetude' and 'more honoured in the breach than the observance', it appeared frequently throughout the early nineteenth century in the villages of south-west Wales where Rebecca would later take place, leading David Williams to state 'with complete certainty that the Rebecca Riots were an extension of the practice of the *ceffyl pren*'. Gareth Elwyn Jones sees Rebecca's links with the *ceffyl pren* as anchoring it (along with the Scotch Cattle) in 'the community of the old Wales rather than in the new Wales of the later nineteenth century', in which 'the law superseded community action'.[33]

Several elements of the *ceffyl pren* were present in Rebeccaite demonstrations: both centred around a public procession and could take place to 'rough music' from pots and pans, bells, guns and rams' horns. The custom further involved the 'riding' of targets, or their effigies or proxies, upon a hobby horse, wooden pole or 'stang', and the symbolic declaration of their offence.[34] In Carmarthenshire *ceffyl pren*, the inclusion of gunshots and participants with blackened faces reinforces its parallels with the ritual and guising used by Rebeccaites.[35] Horses figured in these customs as actual horses on which targets or their proxies or effigies were ridden – often backwards – as well as appearing symbolically as the wooden riding-poles. In an instance at Llechryd in 1837 'a large assembly of men and boys' carried a wooden horse to the house of an individual who had informed on a neighbour for cutting timber.[36] In 1847 a *ceffyl pren* was carried out at St Dogmael's by 'an immense concourse of people' in protest at a wife's infidelity, while the following year at Llanpain eight youths were charged with riot after riding an effigy of a local octogenarian who had been 'tempted to illicit love' with a much younger woman. Over a decade later, at Llandysul, a crowd of hundreds used the *ceffyl pren* against a farmer who had ill-treated his wife.[37] A Glamorgan variant of *ceffyl pren*, known as *cwlstrin*, took the form of a mock trial presided over by a 'judge' who wore the collarbone of a horse around his hat. Local cases of marital discord were brought before this 'court', to be resolved by a procession in which the husband and wife in question were impersonated by actors, the male carrying a broom and the female a ladle, with other participants bearing a petticoat and a pair of breeches on poles. Following a procession around the community, the former garment was pelted and the latter hoisted to symbolically restore established authority.[38]

The above instances suggest the awareness of and appeal to popular authority which the *ceffyl pren* shared with Rebeccaism, along with their common public and collective use of symbol and ritual to expose and correct grievances. The common use of mass gatherings followed by processions, the inclusion of real or hobby horses and the appearance of blackened faces, guising, cross-dressing and other tropes of reversal among participants, reinforce the claim of a connection between them. The *Welshman* complained in 1843 that efforts to obtain evidence against Rebeccaites were failing:

> not merely because [the population is] deterred by fear, but because 'Rebecca' has superseded and, as it were, stepped into the place of the old-fashioned Ceffil-prens, and is thus favourably looked upon by the large mass of the community.[39]

That Rebeccaism could serve the same community function as the *ceffyl pren*, as well as repurposing its repertoire for a different function during protest, is further implied by an incident reported to Edward Crompton Lloyd Hall in October 1843. Noting that

'the Rebeccaites have been interfering with the domestic arrange-
ments of a neighbouring clergyman', he goes on to record that 'a
party of about fifty men armed and disguised' proceeded to the
house of a woman in Bangor who had been living separately from
her clergyman husband. The group compelled her to accompany
them to her husband's house and 'ordered him to receive and to
love and cherish her, and ordered her to stay with him and behave
like a good and dutiful wife on pain of their severe displeasure'.[40]
This appears to be an attempt to regulate domestic and community
conduct in a way that paralleled or blended with the *ceffyl pren*.

The cloaking of economic protest in symbol and ritual associated with the correction of social and moral wrongdoing lent
Rebeccaite activity an air of popular legitimacy as well as familiarity. This popular legitimacy, based on local custom and community
engagement, was in visible opposition to nationally established
constitutional law. The same anxiety which Rebeccaism produced
in local authority figures was evident in letters to magistrates
deploring the persistence of *ceffyl pren*, and stressing that individuals 'should look, not to tumultuous meetings, but to the Law, for
redress . . . and it is by the Law, that those who have offended
against it should be punished'.[41] But part of the context of Rebecca's rise was the growing clash between newly minted laws rooted
in constitutional allegiance – especially those relating to the common ownership of land and the moral regulation of communities
– and adherence to existing custom rooted in popular tradition.

Land use and popular authority

The corrective measures available for breaches of marital or moral
ideals, and the degree of community involvement in the execution
of these measures, expressed collective concern over community
integration and standards. They also, as Owen notes, constituted
'an unofficial legal system deriving its efficacy from the power of
popular feeling'.[42] This was also true of popular reaction in south-
west Wales to increasing private encroachment on common land.
Landed wealth remained the primary guarantor of political and
economic status in Welsh society throughout the nineteenth century. Both rural and industrial Wales in the 1830s and 1840s had
pre-eminent gentry with unassailable economic power and often

vast landed estates, including Middleton Hall in the Towy Valley, the Dynefor estate in Carmarthenshire and the Nanteos estate in Cardiganshire.[43] Large tracts of land in the three counties were owned by the Crown, and its officials and courts increasingly enforced rents and condemned squatting and encroachment on their territories by those lower down the social scale. At the same time, the commons, waste and mountain land in south-west Wales, which lay under contested or indeterminate rights, was subject to increasing encroachment and disputed ownership by all sectors of the population.

In the early nineteenth century, population growth, coupled with the laxity of Crown officials, saw a surge in small-ownership and the creation of new freeholds on commons and wasteland, and the claiming of rights over pasture and sheep-walks by both landlords and groups of parishioners. Also significant were the encroach-ments made on common land by cottagers claiming squatters' rights under the custom of *tŷ unnos* ('one-night house'). This trad-ition entitled a person to the freehold of whatever shelter he or she could build in a night, as long as smoke rose from its roof at dawn, and of the land within a stone's throw of it.[44] Such dwellings were often built as a collective effort by individuals enlisting the help of fellow cottagers, sometimes in order to provide a newly mar-ried couple with a household of their own. The custom annoyed landlords, tenants and parishioners by cutting across the rights of local farmers, interfering with sheep-walks and causing concern that the poorest squatters could become a burden on the rates. The high number of court cases which took place over *tŷ unnos* assumed that if squatters were allowed to remain on the land for more than one generation they had established a legal right to it; before events could take this course farmers and landlords often resorted to direct action to remove *tŷ unnos* and their inhabitants by pulling the houses down.[45]

Land ownership became a volatile issue when changes in its use, occupation or cost resulted in the neglect or overriding of local circumstances or custom. From the 1700s, rural discontent had been provoked in Wales and beyond by the rise of an agrarian capitalism which endangered the subsistence-based peasant econ-omy through accelerating enclosure and privatisation, forcing a conflict between enclosing landowners and their agents and those who traditionally used the land for food, fuel, or living space.[46]

Jones notes that many crimes of theft and violence in rural Wales occurred on newly enclosed or disputed land. An example often invoked at the time of Rebecca was 'the war of the little Englishman', Augustus Brackenbury. This Lincolnshire-born gentleman's attempts to build an allotment at Mynydd Bach in Glamorgan were repeatedly thwarted by crowds, cross-dressed and black-faced, who argued that the land was needed for the poor and were incensed that it could be purchased and privatised by a wealthy outside interest.[47] Other long-standing battles took place in rural Wales over enclosure, encroachments and sheep-walks, in which fences were repeatedly removed and plantations, hayricks and outbuildings set on fire.[48]

By the time of Rebecca the majority of open fields had been privately enclosed, but the residue of common land in towns and lowland parishes was ritually perambulated and its use guarded by parishioners, often with anonymous letters and other protest greeting its attempted appropriation by landowners and large farmers.[49] Alcwyn C. Evans recorded an example of such activity in August 1843, along with its underlying rationale, which was that the wall in question encroached on established 'common rights':

> a wall recently erected at the village of Llandybie across a portion of the Commons or Waste Lands and said to be an encroachment on the common rights of the villagers, was levelled with the ground, and the field which it enclosed was again thrown open, and made part of the common, as it originally stood.[50]

The attitudes surrounding land ownership clarify aspects of Rebeccaite activity. Disputes over the access of farmers and labourers to previously open roads now blocked by toll gates, and the assertion of 'traditional' community-sanctioned rights over those introduced by constitutional law, were rooted in the existence of land of common or indeterminate status and ownership. In testimony given by farmers to the 1844 Commission of Inquiry, their hostility to toll gates stems from the Trust having infringed the 'rights' established by precedent and tradition by erecting new toll gates, and by manipulating their placing in order to maximise the toll exacted. The importance of custom and tradition is apparent in statements such as that recounting how Thomas George, 'a respectable farmer' refused to pay at a newly-erected gate, 'saying "There is no sign or anything here, I will pay at the old gate where I have been in the habit of paying."' A Newcastle Emlyn tenant farmer described the destruction of a toll gate by Rebeccaites who 'said it was not right to remove the gate to the place where it had been removed to'.[51]

In referencing intangible but deeply-felt popular tradition to justify their opposition to toll gates, these farmers displayed the same rejection of official in favour of customary law which characterised Rebeccaism as a whole. Furthermore, the ritualised and collective construction and demolition of *tŷ unnos*, and of other structures considered inappropriate encroachments on land reserved for common use, may have influenced the systematic way in which toll gates were removed and destroyed, usually under cover of night and as a collective effort, lending the action an arguable legitimacy from the perspective of participants. Hywel Francis's study of Welsh protest identifies a continuous extra-parliamentary and extra-legal tradition which juxtaposed natural and social justice with prevailing civil and criminal laws.[52] In its visible and collective elevation of communal laws and codes above the state law, shown in the insistence on the sanctity of customary public rights of way in response to the spread of privately owned toll gates, Rebeccaism adhered to this tradition.

5

'Petticoat heroes':
Rethinking Rebeccaite Costume and Symbolism

The previous chapter outlined the various types of community ritual and civic ceremony which formed part of the social fabric of south-west Wales, providing a symbolic vocabulary on which popular protest could draw. The social and cultural context of Rebeccaism helps explain its emphasis on costume and ritual – the use of these in protest could carry considerable weight in an age which was 'instinctively theatrical in its social behaviour'.[1] The work of several historians has established that symbolic dress and behaviour were intrinsic parts of popular political consciousness in the early nineteenth century, which, besides being able to directly communicate an individual's partisanship, could be used more broadly to lend an activity meaning and legitimacy.[2] The form of symbolic dress most associated with Rebeccaism is that of cross-dressing, and its use by participants forms the basis of this chapter. However, the degree to which the image of Rebecca and her followers as *ersatz* females has gained currency in historical and popular memory of events obscures the more intriguing possibilities suggested by contemporary accounts.

This chapter questions previous assumptions by historians that Rebeccaite costume was purely a case of practical disguise, or of men adopting female dress in order to evade the full weight of criminal responsibility, or even of men acknowledging female jurisdiction over economic issues. Rather, Rebeccaite dress contained a deliberate mixture of masculine and feminine signifiers alongside other binary oppositions, and these oppositions were intended simultaneously to make visible a number of boundaries and to emphasise their blurring and transgression. The symbolic instability and uncertainty thus created allowed the wearer's own identity to be subsumed within the transgressive and transitional figure of Rebecca or her daughter, thereby enabling them to act with enhanced power and potential. The following sections will outline the varying interpretations advanced for cross-dressing in protest, before arguing that its specific manifestation within Rebeccaism is best explained by an alternative analysis which draws on the ways in which symbolic opposition and inversion have been interpreted in other examples of social drama and ritual. We then move on to consider the implications of this for the experiences of protesters.

Interpreting the use of male cross-dressing in protest

The use of feminine dress by men in eighteenth- and nineteenth-century social and economic protest was not unique to the Rebecca movement, and the subject has been widely, if briefly, addressed by both folklorists and historians. Malcolm Thomis and Jennifer Grimmett conclude their book on women in protest with an overview of nineteenth-century popular movements involving elements of cross-dressing, in which Rebecca and Welsh protest in general feature prominently.[3] Apart from this, however, attention to the adoption of feminine dress by men remains a limited subset of work on protest, even in cases like Rebeccaism where it played a conspicuous part in establishing the movement within the popular imagination. Of Rebecca's historians, Williams includes the attire of protesters within holistic descriptions of their activities without singling it out for particular comment or analysis. While Jones gives more detailed attention to the symbolism involved in Rebecca's appearance, he again does not appear to regard it as significant enough to merit consideration on its own terms.[4] Howell's overview of the movement, despite deferring to Natalie Zemon Davis in explaining Rebeccaites' use of masking and feminine dress as 'sexual symbolism and topsy-turvy play' which put to new use ritual and festive tropes of inversion, goes no further in developing this discussion.[5] Beyond this, although cross-dressing is recognised as an integral part of the movement, no more detailed attempts have been made to explore its significance.

The interpretation of cross-dressing in protest as solely a method of disguise, used to obscure individual identity in order to avoid recognition and potential repercussions, has rightfully found little favour with historians. Within Rebeccaism especially, the impractically ornate, highly theatrical and often parodic apparel adopted, and the use of feminine pseudonyms and other forms of female imitation, militate against a purely practical explanation based on the necessity for disguise. Historians seeking to present a more complex logic behind cross-dressing have offered an alternative explanation of it as a display of deference to women as appropriate actors in popular protest. This view rests on the assumption – by no means universally accepted – that pre-industrial social and economic protest, especially over food and pricing, was considered a female preserve.[6] Dorothy Thompson argues that eighteenth- and nineteenth-century protest over economic issues, in sheer physical terms, increasingly required the participation of men, but that in communities where it took place such protest could more clearly be viewed as legitimate if carried out by women, who were able to draw on their gender-determined authority as guardians of family and community welfare and the standard of living necessary to preserve them. These claims have been extensively developed: E. P. Thompson and Olwen Hufton observe that, in times of scarcity, women were disproportionately affected by the need to devise strategies of food acquisition and subsistence; when the means to fulfil their role were visibly withheld or disrupted, it was women who took precedence in the collective expression of hardship and in attempts to remedy it, including through protest and direct action such as food and price rioting. Leaving aside the dogged attempts of John Bohstedt to arrive at a quantitative analysis of female food rioters, the majority of historians have considered the presence of women in social and economic protest on its own terms, seeking to ground it in the role of women in the domestic economy and local community.[7] From this perspective, ritualised cross-dressing is a way to symbolically validate male trespassing on what was perceived to be female terrain.

A. W. Smith has suggested that this awareness of protest by women as 'the ultimate censure' is what underlay the adoption of feminine dress and signifiers by men in eighteenth- and nineteenth-century social protest, as has Kevin Binfield in his interpretation of the various cross-dressed 'Lady Ludds' and 'General Ludd's wives' in social protest contemporaneous with Luddism.[8] Historians who view cross-dressing as the acknowledgement of a feminine 'licence to protest' have also seen the use of feminine dress by male protesters as a comic exaggeration, of a type also present in other occasions of misrule, of what is perceived as an 'upside-down' state of the political or social order.[9] This idea has been explored in Natalie Zemon Davis's work on ritual cross-dressing and other inversion in early modern Europe, in studies covering both festival and social protest. Aspects of her work reinforce the above arguments that one function of cross-dressing was to acknowledge the status of women as appropriate agents in situations directed at the exposure and attempted correction of injustice, in view of their recognised jurisdiction over domestic affairs and the ways in which the female persona sanctioned resistance. The implications of this included the possibility of male protesters evading full responsibility for their actions, since it was perceived to be 'mere women who were acting in this disorderly way'; and conversely the ability of protesters to draw on 'the sexual power and energy of the unruly woman, and on her license (long assumed at carnival and games) . . . to defend the community interests and standards, and to tell the truth about unjust rule'.[10]

Davis also suggests that the cultural logic of men dressing as women in a theatrical and often comic way, which drew on and alluded to customary periods of festive misrule, allowed men to temporarily escape their place in an otherwise rigid hierarchy of gender and socio-economic status, enabling them to participate in 'disrespectful' activities including violent protest. Contemporary observations do indeed hint at a connection between the comic misrule which characterised such occasions and the type of protest which Rebecca exemplifies: Foster observed of the disturbances in summer 1843 that 'There is also mixed up with these outrages a degree of popularity and joke', and the *Carmarthen Journal* similarly noted that the procession to Carmarthen workhouse contained 'much of the ludicrous that was calculated to excite mirth'.[11] The *Quarterly Review* recalled that Rebeccaism was conducted with 'an air of the comic and ridiculous', which made the public 'at first inclined to wink at, if not to sympathise with, excesses carried on apparently in a spirit of frolic and good-humoured insubordination'.[12] The equation of ritual cross-dressing with images of the 'world turned upside down' reinforces the connection between this type of protest and other forms of community ritual and festival which made similar comic or transgressive use of costume and guising. This would, again, make the adoption of feminine garments a deliberate act, intended to express symbolically the way in which protesters viewed themselves and their circumstances, rather than a practical matter of disguise.

However, as we shall see, the signifiers of which Rebecca participants made use were not limited to the feminine and were rather a deliberate mix of feminine and masculine. It is also the case that women and girls were themselves present during much Rebeccaite activity, in supplementary roles which paralleled their participation in charivari and the *ceffyl pren*. During the march to Carmarthen in June 1843, as the *Carmarthen Journal* noted disapprovingly, 'several women were in Rebecca's train' and around two-thirds of street spectators were women and young girls. A clerk to the Board of Poor Law Guardians who witnessed the march's diversion into Carmarthen workhouse recalled seeing at least one farmer's daughter, aged 'three or four-and-twenty', riding behind her father in the march's mounted section.[13] During the workhouse riot itself Frances Evans, a servant girl, was observed urging the crowd onto the building's upper floor and subsequently dancing on the dining-hall table, for which she found herself on trial labelled 'a daughter of Rebecca'.[14] Women also turned out to witness the destruction of toll gates in Porthyrhyd and Pontyberem.[15] During the clash between Rebeccaites and bailiffs at Talog, witnesses reported that 'some women appeared to be encouraging the men', 'running hither and thither and giving the alarm'. The miller Lewis Griffiths, leaving court after giving evidence against the Rebeccaites Thomas and David Howells, found himself 'hissed and hooted' in the street by 'a crowd of women and girls'.[16] Courtrooms were regularly thronged with the mothers, wives, sisters, daughters, and partners of participants.[17]

It is therefore difficult to perceive the need for males symbolically to acknowledge through cross-dressing the jurisdiction of women in protests of this type, if women themselves were already present and not prevented from taking an active part beyond the physical labour involved in the demolition of toll gates. Accounts which seek to explain cross-dressing only through the adoption of feminine dress, then, are unconvincing because incomplete. A more nuanced understanding may be sought by viewing male cross-dressing in protest in the context of its use alongside other types of inversion by participants in community ritual and festival, all of which were deliberately performative and used to convey the impression of transgressed boundaries, supernatural leadership and dual or multiple identities.

Feminine and masculine in Rebeccaite protest

The use of clothing in general, and feminine dress in particular, formed an intrinsic part of Rebeccaism's operation and is perhaps the movement's primary distinguishing feature. The initial demolishing of the Efailwen toll gate in May 1839 was carried out by thirty or forty men, 'all disguised, some having their faces blackened and some being dressed in women's clothes'. The same was true of subsequent attacks at Efailwen in July 1839 and at St Clears in December 1842. At Llanfihangel-ar-arth in June 1843 'about 150 men appeared at the gate, all in female clothes'.[18] The various references to Carmarthen's 'leader in petticoats', and her 'petticoat heroes', are symptomatic of how the riots and rioters were presented in contemporary popular discourse and how they were subsequently remembered.[19] Cross-dressed protesters are portrayed on the cover and frontispiece of Jones's and Williams's major works on Rebecca, and the use of women's clothing forms a main staple of press and popular remembrance of events.[20] Images of cross-dressed male rioters recurred in contemporary prints, cartoons and engravings in the *Illustrated London News* and *Punch*, as well as in publications as far afield as Paris.[21]

Although contemporary observers noted the use of feminine dress and other methods of guising as an identifying characteristic of the movement, they did not tend to stress it as a peculiarity in itself. Rather, cross-dressing was embedded within broader descriptions of processions, riots or other activities, with no separate discussion to suggest it was a novelty, a puzzle or otherwise remarkable. This assumption that readers would have been familiar with the types of costume and symbols, including ritual cross-dressing, which characterised much contemporary protest aside from Rebeccaism, indicates that it was not regarded as a sufficiently unusual feature to merit specific comment. Fraser Easton, in his study of eighteenth-century female cross-dressing, argues that plebeian culture tended to view with approval female imitations of the sexed body of a man for occupational or military reasons, while a more censorious view was taken of women imitating men for specifically sexual purposes. He links this to the paternalist regulation of women's work and sexual identity.[22] This theory may further explain the relatively innocuous way in which male cross-dressing was assimilated into the experience of Rebeccaism, since the protesters' adoption of feminine apparel was considered to be undertaken with a political or practical rather than a sexualised aim in mind, as well as being an acknowledged reapplication of a trope already familiar from festival and carnival.

One result of such assumed familiarity is that comprehensive descriptions of Rebeccaite costume are difficult to come by from contemporary reports. However, although the apparel worn was not identical or uniform, some consistent elements do emerge. Symbols frequently worn or carried by participants included women's 'bed-gowns' and 'smock-frocks', invariably white and worn over work clothes, as well as elaborate hairpieces made of horsehair, and accessories including aprons, parasols, sashes, caps and bonnets.[23] Alcwyn C. Evans recorded the appearance of a crowd which dismantled Carmarthen's Water Street toll gate in May 1843:

> Rebecca and her sister were dressed in long, loose white gowns, with women's caps and turbans on, and faces blackened. Others were dressed in women's clothes. Some had large swords, and the greater part were armed with guns . . . several were mounted on horseback.

The *Hereford Times* in November 1843 stated that 'each man's face was blackened, and the host were clothed in every variety of the gentler sex's outer garments – cloaks, bonnets, caps, hats, gowns, aprons, shawls etc'.[24] During trials, feminine clothing and accessories identified as having been worn by participants, and afterwards discovered in the possession of suspected Rebeccaites, were produced as conclusive evidence of their involvement. In an example of this at the 1843 trial of John Hugh, John Hughes and David Jones for destroying the Pontarddulais toll gate, an arresting officer unfurled a veritable wardrobe of such supporting evidence, including: a woman's cap; 'what appeared to be a white dress'; a pocket handkerchief; a hat or cap covered with white canvas; a flannel sheet; part of a plaid cloak; three straw hats; a black hat; a flannel apron; a plain apron; and a coat with the sleeves turned inside-out.[25]

The dress of 'Rebecca' herself could be conspicuous and ornate, including such accoutrements as jewellery, fashionable bonnets, long horsehair ringlets, and even carriages and gowns.[26] June 1843's procession to Carmarthen featured a Rebecca 'ornamented ... with a profusion of curls, what is generally termed a ladies' front', while the following month Penyrallt toll gate was destroyed by a crowd of two hundred Rebeccaites whose leader 'was, on this occasion, dressed gaily in female attire and sported a parasol'. In Cardigan, the leader of a Rebeccaite attack was reported as 'a tall man, dressed in white, with a very large bonnet'.[27] These representative examples, which underline the elaborate and almost parodic nature of the articles chosen to signify femininity, highlight the performative and deliberate nature of Rebeccaite cross-dressing.

The performance of a feminine identity could stretch beyond the sartorial to include the use of 'female' voices and aliases. Reporting an attack on a Narberth toll gate, *The Times* named two of Rebecca's subordinate figures as 'officers whose *noms de guerre* are respectively "Nell" and "Susan"'. A witness to the preliminary procession towards a Rhydypandy toll gate testified: 'I heard the men calling out on the road, "Lucy", "Mary", "Nanny" and every name'. During the subsequent attack the Rebecca figure, addressed as 'Becca' or 'Mother', 'spoke in Welch, and imitated a woman's voice as near as he could'.[28] At Llanidloes and Rhyader, Rebeccaites engaged in dismantling toll gates were encouraged by Rebecca to 'work away, little wenches'.[29] Recounting the Glamorgan constabulary's defence of Pontarddulais toll gate, Charles Napier reported hearing 'a voice like that of a woman call out "come, come, come", and a voice like the mewing of cats'. Other observers likened the 'feigned voices' to 'a host of old market-women'.[30] These details suggest that participants placed a deliberate emphasis on the use of feminine signifiers which ran deeper than their external appearance, extending to the imitation of female voices, the use of female pseudonyms and the language of female camaraderie. It may further imply that participants adopted the role of 'wenches' or 'market-women' in order to play on recognisable social archetypes of femininity, as will be explored in Chapter 6.

This is, however, only the most seemingly straightforward part of a more complex picture. Close attention to contemporary descriptions suggests that, rather than consisting solely of feminine dress, Rebeccaite costume in fact contained a deliberate blend of masculine and feminine signifiers. The guise of Rebecca was especially salient as a means of invoking this dichotomy. In the majority of reported disturbances, 'Rebecca' appears as a symbolic centrepiece, usually on horseback or placed significantly at the head or rear of a procession. She takes no physical part in the destruction of toll gates, but rather presides over them and orchestrates their beginning and end by giving the word of command. In this emblematic position, Rebecca 'almost without exception [wore] a white shift, bonnet and false beard, and carried both a sword and a gun'.[31] The false beard appears as an indication of involvement in Rebeccaism, and as a specified part of Rebecca's 'uniform', throughout events in 1843 and 1844, but is rarely focused on in the movement's historiography. Williams makes no reference to the use of false beards. Molloy claims Rebeccaite dress was derived from the symbolic and ritual repertoire of the *ceffyl pren* without exploring the implications of this derivation, and refers to the rioters' use of feminine clothing without noting their emphatic mix of masculine and feminine.[32] Jones observes that the Rebecca figure, besides being consistently dressed in a white gown, elaborate bonnet and horsehair wig, also wore a false beard, but does not develop this point.

Press reports and trial records show the false beard to have been present at several notable moments in Rebecca's career, including the destruction of Prendergast toll gate in August 1843 and, two months later, the assault by a large crowd on two bailiffs attempting to execute a distraint warrant on Phillip Phillips at Pound Farm. On the latter occasion, the face of Rebecca's actor was exposed when the beard's adhesive unstuck as 'she' stood too close to an open fire, enabling him – William Harris, a blacksmith – to be identified in court.[33] Nicholl Carne, defending two men indicted for suspected involvement in rioting at Prendergast, made great play of the fact that 'Druids and Oddfellows' wore their beards equally as prominently as his clients were alleged to have done, but hoped the court would 'not think of charging [either group] with being rioters, because they wear beards . . .'[34] Such incidents clearly situate Rebecca as a vessel for the deliberate combining of symbols associated with both masculine and feminine: despite being visibly male, and often emphasising 'her' masculinity through the display of a false beard, sword, or gun, 'she' is otherwise clothed, addressed and speaks as female. The next section will seek to explain the significance of this dual identity.

Festival, carnival, ritual, and Rebeccaite protest as liminal space

Costumes and masks formed a customary part of European festivals and carnivals. Their use could signal the lifting of inhibition and acceptance of folly through the reversal or subversion of the natural order of things, thereby allowing their wearer to disguise their normal, everyday self and to evade personal responsibility for their actions.[35] In several cases of pre-industrial protest, these costumes and masks were repurposed, with similar intentions and effects. Rebeccaism's links with the custom of *ceffyl pren* illustrates one example of the process whereby the established symbolic and ritual repertoire of a locality could be appropriated for use in social protest. The overlap between some techniques present in pre-industrial and early industrial protest, and those of contemporary festival and community ritual, suggests that both categories can be interpreted in similar ways.[36] Barry Reay and Martin Ingram, in their studies of rough music, see ritual regulation of the community through charivari as a specialised application of festive or carnival motifs. Ingram also argues that, just as certain festive activity, such as the Rogation Tide custom of publicly processing to denote parish limits, marked important boundaries of time or space, so tropes of inversion were used during festival to invoke a multitude of boundaries by emphasising their crossing.[37] Alun Howkins and Linda Merricks present the persistence of similar ritual and symbolic elements as evidence of continuity within British popular protest from the early modern to the modern period. Following Ingram and E. P. Thompson, they see these components as having been incorporated from the local festive vocabulary. Significantly for the study of Rebeccaism, they also note that the symbols most visible in charivari are those of reversal and those associated with crossing or blurring boundaries in order to evoke the idea of liminal or transitional states.[38]

The 'liminal' state of being was identified by Victor Turner as one in which usual social expectations are suspended, deriving power from its resistance to classification and its 'interstructural' location outside the familiar bounds of society.[39] Turner's work on ritual also explores a liminal or transitional stage within rites of passage, in which the participant has left a prior state of being or consciousness without yet having entered the next.[40] Mary Douglas has further defined this transitional stage as a moment of social and psychological liminality, making it both dangerous and powerful.[41] Utilising these anthropological ideas, Natalie Zemon Davis suggests that themes of inversion, polarity, and transitional boundary-blurring – including cross-dressing – were used similarly during carnival, festival and collective violence, to express visibly a situation's removal from familiar social structures and to enable its participants to carry out actions which would be far less feasible when in their ordinary, everyday guises.[42] The use of feminine dress by male Rebecca protesters, then, was related to the customary use of cross-dressing to enable misrule and subversion during charivari, carnival and festival. In protest, the anonymity allowed by the use of masks and costume, and its symbolic presentation of a 'world turned upside down', enabled participants to cast off personal responsibility in favour of assuming a de-individuated collective identity for the duration of protest. The specific form taken by this collective identity, however, was defined by the attempt to bring together clashing or opposing signifiers in order to create a 'liminal space', which would allow protesters a wider range of possible actions by lifting the inhibitions imposed by their everyday identities.

Cultural studies of ritual cross-dressing emphasise that the process is about 'deliberately traversing meaningful boundaries'.[43] Several cultures contain spiritual, carnival or festival traditions in which an altered state of consciousness is assumed to be achieved by either individuals or collectives, induced by public or private performances involving dancing, costume and masking. These performances frequently include the use of double, opposite or composite signifiers such as horse/rider, man/animal, black/white, which 'exist to bring together, jarringly, the culture's traditional polarities'.[44] Thus, in various forms of folk drama, ritual, festival and carnival, cross-dressing was used to invoke the perceived dichotomy of male and female, as the equally prevalent use of animal masks, hides, or hobby horses invoked the contrast between human and animal or horse and rider. The majority of work on rituals in which such dichotomies are brought together agree that the purpose of doing so was, ultimately, to reinforce the stability of separate categories (man/animal, man/woman, man/child) and the relative place of each in a social hierarchy, clarifying the perception of such a structure through the process of reversing it. However, Natalie Zemon Davis's work on 'misrule' suggests that comic and festive inversion, of the type also present in Rebeccaite costume and ritual, could serve subversive as well as conservative purposes.[45]

The hobby horse and rider offers one example of a process in which performative signifiers were used firstly to invoke dichotomous identities and then merged into a single figure. The corresponding merging of masculine and feminine performative signifiers in a single figure has been used to indicate, in some historical contexts, the idea of an integrated, synthesised, gender-neutral figure, and, in others, the state of instability produced by the impossibility of reconciling masculine and feminine elements.[46] The symbolic transgression of boundaries inherent in this process, and the liminal state that it produced, invested such a figure with enhanced possibilities for action.[47] It is possible, then, that a comparable belief system informed the combination of masculine and feminine symbols in the figure of Rebecca and her followers. The function of this for Rebeccaite activity would have been to make visible the liminal state in which it took place, and which enabled participants to carry out extraordinary acts of lawlessness and destruction while abstracted from their everyday, 'respectable' selves. From this perspective, Rebeccaite costume had less to do with one gender adopting the clothing of the other, and more with the attempt to convey an altered state of being. By presenting a transitional identity which symbolically blurred the boundaries between dichotomous genders, individuals could become invested with the heightened power and abilities customarily accruing to such liminal spaces and figures.

Other boundaries and binaries in Rebeccaite activity

Participants in Rebecca appear to have stressed the fusion of opposites in terms other than gender. False beards may have been intended as a signifier of age and virility, as argued by Will Fisher in his study of the beard – both real and false – in Renaissance culture.[48] In this respect, they could have been set against the signifier of youth inherent in a participant young enough to have no beard of his own. Anthony Synnot identifies facial hair as a symbol of 'double opposition' for men, distancing them in appearance from both women and children.[49] The women's frocks and 'bed-gowns' used by rioters were not worn alone, but 'thrown over' masculine work clothes including 'fustian trousers' and work boots.[50] Rioters at Bwlch-clwyd in August 1843 wore 'long white gowns, girded about with sword-belts' and accessorised with 'large straw hats'.[51] The bed-gowns – usually nightdresses borrowed from the wives or mothers of participants – were already symbols of inversion by virtue of their inappropriateness for outdoor activity, and they may also have allowed male protesters to emphasise their own integral masculine qualities through contrast with the feminine fragility and vulnerability implied by their wearing of night attire. A costume was thereby created which combined domestic and private dress with outdoor and public pursuits, as well as combining overtly feminine with overtly masculine garb.

Also significant is the rioters' choice of white for the most visible part of their outfit, in the form of gowns or white shirts, which contrasted with their invariably darkly veiled or blackened faces.[52] This too was a motif common to English and Welsh social protest, appearing as early as 1450 when the Duke of Buckingham's deer park was raided by a troop of men in blackened faces and white gowns, claiming to be under the leadership of the Queen of the Fairies.[53] The parasols, bonnets and ringlets worn or carried by protesters, although their primary meaning may have been a further display of clashing sexual symbols, may also suggest an attempt at class appropriation or mockery through the imitation of women of a higher status than that of the participants. Stage and print satire at the time of Rebecca portrayed fashionable 'dandizettes' wearing extravagant headgear, wigs and parasols, while cartoons and broadsides frequently mocked the fashion among upper-class women for powdered and frizzled hair.[54] Elaborate wigs and bonnets in particular may have been intended to convey class status, since long hair on women was regarded as a symbol of wealth and leisure because of its impracticality and expensive upkeep.[55] The author of an 1854 pro-Disestablishment pamphlet attacked the preference for bonnets over caps as a symbol of those who 'awkwardly aped' their churchgoing social superiors.[56]

Behaviour during protest was also informed by the clashing of signifiers, with attacks often prefaced by the exaggerated performance of frail elderly or maternal qualities by the Rebecca figure. A typical incident was the precursor to the destruction of a gate at

Pwll-Trap in April 1843, involving dialogue between Rebecca and her daughters suggestive of both ritual and pantomime:

> The old lady, leaning on her staff, was greatly surprised that her progress along the road seemed to be interrupted. 'Children,' said she, 'there is something put up here; I can't go on'.
> 'What is it, mother? Nothing shall stop your way'.
> 'I do not know, children. I am old, and cannot see very well'.
> 'Shall we come on, mother, and remove it from your way?'
> 'Stay a minute. Let me examine it (feeling the gate with her staff) it seems like a great gate put across the road, to stay your old mother's progress'.
> 'We will break it, mother! So nothing will hinder you on your journey'.
> 'No, let me see. Perhaps it will open – no, children, it is bolted and locked, and I cannot go on. What is to be done?'
> 'It must be taken down, mother, because you and your children MUST pass'.
> 'Off with it, then, my dear children. It has no business here'.[57]

The emphasis on Rebecca as matriarch – as 'mother of hundreds' – may have been a function of her ability to represent qualities at that time chiefly associated with opposing genders: the beard and sword associated with men, procreation with women.[58] This choice of symbols fits logically into the theme of high contrasts in Rebeccaite costume. The use of opposing masculine and feminine signifiers in a single figure was part of the attempt to present a dual or amalgamated identity involving conflicting or synthesised opposites – a more sophisticated operation than men straightforwardly 'dressing as women'. The performance of stylised elderly and matriarchal virtues also heightens the contrast with the actual qualities of the 'actor' who would have assumed such attributes. In combination with the display of masculine and feminine signifiers, this suggests a deliberate clash of performative signs through which to emphasise the blurring and transgression of a set of boundaries wider than those relating to gender. It is this mixture of signifiers – at once invoking the existence of a sexual dichotomy with clearly defined boundaries *and* visibly implying the transgression of these boundaries – that is more significant than the use of feminine dress in itself. To view Rebeccaite costume purely as the adoption of feminine dress is to overlook the subtlety and range of Rebecca's symbolic repertoire.

Abstract and practical gendered views of Rebecca

This section considers how the blend of signifiers used in Rebeccaite costume can contribute to debate on the historical perception of gender. Anthony Fletcher's history of the construction of gender in English culture claims that:

> the period between 1660 and 1800 saw the fruition of an ideological construction of gender which, breaking with the simple didacticism of preceding years, built upon its sure foundations in the concepts of 'manhood' and the 'weaker vessel' to create masculinity and femininity in something like a modern sense . . . eighteenth-century ideologists [were] intent upon fixing men and women in a framework of polarity.[59]

Other analyses of the construction of gender, such as those by Marjorie Garber and Will Fisher, rest on the conception of sexual signifiers as non-essential, unfixed and in need of continual reinforcement.[60] The signifiers used in Rebecca – false beards, wigs, 'feminine' voices, swords and parasols – are significant in that they are detachable and that they represent masculinity and femininity through secondary sexual characteristics. Their detachable nature illustrates Fisher's theory that historically gender 'was materialised through an array of features and prosthetic parts [including] the beard . . . clothing, the hair, the tongue, and weapons such as swords or daggers'.[61] The symbolic expression of masculinity and femininity through secondary characteristics, the hair and beard in particular, implies a conception of gender as marked by external characteristics as well as by genital difference.[62] However, Fisher's related argument, that the false beard's detachable and malleable nature suggests that the masculinity which it confers is equally prosthetic, is not borne out by the use of signifiers in Rebeccaism.

The deliberate clashing by protesters of masculine and feminine signifiers, in order to present an unstable and liminal dual identity, may initially suggest a view of the body as a neutral canvas which the use of sexual signifiers could tip one of two ways, and a corresponding view of gender as inherently fluid and apt to dissolve under a change of clothing. However, the ways in which cross-dressed male rioters were perceived by contemporary observers implies that they were considered to retain an inherent and essential identity which their adoption of feminine signifiers in protest did little or nothing to compromise. A disjuncture exists between references to Rebecca as an abstract concept, a leadership figure representing the movement as a whole, in which 'she' is characterised as unequivocally female, and references to the individual men who temporarily adopted her role for the duration of a particular protest. Contemporary reports consistently use feminine pronouns in reference to both 'Miss Rebecca' and 'her daughters', despite describing them in the same reports as groups of men.[63] This disparity is reinforced by the attitude of participants themselves towards the character of Rebecca and to the men chosen to perform it.

Press reports or editorials on the movement are notable for their use of feminine epithets to describe participants in action. Rhetorical references abound to 'this renowned lady', 'this notorious lady', 'that rustic queen', 'Miss Rebecca', 'Sister Rebecca', 'her Ladyship' and 'her fair daughters'.[64] The *Welshman* sardonically concluded its report on the destruction of a Lampeter toll gate by reflecting that 'this wonderful lady has distinguished herself so much of late'.[65] The *Swansea Journal* retained the feminine pronoun throughout its description of the return of an illegitimate child to its father, a freeholder living near Newcastle Emlyn, by Rebecca in her 'black footman' incarnation and an accompanying crowd of 'daughters':

> She entered the house and introduced herself to the farmer, by the name of Rebecca [and extracted his promise to bring up the child 'under her sharp eye']. Rebecca then expressed herself satisfied, shook hands with the farmer, stepped back into her carriage and rapidly drove off.[66]

The same reports and editorials which employ this conceit, however, contain no suggestion that the writers believed participants in fact to be female. Reports of Rebeccaite crowds as 'a large mob of men' or 'a large assemblage of men and boys' are supplemented by more detailed observations that 'the majority of them were young men, although there were several men aged about sixty'.[67] A witness at the trial of four Rebeccaites for rioting at a Bolgoed toll gate identified 'both old and young men present', while the Glamorgan constabulary's chief, Charles Napier, reported that the 'number of men' with whom he clashed at Pontarddulais in August 1843 'appeared to be dressed as women'.[68] The separate use of masculine and feminine pronouns in the same article, letter or report indicates the distinction made by external observers between protesters' everyday identities and those which they performed in protest.

The attitudes expressed by male participants themselves towards Rebecca suggests that they too viewed her as a character who could be temporarily 'acted' or 'personated' without compromising their underlying identity. Associates and neighbours of Daniel Lewis were informed that he was 'to act Rebecca's character' during the destruction of Bolgoed toll gate.[69] Several accounts by participants or observers refer to Rebecca in the third person as an abstract figure, even in cases where her actor is identified by name or personally known to the witness. Occasionally this involves a shifting of primary responsibility for actions onto 'Rebecca', allowing the individual participant to distance themselves or deny their own complicity: the Rebeccaite Thomas Howells, directly after his participation in the destruction of the tollhouse inhabited by William Rees, commented sheepishly to the now homeless Rees that 'Becca has done bad work to pull the house down ... you had better have a damper of ale'.[70] The presentation of Rebecca as a character separate from her actor implies that the costume necessary for her portrayal was no more than that, and that the assumption of feminine guise was not considered to have lasting effects on a fixed male identity. The reliance of Rebeccaites on detachable signifiers, and the ease and alacrity with which they could discard them, is vividly demonstrated by the evasive action taken by Michael Bowen, who was caught 'in character' as Rebecca during the military's expulsion of protesters from Carmarthen workhouse:

> A person who personated Rebecca, and was ornamented with a profusion of curls about his face, entered the workhouse, but when the dragoons advanced he clapped his curls in his hat, jumped over the wall [and made off across the surrounding fields].[71]

These distinctions between the everyday identity of protesters and their chosen identity for the length of their participation in protest indicates that the use of feminine dress and accessories, if visibly constructed as an alternative persona with a specific purpose, need not undermine an individual's male identity. In fact, the men chosen to play Rebecca were usually notable for their 'masculine' qualities of imposing physical stature, height and strength. The first recorded Rebecca, Thomas Rees of Mynachlog-ddu, was an agricultural labourer renowned in his parish as a pugilist and prizefighter. In early 1843 the *Welshman* reported that Rebeccaites at St Clears were 'headed by a very tall man', and Thomas Cooke reported an attack on a toll gate headed by 'a tall stout man' who, despite riding side-saddle 'like a woman', 'looked well on horseback'.[72] Michael Bowen, who played Rebecca's role in the procession to Carmarthen, was a notably handsome 'fine tall man' of twenty-four.[73] The Rebecca who appeared at Llandeilo-yr-Ynys gate was described as 'at least six feet high', while John Hughes (Jac Ty Isha), 'a hale, powerful and good-looking farmer', took the part of Rebecca in the destruction of Pontarddulais toll gate.[74] These physical qualities, considered overtly masculine, would have been emphasised in protest through incongruous contrast with 'feminine' dress and accessories, enhancing the impression of unstable polarity while at the same time underscoring the fundamental 'masculine' identity of Rebecca's actor.

Rebecca as a masculine role model

Rebecca's presence in the public imagination could expand or alter available discourse in sometimes surprising ways. In an instance of this in 1846, evidence given at the divorce trial of the ninth Earl Ferrers made mention of his habitually dressing up 'after the fashion of the tollgate breakers'. According to the witness statement of a friend, after dinner the Earl 'used to put a night-cap over his whiskers, and tie his pocket handkerchief over his hat, and then he used to go out at night'.[75] This suggestion that Rebecca's image may have become embedded in public consciousness as a synonym or shorthand for more escapist, playful or transgressive forms of cross-dressing was foreshadowed in 1843 at the trial of John Archer of Ludlow, who was reprimanded and discharged for having worn women's apparel during Sunday evening service at his local church, before 'taking the arm of a young gentleman for a walk through the streets'. Although the court records contain no suggestion that he intended specifically to impersonate Rebecca, the *Hereford Times*'s account of Archer's trial consistently referred to him as 'Miss Rebecca' and by use of the feminine pronoun. In court Archer caused amusement by producing his hairpiece, cap and bonnet and donning them 'for their worships to see what a sweet pretty bewitching damsel she was'.[76]

Whatever Archer's reasons for dressing up, what becomes apparent in his trial is the degree of performativity involved in adopting the guise of Rebecca. Signifiers like the 'ladies' front', cap and bonnet could be easily and visibly detached in order to assume a particular role before a knowing audience or to divest oneself of it. In the process, the signifiers used to assume the identity of Rebecca could be acknowledged as artificial and observers could become complicit in an individual male's performance. Alcwyn C. Evans's recollection of his involvement as a fifteen-year-old in the march to Carmarthen, in which the role of Rebecca was taken by his acquaintance Michael Bowen, displays acute awareness of the distinction between actor and role. His admiring description of Bowen prior to the march setting off is written with all feminine pronouns underlined, as if ironically to emphasise the artificial nature of Bowen's femininity and Evans' collusion in its performance:

> I was anxious to have a peep at 'Rebecca' for the occasion, and soon found <u>her</u> a stalwart young person, adorned with a horsetail beard, and horse-mane wig, and whose bright brown eyes laughed as it were with mischief and fun, one of which winked at me as I stood gazing. I winked back in return, for I recognised <u>her</u> name as Mike Bowen.[77]

In the subsequent procession, no participant other than Bowen appears to have been in costume; the *Carmarthen Journal* identi-fied 'a man in disguise to represent Rebecca', walking behind a man bearing a placard and followed in turn by the mounted part of the march. Bowen's role, therefore, was explicitly representative and symbolic. This acknowledgement of Bowen as an actor play-ing an abstract role is similar to the recognition of Daniel Lewis's friends and neighbours, noted above, that he was 'to act Rebecca's character'. Such a perspective would have allowed Rebecca's male actors to adopt her guise without experiencing anxiety over their own gendered identity.

The most effective way of retaining a 'masculine' identity while engaged in protest may have been to make the adoption of 'feminine' signifiers explicitly performative, by making the signifiers adopted as exaggerated and artificial as possible. The frequency and emphasis with which Rebecca's actors donned wigs, bonnets and hairpieces suggests that these were intrinsic in the expression of a dramatic – and therefore inauthentic – persona. By the time of Rebecca, theatrical comedy and print satire had established the wig as the epitome of extravagant artifice.[78] Amelia Rauser argues that the artificiality associated with the wearing of elaborate and oversized wigs made them an obvious 'icon of inauthenticity' which could be embraced as a performative or parodic form of self-expression.[79] The use of 'feminine' signifiers indicative of exaggeration and artifice ties in with the choice of emphatically physically 'masculine' men to adopt these signifiers as Rebecca. The need to make their performance explicit may have led to the mocking or ironic adoption of 'feminine' styles of speaking, address or comportment, in a way similar to that described in Peter Bailey's analysis of the 'knowingness' involved in Victorian music-hall.[80] Several of Rebecca's appearances involved the presentation of a parodic persona made familiar through cultural archetypes, whether that of Lady Bountiful attended by her black footman, spirited matriarch or 'old market-woman'. The need to appear exaggeratedly, artificially female in dress, voice and behaviour brought the comic and theatrical elements of Rebecca's image to the fore. Acknowledging the high level of performativity and knowingness involved in acting the part of Rebecca enabled participants to adopt stylised 'feminine' signifiers without compromising their 'masculine' identity. However, this lack of compromise depended on maintaining an 'unreal' appearance through stressing the artificial or parodic in their performance.

Despite its frequently comic nature, the assumption of Rebecca's guise could be empowering and strengthening, conferring greater social standing upon her actor. Daniel Lewis, the young weaver who took the part of Rebecca at the destruction of Bolgoed toll gate in July 1843, let his upcoming adventure be known in advance to his fiancée, family and 'all the neighbourhood' as a matter of pride – with community gossip consequently making it general knowledge 'a week or fortnight before' the attack actually took place.[81] Rebecca's growth into an aspirational figure is perhaps unsurprising, given the grudging admiration detectable in much contemporary press and the leadership status bestowed upon her actor during protest. The idea that playing Rebecca was an enviable privilege which carried kudos and status is further suggested by an incident prior to the attack on a Prendergast toll gate in September 1843. There John Davies, having been asked by his party's original Rebecca to remain in charge while 'she' went ahead alone to scout for any military presence, chose to usurp the leadership role by donning Rebecca's abandoned bonnet and gun, and led his fellow daughters on to attack the toll gate himself.[82]

Rebecca's impact on the contemporary imagination received colourful expression in the several instances of 'spoof Rebeccas' perpetrated by young men in south-west Wales in the summer of 1843, caught up in what the *Swansea Journal* termed 'Rebecca mania' and David Williams dubbed 'Midsummer Madness'. These incidents, seemingly in keeping with the high-spirited 'air of the comic and ridiculous . . . frolic and good-humoured insubordination' which defined Rebeccaite activity proper, both demonstrate the depth to which awareness of Rebecca's characteristic image and conduct was now ingrained in public consciousness, and highlight which signifiers were thought to render an individual instantly recognisable as Rebecca. They also lend further weight to the concept of Rebecca as a model of aspirational masculinity. The escapade of William Williams, a mason living in Swansea, is typical: the town's mayor relates that around 9 p.m. he saw a crowd of people approaching the centre of Swansea from surrounding fields:

> He perceived a man lifted upon other men's shoulders, having his apron tied over a straw hat, so as to resemble a bonnet and veil, when, as the crowd drew near him, the man with the straw hat and veil called out 'Rebecca for ever' and began shouting.

Subsequently arrested and charged with exciting a tumult, Williams expressed regret and explained his behaviour as 'a hayfield lark'. His judge dismissed the case after disapprovingly deeming it 'a very foolish "lark"'.[83] Other instances of individual men autonomously impersonating Rebecca, without doing so for political ends or petty criminality, were more often than not occasioned by drink. William Davis, a farmer at Pantyfen, arrived at the Pen-y-garn toll gate too drunk to remain upright on his cart, and threatened the gatekeeper with physical violence before leaving with the parting shot of 'I am Becca; if anyone asks you who is Becca, say I am Becca'.[84] A similar mixture of belligerence and self-aggrandisement in performance was displayed by Shoni Sguborfawr, on his first recorded appearance in Rebecca's country at New Inn, Pontyberem in September 1843. Witnesses describe him being heavily drunk in the street, dressed in a white gown, tartan cloak and straw bonnet, firing a gun indiscriminately through windows and shouting: 'By god, I am Rebecca, and I will have justice done'.[85]

These occurrences, vividly depicting how widespread awareness of the movement had become, and the growing sense of panic over Rebecca's potency and reach, also demonstrate that the identification of the figure of Rebecca was reliant on symbols and signifiers, the most important part of which was the use of feminine apparel. The frequent focus on isolated signifiers of femininity – hair and headgear – by those impersonating or considered to be impersonating Rebecca illustrates how Rebecca's image in public discourse was becoming increasingly stylised through familiarity, until she could be represented by a single facet or isolated pieces of her costume. These incidents suggest too that the leadership, daring and virility associated with the figure of Rebecca, both by her supporters and in general consciousness, made the adoption of her identity a desirable act for individual men. As such, it involved no compromising of their own identity, but rather strengthened it – both through heavily stylised contrast with its opposite, and through the heroic and empowered associations which Rebecca's image was amassing in the popular imagination.

'Six hundred children and more every day': The New Poor Law and Female Sexual Agency

The contexts in which women could appear in eighteenth- and early nineteenth-century politics drew on traditional associations of the female body with allegorical representation.[1] They also, as James Epstein notes, drew on the emerging perception of women as predominantly associated with the domestic sphere, which could, in some cases, equip them with the ability to present a radical political agenda within an otherwise conservative discourse of family welfare or paternalist responsibility.[2] The ways in which Rebecca was presented as an abstract figure in press and popular imagery will be more fully explored in the following chapter, but an examination of the social and cultural feminine archetypes which were also available to participants in Rebeccaism will illuminate the factors which informed their choice of her as a symbolic leader. The images of women present in contemporary society and culture both influenced the presentation of Rebecca and helped to ground 'her' as a figurehead with popular appeal. In the specific variant of Rebeccaite activity known as the 'black footman', the actions of protesters may be read as a response to the clash between older forms of community regulation of sexuality and marriage and newer attempts, generated by the New Poor Law, to more stringently police the sexual agency of women.

Female archetypes in contemporary society and culture

In south-west Wales at the time of Rebecca, several factors existed which may have helped to construct highly visible and powerful female archetypes. Society in the region was predominantly female: across Wales as a whole, the numerical superiority of women over men persisted everywhere apart from the industrialised south-east, to which large numbers of young single men migrated in search of employment.[3] Men in rural areas proved more vulnerable than women to debilitative injury and lower life expectancy, due to their higher level of participation in outdoor work and greater susceptibility to childhood illness. The male:female ratio across the three south-western counties was 47:53, and almost half of all women over twenty were either single or widowed.[4] Conditions in rural areas were often conducive to female independence, with widowed or unmarried women commonly living in their own small cottages and renting or owning small plots of land. The characteristic female employment was domestic service, followed by weaving and dressmaking, with smaller numbers of women engaged in brewing, laundering, handicrafts or the sale of eggs and milk.[5] The predominance of agriculture in south-west Wales offered employment outside the home to a greater proportion of women than was the case in urban areas, giving many women a high profile in their community as producers, buyers and sellers. A nineteenth-century sketch of typical travellers in rural Wales included 'Aunty Betty Fowl Feathers' among caricatures of 'pretty regular, and very independent market goers'.[6]

In addition to their economic roles, women were active and visible in social and political life. They took part in the *ceffyl pren* and similar instances of community discipline, and were present at fairs and festivals.[7] An 1850s writer on the history of Carmarthen, praising the area's history of lawful protest, recalled an occasion when a minister 'erred' in local factional politics by voting with the 'Reds' against the 'Blues', whereupon 'the noble and spirited women of Carmarthen the following Sabbath bravely went to his chapel with blue ribbands in their caps to shew that they were more firm than ever'.[8] The Welsh system of trial marriage, besides alleviating any social stigma attached to divorce, allowed women to retain their property and maiden name while 'cohabiting'. Property rights favourable to Welsh women extended to official marriage, with wives able to 'keep their property separately from that of their husbands, from generation to generation'.[9] Welsh women were able to keep their maiden names throughout married life even in the late nineteenth century, and children normally took their mother's surname.[10] It is worth considering whether these examples of female social and economic prestige contributed to the creation of matriarchal cultural archetypes which influenced the portrayal of Rebecca, as well as contributing to a tradition of female agency and autonomy which soon found itself up against the legislative strictures of the New Poor Law.

The 'riding wedding' customs outlined in Chapter 4 included female participants on an equal footing with the men in their party, as a contemporary observer recorded:

> The appearance of such a number of men and women, all smartly-dressed, and galloping about in every direction, gave the whole scene a most singular appearance, especially as the women were such bold and expert riders, kept up, and mingled with the foremost of the party, and entered into the spirit of the tumultuous procession in a most animated manner.[11]

Familiarity with women as horse-riders in early nineteenth-century culture seems significant in view of the frequency with which the figure of Rebecca appeared on horseback, both in protest and in popular representations of it. A pseudonymous poem of 1843 depicts her 'athwart her prancing milkwhite steed'.[12] While Jones compares Rebecca's recurrent appearance on 'a splendid white horse' to that of 'the Holy One in Revelation, or a latter-day Captain Swing', similar images were commonly used in popular ballads and poems to signify female agency and heroism.[13] The horse was a symbol of the goddess Rhiannon, whose legend in the *Mabinogion* describes her appearing to her future husband on a white steed on which she outpaces his fastest horsemen.[14] The broadside ballad 'Lord Thomas and Fair Eleanor' presents its titular heroine riding off to interrupt her lover's wedding to another, cutting a commanding and imperious figure at the head of a crowd of followers which is reminiscent of reports of Rebecca's appearances:

> [Eleanor] clothed herself in gallant attire
> And her merry men all in green,
> And as she rode through every place
> They took her to be some Queen[15]

A comparable insouciance and untouchability is conveyed by Levi Gibbon, a contemporary Carmarthenshire balladeer to whom is attributed one of the surprisingly few ballads written on Rebecca:

With no fear of soldier, nor lawyer, nor law,
Proud Beca rides on, her white horse at the fore.[16]

The idea of Rebecca as proficient on horseback, with its connotations of authority, status or romance, formed an integral part of her representation. The *Quarterly Review* envisioned 'the mounted Rebecca heading the charge of her sylvan cavalry' while 'T.L.' in the *Welshman* imagined her as an 'amazonian' heroine:

Her heels well spurred – her brows adorned
With graceless curls, and ringlets brown,
And in this state she gallops night by night
O'er Wallia's mountains and through Wallia's vales[17]

As her renown as an abstract figure increased, Rebecca's daring, leadership status and imperviousness to the law may have suggested a connection with images of female authority and independence made familiar through popular literature, ballads and theatre. Female characters who appeared in Welsh theatre throughout the early nineteenth century ranged from Shakespearean heroines to the stock figures of pantomime, comic opera and Jacobean tragedy.[18] Although generally cast as wives and daughters, the adjuncts of patriarchs, there was also scope for female agency. *The Miller of Mansfield*, a play performed in 1790 at the private theatre of Sir Watkin Williams-Wynn in Wrexham, has the protagonist's daughter insulting her lover before fighting him with shears.[19] The insolent and vituperative nature of Welsh women was proverbial, and may have influenced playful portrayals of Rebecca as 'a Scold' who is 'always inclined To tell her own mind, / But can not bear being *Toll'd*'.[20] Eighteenth and nineteenth-century Welsh as well as English ballads contain many images of active, powerful and independent women, who are portrayed challenging men to duels, cross-dressing as soldiers or sailors, remonstrating with husbands over their vices, engaged in extravagant spending, or drinking copious amounts of tea or liquor.[21]

The existence of visible and recognised female power and agency in the spheres of community life, local politics and popular culture would inevitably have played a part in shaping the image of Rebecca as a female leadership figure. This connection between social and cultural female archetypes and the stylised and symbolic images of femininity constructed in protest illustrates the ways in which Rebeccaism was interwoven with aspects of contemporary society. By referencing or alluding to such aspects, Rebeccaites were able to establish their chosen symbol – 'Rebecca' – as a representative of the society and culture from which they sought support. A further example of their appeal to popular authority was the upholding of notions of justice and fairness on behalf of unmarried mothers against the constitutionally enforced New Poor Law. The following section considers contemporary attitudes to sexuality, marriage and courtship, how legislative changes – namely the New Poor Law of 1834 and its bastardy clauses – affected these circumstances over the course of the early nineteenth century, and how they related to a specific form of Rebeccaite activity referred to as the 'black footman'.

Poor Law reform and shifting sexual culture

The Poor Law Amendment Act of 1834 sharply reformed the existing system of poor relief in England and Wales, introducing a more restrictive system of application and creating a centralised bureaucracy to administer it. Whereas the previous system of relief had relied on local administration, on the basis that parish officials were best placed to assess the circumstances of their local applicants, the new system not only took these decisions out of local hands but also, by introducing a uniform system of relief, challenged the idea that support should be provided according to the particular needs of an individual.[22] For many who opposed these changes, the New Poor Law exemplified a shift in rural relations over the early nineteenth century. This shift involved the removal or withdrawal of local authorities from their pre-industrial social responsibilities, and the restriction of common rights through processes which included the enclosure of common land, laws against poaching and gleaning, and, finally, the tightening of access to poor relief. We have seen how participants in the Rebecca riots intervened to oppose these removals and restrictions in the public arena of toll gates and enclosures. They also opposed the private individual effects of the New Poor Law, most visibly through insisting upon the right of unmarried mothers to public support. In doing so, they referenced and attempted to uphold established customs based on a more permissive view of female agency and independence, against the proscriptive view of female sexuality, and attempts to police it through centralised regulation, which the New Poor Law enshrined.

The reforms of the New Poor Law, besides reducing the amount spent on poor relief by the property-owning classes, were also designed to act as an instrument of social discipline. They were introduced in the context of attempts by an increasingly centralised state to regulate the behaviour of poor women and the functioning of the patriarchal family. Political and ecclesiastical authorities in early modern Europe had expressed increasingly proscriptive concern with the behaviour of both men and women, including the outlawing of leisure activities, like dancing and fair-going, which presented alternatives to church worship. Many campaigns for moral reform, however, focused particularly on the young female poor, with their supposed promiscuity and sexual laxity becoming the subject of laws against 'vice'. Legislation against bastardy and infanticide passed in 1576, 1610 and 1624 was openly class- and gender-specific, indicating concern over uncontrolled female sexuality among the poor, and establishing this social group as a threat to society's values and interests, and therefore the target of public regulation.[23]

As we have seen was the case in Rebecca's country, many women retained opportunities for involvement and agency in areas of the local community and economy, which qualifies to some extent the argument that the introduction of industrial capitalism and a wage economy saw women increasingly marginalised and confined.[24] Despite this, as the nineteenth century progressed, female morality and behaviour was increasingly stringently policed in politics and society. As industrialisation and urbanisation spread, wealthy women withdrew from productive labour, while poor women increasingly filled lower-waged roles in the workforce in contrast to their previous roles as independent producers in an agricultural economy.[25] Married women lost legal rights over their dowries and possessions, and were becoming less directly involved in local and national politics as men were defined as public agents and representatives, with women as supporters and dependants. Within political and cultural discourse, the relation of wife to husband, and of children to father, was used to express the general relation of subordinates to their superiors. In the writing of

Locke, for instance, the wife's relinquishing her right of decision to her husband was philosophically analogous to the individual's relinquishing his natural liberties of decision and action to the legislative branch of government. Contemporary proscriptive literature was concerned with women's 'supposed sexual voraciousness, pride, shrewishness and tendency to scold', with remedies for female unruliness centring on religious training to impart modesty and humility, education on the moral duty of women, and legal changes that made women subject to their husbands.[26]

Anna Clark, Ellen Ross and Rayna Rapp count the bastardy clauses of the New Poor Law among several factors which influenced a shift in popular sexual culture in early nineteenth-century Europe, in which an earlier tradition of sexually assertive femininity, as traced in ballads and folktales, gave way by the 1860s to a more cautious and prudish image of womanhood. This shift was inextricably linked to the changing legal and political environment – whether the altered system of poor relief in Britain, or the French Civil Code of 1804 which forbade searching for the putative fathers of illegitimate children and made unmarried women solely responsible for their support.[27] U. R. Q. Henriques claims further that changes to bastardy laws were part of an anxiety induced by Malthus's *Essay on the Principle of Population* over the growth of an impoverished population, and formed part of efforts to restrict it by discouraging large numbers of illegitimate births and improvident marriages. The reforms were an uneasy blend of attempts at state regulation of family development and at enforcing female virtue and self-control, and the economic burden of these political exertions fell primarily upon women.[28]

Under the system of poor relief which the New Poor Law replaced, any man named by a woman as the father of her child had either to marry her, or to contribute financially to the child's upkeep. If he refused or reneged, local parish officials intervened and could impose a prison sentence. According to the Poor Law Commissioners' Report of 1834, such a system provided unscrupulous or scheming women with the temptation to indict not the real father of their child, but the wealthiest man upon whom the charge could be plausibly pinned. The report claimed further that the existing system undermined modesty and self-reliance, since the mother 'lost all sense of shame, and soon looked on the parish payments as a right'. Since mothers of illegitimate children were frequently allotted higher payments than widows with children born within wedlock, the report argued that such allowances encouraged sex outside marriage. The commissioners regarded the availability of maintenance payments as discouraging women from exerting self-control over their sexual behaviour.[29] As a remedy for these social ills, the commission proposed that all responsibility for the maintenance of an illegitimate child should be placed on the mother or her parents if single, and upon her husband if she married. If destitute, she was expected to appeal to the parish – which increasingly meant her committal to one of the proliferating number of workhouses, in which conditions were frequently designed to be so harsh as to discourage applicants from seeking relief there.

The alterations to the bastardy clauses, and the resultant committal of women and children to workhouses or else to destitution, were among the most criticised in the whole of the Poor Law Amendment Act.[30] Part of the new system's unpopularity lay in the change it required in both attitude and practice from the existing sanction for female sexual agency, including sex outside marriage and the rights of unmarried mothers to support and protection from stigma. We have seen in the previous section that women in Rebecca's country could possess a significant amount of agency, authority and independence, even after they married. Like many areas of late eighteenth- and early nineteenth-century Britain, the region also had a high tolerance of clandestine and common-law marriage as opposed to official state-licensed ceremonies.[31] The particular situation in south-west Wales was outlined in the 1847 report by the Commission of Inquiry into the State of Education in Wales – the infamous 'Blue Books' – which provoked a significant debate on views of Welsh society.[32] A large part of the hostility with which the report was received within Wales stemmed from its condemnation of the 'immorality' which the commissioners saw in Welsh attitudes to courtship and marriage, especially in rural areas. Factors contributing to this impression included the tendency of couples to marry only in their late twenties, and the fact that a 'sizeable part of the Welsh labouring classes' favoured secular unions or trial marriages which did not conform to the full requirements of Church and law.[33] Observations by John Evans in 1803 established these 'little weddings' – private, unofficial and less effectually binding than official ceremonies – as part of the popular culture of rural Wales. Reasons for the popularity of trial marriage included its cheapness, its facilitation of quick and convenient ceremonies and its enabling of couples to circumvent external objections.[34]

The forms of trial marriage sanctioned in rural Wales included the custom of 'bundling', or courtship in bed. Community understanding and licensing of the practice was described in statements to Commissioners and accounts such as that of a Cardiganshire doctor who was accustomed to people courting 'on the beds . . in the sight and with the approbation of their mutual friends and relations'.[35] This collectively regulated courting among the youth of the community was referenced during the trial of a man accused of pulling down a *tŷ unnos*, who produced as alibi a female witness who swore he had been 'courting her all night as is the custom of the country'.[36] 'Besom marriages' were another common form of trial marriage, accomplished by the couple jumping over a broomstick placed across the threshold of their house. The performance of this ceremony often required neighbours as witnesses, with a community elder also present – components which, again, reflect the authority accruing to community involvement in the conduct of individuals.[37] If the trial proved mutually agreeable it was often followed by an official ceremony; if not, it could be made void within its first twelve months by the couple jumping back over the broomstick from the house into the open. Both husband and wife were then free to remarry, with the female subsequently 'not worse looked upon . . . than if she had been an unspotted virgin'.[38] A natural result of the prevalence of trial marriages and courtship, and the lack of social censure or financial penalisation for sexual engagement by women, was the high levels of illegitimate births and subsequent infanticide or child desertion experienced in southwest Wales which the 1847 Commission strongly criticised, but which the New Poor Law had done little to reduce and in some cases may have exacerbated.[39]

Whereas existing marriage and courtship patterns had condoned premarital pregnancy and allowed mothers to collect regular support payments, the New Poor Law undermined the legal obligations of putative fathers – and, when men no longer feared imprisonment or other penalties, women found themselves with less prospect of marriage or assistance. The removal of outdoor relief for mothers and children further changed the sexual balance of power. The impact of these changes in south-west Wales was acknowledged in evidence given by both supporters and opponents of Rebeccaism to the 1844 Commission of Inquiry, in which witnesses excoriated the bastardy clauses as having 'altogether failed of the effect which sanguine persons calculated they might produce on the caution or moral feelings of the weaker sex'. In Rebecca's country, where premarital sex had attracted little stigma since 'subsequent marriage . . . almost invariably wiped out the light reproach which public opinion attached to a previous breach of chastity', subsequent marriage was becoming rarer. The commissioners were told that the new system left women exposed to 'all the temptations of a life of vice', while 'the man evades or defies the law, with a confidence and effrontery which has outraged the moral feeling and provoked the indignation of the people to a degree that can hardly be described'.[40] There were reports of mothers and children being left destitute, begging from house to house and even starving due to lack of assistance from either alleged fathers or parish authorities, and of increasing numbers of children deserted, or abandoned at the doors of workhouses, by mothers who could no longer support them. One female interviewee's opinion that 'It is a bad time for the girls . . . the boys have their own way', is echoed by several of her peers, male and female.[41] Russell Davies's collection of quarrels, brutality, abuse and violence – up to and including murder – among married couples in south-west Wales in the later nineteenth century suggests the extent to which women remained in unhappy relationships, refusing to acknowledge their failure, through lack of any practical alternative, lack of sympathy from Poor Law officials, and fear of the workhouse.[42]

The new poor relief system's unpopularity in principle, and its negative effects in practice, gave rise to widespread protests across Britain, in which organised public protest in rural areas frequently intertwined or merged with established forms of rural protest including arson, intimidation and assault. Some locations, including south-west Wales, witnessed an 'institutional revolt' in the 1830s and 1840s by those refusing to accept workhouse rules and discipline. In much of Wales, the New Poor Law faced not only popular opposition from those suffering from its strictures, or who feared they might fall subject to them, but also official resistance from local authorities who were reluctant to cede their decision-making powers to a centralised administration. Opposition was intensified by issues of language, religion and community closeness, with the high-handedness of English Poor Law officials alienating not only the labouring poor but more respectable tiers of the local community. Letters from Poor Law Commissioners in Wales describe 'popular manifestation against the law', including petitions and letters to Parliament, but also the refusal of local Boards of Guardians to erect workhouses. The commissioner Edmund Head attributed this recalcitrance to the lack of gentry influence or control over parish affairs, and to the language barrier impeding communication. In Cardiganshire, opposition to the New Poor Law was attributed to a reluctance to exchange relative licence in the operation of the law for stringency.[43]

The *Carmarthen Journal* had long been hostile to the New Poor Law, criticising particularly its separation of families within workhouses, and the new system was also a target of Welsh Chartism.[44] Resentment of it played a catalytic part in the 1843 assault on Carmarthen workhouse, prior to which marchers had called for 'the alteration of the present poor law, towards which they expressed the most bitter hostility'.[45] Other workhouses were attacked in Pembrokeshire and Carmarthenshire, and in Cardiganshire they were threatened with destruction. At Narberth workhouse, letters were received promising a visit from Rebecca unless better-quality food was given to the inhabitants.[46] Rebeccaism, then, coincided and overlapped with the broader campaign against the New Poor Law, in which public awareness of the altered political and legal situation, and its faults, made the new system's administrators and the negligent fathers of illegitimate children as valid a target for Rebecca's intervention as tollkeepers, landlords or bailiffs.

'Rebecca's black footman' and the New Poor Law

In light of the social and legal clash produced by the imposition of the New Poor Law on an older, more permissive tradition, the popular representation of Rebecca as sexually free and prolific is significant. In a contemporary ballad, Levi Gibbon used the metaphor of childbirth to show Rebecca's growing popularity and support (as did the very notion of 'Rebecca and her daughters'), but linked this graphically with sexual appetite and fecundity:

Her name it is Beca, I'll tell you no lies,
There's no woman like her for men in her thighs.
She's worse than a rabbit for breeding, they say,
With six hundred children and more every day[47]

This attribution to Rebecca of an active and independent sexuality seems thematically linked with the sympathy accorded to unmarried mothers by Rebeccaite participants. Subliminally or deliberately, such a presentation strengthened 'her' campaign by configuring her symbolically as not only a sympathiser and defender of the customary rights of an oppressed group, but also as a member of that group herself.

The actions of Rebeccaites against the new bastardy clauses were also presented poetically in the mock-heroic address 'Rebecca Regina!', which was published in the *Welshman* in September 1843:

Sometimes with prattling baby on her lap
. . . she calls on worthless Pa . . . the child is warmly prest
And sheltered 'neath his own paternal roof
Too much for Bec – she drops a tear
At her success – and then retires.

A month earlier, the same paper had reported this type of intervention more prosaically, under the headline 'Rebecca and the Poor Law':

It is said that Rebecca has stated that if the government will not take the Poor Law in hand, she and her followers are determined to do so, and in order to carry out her intention, she is taking most effectual steps to prevent the operation of the Bastardy clauses. Some short time since she presented a freeholder for the county, in the neighbourhood of Llandysul, with an illegitimate child which he had refused to maintain, and told him he must keep the child and bring it up with his own carefully avoiding any harshness or he could expect another visit from her . . . On Wednesday a man called at the house of a woman on the castle green, in this town, and requested her to give him an illegitimate child which she was nursing for its mother. She did so, and the child was taken to a place near Nantgaredig, where there was a large meeting of Rebeccaites, disguised and armed, who proceeded to take the child

to the Father's house . . . Arrived at the house, Rebecca entered and taking the child with her, she introduced him (a fine boy about four years
old) and requested the father to kiss him. This he refused to do, but was
ultimately compelled to obey, being threatened with instant death if he
did not. A drawn sword was held over his head, and he was made to
caress the child and promise to maintain it as his son. Rebecca then told
him that she should keep her eye on him, and she warned him that if he
attempted to ill–use his child, speedy vengeance would be taken by her
followers. The whole party having given three cheers, then separated.[48]

In December of the same year in Narberth, Martha John, the
28-year-old mother of an illegitimate child, induced a local schoolmaster to write in the name of Rebecca to the child's father, a
farmer whose service she had left while pregnant. The letter
warned him that 'unless he would contribute towards the maintenance of the child of Martha John, that she, "Becca", with "Nelly"
her eldest daughter, would visit him, and set on fire himself and
all his possessions; that he should be like Martha John, without
bread and cheese'.[49] For this, the mother received six months of
hard labour and the schoolmaster four months of imprisonment.
The case demonstrates how the previous actions of 'Rebecca', and
public awareness of them, could empower individuals in similar
circumstances to act under 'her' auspices, without needing her
official contact or sanction. Again, one is reminded of the ease
by which a contemporary individual can obtain membership of
the Anonymous collective by taking action under their auspices
against a designated target, or merely by putting on a stylised Guy
Fawkes mask.

The idea of Rebecca as a protector and benefactor of women
considered to have been badly treated under the terms of the New
Poor Law was expressed both in threatening letters and in the visits of protesters to the fathers of illegitimate children. The latter
was an enigmatic incarnation, reported in the press as 'Rebecca
And Her Black Footman'. Two such incidents are recounted in full
by the *Welshman* and the *Swansea Journal*, both in August 1843,
with the latter report implying 'several other cases' to be dealt with
similarly in the future. Both reports describe the visit of Rebecca,
'very gaily' and extravagantly attired, accompanied by a crowd of
followers and attended by a figure, referred to as her 'black footman', who takes down the steps of her carriage. In each instance,

she presents an illegitimate child to its father and obtains his promise either to bring the child up himself or to pay the mother for its upkeep.

The first account is headlined 'Rebecca and the Black Footman, and her Method of Correcting Poor-Law Evils'. It begins by recounting the plight of a girl who is now an inmate of Newcastle Emlyn workhouse, having been abandoned by the father of her two-year-old child, until 'Last week the facts of this case reached the ears of that now renowned Welsh outlaw Rebecca, who at once resolved on befriending the betrayed and deluded girl'.[50] At midnight on Friday, the child's father, woken by a knock at the door, 'on opening his front door, saw a black footman taking down the steps of a carriage, and opening its door, when out came a lady, very gaily attired, with a child in her arms'. Entering the house and introducing herself by the name of 'Rebecca', she made him promise to bring up the child under her 'sharp eye'. The father having conceded, 'Rebecca then expressed herself satisfied, shook hands with the farmer, stepped back into her carriage and rapidly drove off.' The second report, published on 30 August and headlined 'Rebecca and her Black Footman Again', details the return of an illegitimate child to its father, a farmer at Cothy Bridge, by the husband of its nurse, overseen by Rebecca and a crowd of two hundred 'daughters'. The report concludes: 'We understand that several other cases of Bastardy are to be disposed of by "Rebecca and her black footman" in the course of next week.'

The mention of the 'black footman' as an identifying figure in these reports is intriguing, but the lack of any further information from participants makes it difficult to divine any more precise meaning. Footmen, the highest-ranking indoor liveried male servants, customarily served as escorts when upper-class women paid calls. Black domestic servants, meanwhile, were increasingly depicted in prints, textiles and ceramics of the early 1800s, providing evidence in visual culture of the black presence in Britain, albeit 'merely to reflect the wealth and fashionable tastes of their "owner" . . . within the growing empire' – despite the diverse numbers of black people present in nineteenth-century Britain and their variety of occupations and lifestyles.[51] Black servants, grooms or pages were typically depicted in eighteenth-century portraits and group pictures as boys or young men wearing a form of 'exotic' dress – luxury materials, jewellery, feathered turbans – which often had less to do with their own ancestral cultures and more with an orientalist perception of them.[52] Hogarth frequently included black servants in his satirical images of eighteenth-century life, including Plate II of *A Harlot's Progress* and *Taste in High Life*, in order to suggest the inequity and exploitation underpinning the worlds of contemporary marriage and fashionable consumption. The use of a 'black footman' to accompany Rebecca, then, reinforces the elaborate pomp of this particular aspect of Rebecca – the presentation of upper-class femininity – and may have included some additional element of satire and subversion.

This aspect of Rebecca, in which she appears imposing, solemn and imbued with an authority stemming from ostentatious wealth, seems very different from the sexually voracious girl-about-town depicted in Levi Gibbon's ballad, but 'she' is clearly interceding on behalf of the latter group even if no longer presented as a member of it. Instead, her appearance seems almost to parody the 'Lady Bountiful' archetype sceptically depicted by near-contemporary writers including Amy Dillwyn, whose novel *The Rebecca Rioter* portrays contemporary public awareness of and hostility to this stereotype of upper-class female philanthropy.[53] The way in which this particular issue was addressed by Rebeccaites suggests an acknowledgement that the mothers of illegitimate children were operating in an altered legal and political environment, the social impact of which necessitated the help of an external agency. It may even have been intended to serve as a reminder to the local gentry of their lately abandoned paternalist duties to the unfortunate poor, by portraying them in an exaggerated, pantomime manner. Rebecca's intervention in her guise as a dazzlingly wealthy 'Lady Bountiful' mirrors the actions of parish authorities in west Wales, who had previously administered maintenance payments from fathers to mothers, recognising that enforcing marriage on couples who could not easily afford their own home would prove a greater burden on rates and property through overcrowding or the construction of *tŷ unnos* on disputed land. A parliamentary report identified this system in Cardiganshire as one 'not of administering relief, but of providing redress to the woman under the grievance sustained, or rather of forcing the two parties to combine in the maintenance of the child'.[54] This is the principle and objective upheld by the 'black footman' incidents, strengthening the argument for viewing them as a response to the changed circumstances brought about by the New Poor Law. They constitute a ritualised response to the receding of female sexual autonomy and the emergence of a legislative rather than a communal approach to child maintenance. From this perspective, the 'black footman' aspect of Rebecca, besides illustrating the movement's variety of targets beyond toll gates, reinforces the argument that ritual in protest must be understood in relation to changes in other areas of social life and politics, rather than as part of a free-floating 'popular culture'.

'Maid, spirit or man':
Rebecca's Image in Public Discourse

Chapter 5 examined the disjuncture between the feminine identities assumed by male Rebeccaites during protest, and the
masculine descriptors employed for the same participants in press
and court reports. This discussion established that protesters were
seen as retaining a male identity which was not compromised by
their temporary performance as Rebecca or one of her daughters.
By contrast, contemporary representations of Rebecca in the press
and other popular imagery tended to present her as an abstract
female figure who could be shown in the guise of a host of social
and cultural archetypes. Chapter 6 considered the changing image
of female sexual agency in the 1830s and 1840s, and its relationship with images of Rebecca. This chapter will explore the wider
array of identities which the figure of Rebecca assumed in the public imagination and political discourse, and how these identities,
too, reflected or reinforced contemporary ideas about women.

   The nature of womanhood was an ever-present topic of discussion in both working-class and middle-class society at the time
of Rebecca. Debates on the moral character of women and the
proper nature of women's work permeated political, religious and
scientific discourses as well as the fields of literary and visual representation.[1] The presentation of Rebecca in the press as a stylised or
allegorical figure also fits within wider currents of early nineteenth-
century politics, in which the female body was conspicuous in state
and civic occasions. Women and girls were featured in national and
local celebratory parades and ceremonies, including the coronation
and opening of Parliament, dressed to represent allegorical virtues or symbolically to evoke purity and reproductive power. The
female body, as Nicolas Rogers argues, 'served as the symbol of the
nation's health and, indeed, in the figures of Britannia and Liberty,

as the symbols of national unity, patriotism and independence'.[2] Rogers and Epstein illustrate how the depiction of women as symbols in themselves, and as vehicles for symbolic display, could be co-opted by radical as well as loyalist pageantry.[3] Popular politics at the time of Rebecca, then, granted the female body and female dress significance in political communication and mobilisation and in the occupation of public space. This significance combined the female body's established associations of allegorical representation with the greater leniency afforded to women in public protest, which was based both on the presumption of their lower level of political awareness or engagement and on their capacity for irrational and unruly behaviour.[4] All these tropes contributed to the popular conceptualisation of Rebecca.

The prominence of Rebecca's image in the press indicates the contemporary importance of print culture in creating an enhanced sense of familiarity between leaders and led, through printed public addresses, portraits and cartoons. James Vernon's exploration of the roles and personae adopted by nineteenth-century male political leaders, and projected onto them by their audiences and constituencies, finds that they 'turned upon a relatively small number of familiar and popular narratives'.[5] Analysis of the words and imagery used in press reports reveals that Rebecca was similarly portrayed, but through a much wider range of personae, some of which were explicit, theatrical and stylised while others were conveyed through subtleties of language and association. 'Her' identity was fluid, transcending age and socio-economic status as well as ideas of gender-appropriate behaviour, and 'she' could appear sexualised or desexualised, imperious and commanding, or wanton and frenzied. Each of these multiple representations was surrounded by particular sets of associations, catered to varying constituencies, and drew on – or projected onto Rebecca in particular – various contemporary ideas about women in general.

The identities given to Rebecca included types which I have categorised here, in loosely descending order of respectability, as follows: the Lady, a figure commanding implicit respect, in which image she was often presented as a foil to Queen Victoria; the Performer, a figure conveying femininity through a self-consciously theatrical image which could be grotesque, camp or comic; the supernatural or mythical Heroine, a construct which drew on emergent Romantic ideals of Wales and on wider literary or poetic allusions; the Girl Led Astray, which employed biblical associations, moralising and paternalist attitudes, and suggests the influence of broader shifts in sexual culture; and, finally, the Unruly Woman, in which guise Rebecca and her followers were presented as a violent and subversive threat to established authority. These identities enabled a corresponding range of narratives in which Rebecca could be discussed, approved of or condemned in a way that also pronounced implicitly on the behaviour of her followers and supporters, and which could allow a comic or critical portrayal of her opponents in the local and national political scene. These uses of her image indicate Rebecca's acceptance into a pantheon of folk heroes and publicly recognised characters, as well as reinforcing her status as a personification of alternative popular authority.

Rebecca's establishment as an abstract character

Throughout 1843 and 1844, Rebecca appeared in press reports, editorials and readers' letters on the state of south-west Wales as an abstract and multivalent figure. There was little attempt or encouragement to identify a single or named individual as Rebecca – indeed, by the summer of 1843 the *Cambrian* had deduced that the destruction of several gates over a wide area on a single night was proof 'that Rebecca may be in several places at one time, or rather [it is more likely] that there are several Rebeccas'.[6] The *Quarterly Review* criticised the 'disposition to personify and fix on some individual agent the spirit which prompted and organized the various enterprises'.[7] *Blackwood's Magazine* – with greater perception than its dismissive tone may suggest – noted:

> It seems well-known that . . . the Rebecca is no other than some forward booby, or worse character, who ambitiously claims to act the leader . . . The 'Rebecca' seems no more than a living figure to give effect to the drama, as boys dress up an effigy and parade it as the Guy Fawkes.[8]

This abstract concept of Rebecca, widely recognised and accepted, was used in contemporary discourse not only to represent the entire movement as a single entity, but also to embody wider collectively held sentiments. The *Carmarthen Journal*, for instance, viewed Rebecca as personifying a troubling 'spirit of political disaffection':

> We are everywhere asked, Who is Rebecca? We answer, Rebecca is an impersonality – a mere political abstraction, or if she has any corporeal form or essence, we say that she is AN EMBODIMENT OF THE PRINCIPLES OF REVOLUTION . . .[9]

During the course of Rebecca mania, her image and its associations gained sufficient familiarity with the reading public that 'Rebeccaism' – acts of resistance or hostility to various types of authority and specifically to toll gates – could be used, as Rogers described popular Jacobitism in Georgian England, as 'an idiom of defiance…a mobile script [which was] deployed in a variety of contexts and could generate multiple meanings' often far removed from its original time and locality.[10] This most often occurred in circumstances which directly related to the destruction of toll gates, but which took place outside south-west Wales. This covers the twenty people charged with riotous assembly in Mark and Wedmore parish, who appeared in the *Welshman* under the heading 'Rebecca In Somerset'; the reported assault on a female tollkeeper by a farm servant for whom she had refused to open her gate, headed 'Rebecca At Bromsgove'; or the *Swansea Journal*'s reminiscence on the destruction of turnpikes in Bristol over a century earlier, entitled 'Rebecca in 1727'.[11] The stylised image of Rebecca and her typical actions were clearly sufficiently imprinted on popular consciousness to be further recognised in amusing or outlandish forms. The *Cambrian* reported an elephant keeper's attempt to take his charge through an Aylesbury turnpike, which resulted in the elephant lifting the gate off its hinges, under the heading 'One of "Rebecca's Daughters"'.[12] In October 1843 a mock Rebecca letter was sent to the porter of University College, London, 'declaring it to be the intention of herself and others to remove the "obstruction"' of the college gate. The gate was later taken off its hinges at midnight by persons unknown and hidden in nearby bushes.[13]

The previous month, a notice stuck up in Pemboyr parish had engaged 'Rebecca' in dialogue with an everyman farmer, in which she dispensed advice on how to 'lighten your heavy burdens' through the collective petitioning of landlords for lower rents.[14]

In its use of familiar and homely language and arguments to pro-
mote a moral or political objective, Rebecca's engagement with the
farmer fits into the didactic tradition of dialogue found in evan-
gelical repository tracts, themselves modelled on the form of other
cheap popular literature sold by itinerant hawkers and chapmen.[15]
Such appearances suggest that Rebecca's image was becoming sufficiently familiar not to require 'bringing to life' by a human actor,
indicating rather that she was entering the popular imagination
and popular culture as a stock character with an associated set of
opinions and behaviour.

Rebecca's range of feminine guises

The Lady

Press reports of her activities frequently depicted Rebecca as a
'Lady' of elegance and renown, commanding well-deserved respect,
the term detaching her from the less overtly refined connotations
of 'woman'. Allusions to a gracious and respectable Rebecca are
particularly associated with her 'black footman' incarnation,
where such an image was deliberately emphasised by participants
themselves, but they appear frequently in descriptions of all her
activities. Common epithets include 'the renowned Lady', 'this
noted lady. . . this wonderful lady', accompanied by her 'respectable family' or 'her faithful and obedient children'.[16] A major
aspect of this image, further reinforcing its implicit feminine qualities, was the frequent ironic reporting of Rebecca's appearances in
the terminology of social engagements. She and her daughters were
said to have 'visited' or 'paid a visit' to toll gates, and Rebecca's
public opponents or tollkeepers in receipt of threatening letters or
notices, informing them of her intent to destroy a particular toll
gate, were referred to as having 'received Becca's compliments'.[17]

An 1843 poem, preserved by Alcwyn C. Evans, depicts Rebecca's daughters as debutantes, 'of ages quite fit to come out',
dancing 'with matchless *éclat*' with their military antagonists.[18] A
correspondent at Glasbury reported that 'the unexpected visit of
the daughters of Rebecca . . . has caused a considerable degree of
excitement and bustle in this quiet and picturesque hamlet', while
the *Hereford Times* in November 1843 noted 'Rebecca's arrival

in this ancient and loyal borough'.[19] In August 1843, her visit to
a Haverfordwest farmer suspected of hoarding corn was reported
in the following ironically understated terms, redolent of delicacy
and refinement:

> Having with part of her retinue been admitted to a *tête-à-tête*, she
> informed him of her desire [that he should sell his corn immediately at a
> moderate price] otherwise she would in a few days assist in its removal.
> The farmer promised explicit obedience.[20]

Similarly wry language was used in October 1843 in reference to a
bailiff stationed at Towy, who, upon hearing Rebecca's approach,
hid under his bed 'to avoid a *tête-à-tête* with a lady of whom he
had heard too much'. Rebecca, however, 'insisted on an interview'
and 'received him graciously' before dispatching him out of the
house towards Carmarthen.[21]

This understated language of polite interest and mild veneration
formed an ironic counterpoint to the level of violence and threat
which it was employed to describe. The *Cambrian* closed its report
on the demolition of several Lampeter toll gates with the observation
that local toll collectors 'begin to fear more visits than will be agreeable ...'.[22] Occasionally this arch mode of communication could
be attributed to 'the Lady' herself: in September 1843 the *Hereford
Times* carried a letter purporting to be from Rebecca, which noted:

> Some of my Daughters in Herefordshire inform me that their [*sic*] be
> some needless Hindrance in that County called Turnpikes, and as some
> of my Daughters be very much Rose in their Tithes; and be looked after
> so sharp in the Game way, I beg to announce to them, through your
> paper, that I intend visiting Herefordshire.[23]

The presentation of Rebecca as a 'Lady' of renown and sophisti-
cation illustrates the contemporary importance of social class and
the amenability of this trope to overt and implicit use in political
rhetoric. As we have seen in previous chapters, the extravagant
attire used in Rebecca's 'black footman' incarnation can be interpreted as a deliberate mocking of upper-class femininity through
the appropriation and subversion of its sartorial trappings. It is
possible that a similar mocking or subversive compulsion underlay this press portrayal of 'the Lady' Rebecca. The most direct

comparative use of such language, drawing on the subject's implicit celebrity and the consequent honour bestowed on the place or person chosen for a visit, is that used in reference to Queen Victoria.[24] Rebecca was frequently presented as a foil to the current Queen in the guise of 'Rebecca Regina', 'Regina Rustica, Rent Reducer', 'that rustic queen' and 'her most graceless Majesty'.[25] The same allusion informs the Swansea magistrate Lewis Weston Dillwyn's letter to the Marquis of Bute, describing Irish Chartist leader Feargus O'Connor's 1843 tour of south Wales in which O'Connor 'is supposed to have gone on to Carmarthenshire with the hope of becoming Rebecca's Prime Minister'. An 1854 squib against Church rates, which utilises Rebecca's image, has her taking 'the advice of my Privy Council' and warning opponents not to 'dispute my Imperial Power' or 'incur my Royal displeasure'. The squib was preserved by one contemporary source as 'Rebecca's Proclamation of 1854'.[26] Such references suggest the popular subversion or appropriation of Victoria's highly visible feminine image, perhaps to project an increasingly self-aware Welsh national identity by employing Rebecca as an allegorical counterpart to Victoria. In Amy Dillwyn's novel *The Rebecca Rioter*, this comparison is drawn with more serious intent, as Dillwyn explicitly juxtaposes Rebecca with the existing Queen and constructs 'Rebecca' as an emblem of roused nationhood, gendered as female and implicitly held up as an alternative ruler of the Welsh.[27]

The Performer

Press descriptions of Rebecca were often imbued with the same 'knowing' awareness of performance and self-conscious theatricality as that emphasised in protest by Rebeccaites themselves. A *Welshman* editorial in July 1843 caricatured the national press attention and military presence in Carmarthen, and the inaction of local authorities, using theatrical and operatic terms including a satirical cast list which described Rebecca as 'Ignis Fatuus', a collective delusion:

> A company of foot garrison the workhouse – almost recalling Commandant de Launy and his *Invalides* in the Bastille . . . the anxious public, like the chorus of a Greek play buzzes *gossipo* – tremulous about the principal actors, uttering mere platitudes.[28]

The paper proceeded to print a doggerel 'rhythmical effusion' from an anonymous correspondent, which put defiant dramatic rhetoric into Rebecca's mouth. Again she was depicted as a performer whose 'soprano, with the full chorus of her followers ... must be electrifying and wonderfully powerful'. In such overtly arch commentary, the theatrically feminine image often adopted by 'Rebecca' in protest was reinforced by association with the overblown conventions of opera and pantomime. This type of image served in turn to reinforce the satirising of current circumstances – in this case, the perceived overreaction of local and national authorities and a resultant overbearing and unwarranted military presence in south-west Wales.

The stage and social or political commentary was not an uncommon coupling at this point in time. Pantomime had, since its eighteenth-century inception, dramatised or satirised the ceremony of government and the rowdiness of electioneering culture, as well as commenting on specific political issues including the New Poor Law.[29] Sara Hudston notes more broadly the links in 1830s and 1840s Britain between stage drama and social unrest, the latter of which was 'theatrical in the most immediate sense ... being extravagantly histrionic, stagy and calculated for display'.[30] This 'stagy' incarnation of Rebecca persisted after the riots' conclusion. A 'squib against Church rates' of 1854 called her into service as its nominal protagonist, no longer concerned with toll gates but with another perceived oppression to be urgently addressed. Like the *Welshman* editorial above, it conceptualises Rebecca through dramatic conventions, drawing on the technique, common to several nineteenth-century broadsides, of including a playbill-style 'cast list'.[31] The squib's portrayal of Rebecca is highly theatrical, redolent of pantomime in its self-conscious narrative voice and its focus on stylised feminine signifiers: 'Yes, my darlings! From information received, it is probable my services will soon be wanted again, so rig on your Bustles, get your Petticoats ready and Bonnets trimmed!'[32] This incarnation of Rebecca may be an extension or reflection of the comic exaggerations of femininity used by participants, or a co-option of Rebecca's identity into familiar tropes of dramatic or comic artifice – or indeed both. The vivid and absurd nature of this particular presentation may have enabled it to survive longer in the public imagination than other more subtle or particular aspects of her appearance.

The Heroine

In contrast to her comically theatrical incarnation, other dramatic presentations of Rebecca imbued her activities with a somewhat incongruous glamour and romance. By 1843–4, Wales had undergone a shift in cultural perceptions from an unexciting cipher to a romanticised reminder of the ancient British past and of ideals of resistance to foreign enslavement.[33] It is possible that this affected views of Rebecca inside and outside Wales, making her image a mechanism by which the country she was held to represent could be de-ciphered, or her actions exalted as the deeds of an exotic heroine. Raphael Samuel and Paul Thompson claim that heroic myths are based on overwhelmingly male qualities of 'courage, daring, self-determination and independence', but in contemporary sources we also find these qualities unhesitatingly applied to Rebecca, and her exploits directly likened to the acts of classical or literary females.[34] The *Quarterly Review*, struck by Rebeccaism's chivalric and Romantic aspects, compared her to 'the beautiful heroine of the Volscians' or 'Madge Wildfire, the redoubtable assailant of the tollbooth, as described in a scarcely less classic page'.[35] The article imagined Rebecca 'heading the charge of her sylvan cavalry, rallied in an instant from their mountain ambush, and dispersing again with the rapidity of ghosts at dawn', and marvelled at this being the creation of 'the plodding and unpoetical Welsh farmer'.

Within Wales, writers of poems or ballads on Rebecca, most of which appeared anonymously or pseudonymously, tended to strike a similarly admiring note. They reinforce the tendency for poetic presentations of Rebecca to draw on existing literary or stage representations of heroic, bold or daring women. The lengthy poem 'Rebecca Regina!', sent to the *Welshman* by 'T. L.' in September 1843, depicts Rebecca as 'Queen Bec', a play on Queen Mab. The writer's pastiche of the Shakespeare passage in which Queen Mab appears lauds Rebecca as 'our heroine', 'in shape, alike the amazon heroines of old', her fame extending beyond 'England's throne' to Europe.[36] The poem stresses the original passage's hallucinatory or dreamlike qualities in a way perhaps reflective of the nocturnal setting and altered state of consciousness in which Rebeccaite activities were conducted, and draws on overtly feminine connotations of Rebecca's public image – the supernatural, irrational and seductive. Its references to Wales on a national and European stage may signify the ways in which Rebecca's growing fame facilitated the creation and external projection of a self-aware Welsh identity, with her feats lending Wales a certain glamour and renown by association.

The long, arch and pun-filled poem preserved by Alcwyn C. Evans glorifies Rebecca through comparison to 'famed Amazonians' and 'Great Joan of Arc'. Inhabiting both 'the halls of the rich' and 'the cots of the poor', she is portrayed as mythical and supernatural, 'Hydra-headed' and with more eyes than Argus, and likened to Terpsichore, the Greek muse of dancing. Unusually, the poem acknowledges the sexual ambiguity of her identity, addressing her as 'maid, spirit or man' and declaring:

> 'Twould puzzle the brains of a Newton or Secker
> To trace out thy epicene nature, Rebecca![37]

However, the poem derives its overwhelming impact from showering the reader with multiple and all-encompassing images of Rebecca as explicitly and extravagantly feminine – she is at once 'daughter of mystery' and 'the mother of hundreds', both respectable (if comic) old 'Mother Hubbard' and disreputable 'miscreant Jezebel'. This multivalent heroic guise, spanning the spectrum of age, culture and status, allowed Rebecca's image to be positively strengthened through the assumption of multiple feminine attributes not tied to a single or specific female identity.

The Girl Led Astray

Mentions of Rebecca and her daughters which cast them as supernatural or mythological figures – witches, 'elvish troops', 'myrmidons', 'amazons' and the fulfilment of a prophecy by Merlin of violence and bloodshed – implicitly questioned or condemned Rebeccaism by associating it with the irrational, malevolent and remorseless.[38] A more sympathetic, if condescending, treatment was provided by the presentation of Rebecca as a girl led astray, whose individual misconduct – and therefore the general misconduct of her followers – resulted not from an irredeemably bad nature but from ignorance and yielding to temptation.

In September 1843 the *Welshman* carried 'Deborah's Address to Rebecca', ostensibly advice from one biblical heroine to another, which presented Rebecca as youthfully reckless, 'self-willed' and subject to immoral blandishments. 'Deborah' criticised 'the guardians of Rebecca's early youth' for not having instilled 'the moral principles necessary to counteract in after life the evil suggestions of an evil world', and hoped that her 'young charge' would 'take warning from the shameful abuse of her once respectable name . . . consider her ways, and be wise in time'.[39] Deborah's injunction is echoed in the advice to 'change and be honest' issued by the author of Evans's poem, in order that Rebecca be saved from 'ending her days' on the gallows.[40] The relevance to contemporary women of biblical models of female leadership, including the example of Deborah, formed part of a broader debate on methods of female political mobilisation in the mid-nineteenth century.[41] As a whole, the *Welshman*'s address echoes contemporary prescriptive literature which advised women against wantonness and immoderation, encouraging them to 'turn their natures to good account' through compassion, piety and modesty.[42]

Like the 'black footman' incidents discussed above, the image of Rebecca as a girl led astray and bereft of protectors may reflect contemporary public awareness of the shifting legal and social environment produced by the operation of the New Poor Law and its impact on women in particular. Although still displaying the multivalency and fluidity of Rebecca's image, this portrayal conflicts with the heroic and theatrical images of Rebecca, which, in their connotations of aggressive or assertive female agency, power and independence, seem more indebted to the older tradition of 'lively female sexual assertiveness' identified by Ross and Rapp.[43] Depictions of Rebecca as dependent on external protection, defenceless against the loss of her 'once respectable name' produced by sexual laxity or independence – versus the older tradition which hesitated to stigmatise unmarried mothers or sex outside marriage – may also provide an example of how contested attitudes to female sexuality were projected onto a particular and highly visible female symbol.

Rebecca's image as a channel for political satire

The various characterisations of Rebecca could provide opportunities to portray the political response to 'her' actions comically or critically. Editorials utilised the concept of Rebecca as a girl led astray when depicting the turnpike-centred movement's 'perversion' by the adoption of more diverse and violently pursued objectives, presenting this narrative as the story of a politically 'pure' Rebecca's temptation and ruin. The *Welshman* developed a recurring joke in which it depicted Robert Peel as Rebecca's grandmother, fixated on condemning and punishing Rebecca's flighty and 'mischievous' behaviour without examining its underlying causes. In September 1843, at a stage of increasing military presence and government intervention in south Wales, an editorial complained: 'Beccy's Granny . . . is always scolding her granddaughter, and never says a word in condemnation of those persons who have made poor Beccy what she is.'[44] The paper also caricatured Peel by linking him to the image of Rebecca as an elderly woman, with attendant associations of impotence and emasculation. In August 1843 an editorial asked rhetorically: 'if there has been a leader in petticoats in Carmarthen, has there not been an undoubted old woman in the Cabinet?'.[45] A month later, the paper satirised what it perceived as an overblown military response to the threat of Rebeccaite attacks in Haverfordwest:

> Here we are . . . with a military force sufficient to frighten a foreign regiment, merely because two old women chose to have a scuffle, namely Granny, or Grandmother, and Rebecca. We have a detachment of marines, a troop of cavalry, and the militia, patrolling our quiet streets everyday, looking as cheerful as possible, as well they might, having nothing whatsoever to do but eat, drink and be merry, and laugh at the truly ridiculous scuffle of Granny versus Rebecca, or much ado about nothing.[46]

In further attempts at satire or criticism, commentators attempted to undermine or question the masculine qualities of authority figures through contrasting them with Rebecca. In such cases, Rebecca was reported as having 'unmanned' constables, bailiffs, gatekeepers and local officials by displaying superior strength, courage or, frequently, 'daring' and 'valour'. Qualities emphasised in descriptions of Rebecca's appearance and conduct included martial prowess, physical strength and height, leadership and command. Her 'unlimited authority' over her followers, and the more general loyalty commanded by the movement, was often described in the language of military and aristocratic masculine potency. Rebeccaite 'officers' and 'commanders' adopted *'noms de guerre'* and the report of several Rebeccaite operations at Narbeth concluded with the view that participants had 'asserted their own supremacy over the laws by which other less potent and particular *seigneurs* feel themselves bound'.[47] In contrast to this, press reports constantly lampooned gatekeepers who, finding that 'the better part of valour was discretion', stayed indoors with 'ready obedience' rather than confront a visiting mob, and bailiffs and constables set upon by Rebeccaites in the course of their duty who, 'terribly afraid', were compelled to 'bolt away' and hide in hedges and ditches. The three parish constables guarding Llanddarog gate were reported to have 'showed the white feather' at 'the Lady's' appearance, and those at Croeslwyd similarly:

> no sooner saw what was going on, than they incontinently took French leave, and scampered in a hurry-scurry down the road towards Carmarthen and if there be any truth in Hudibras, they were victorious, for
>
>> 'When the fight becomes a chase
>> They win the fight who win the race,'
>
> and it is an undoubted fact that they were the ones who were the first to arrive at Carmarthen.[48]

The portrayal of local and national authorities as supine, inept and lacking in valour, in contrast to Rebecca's 'daring', 'coolness', 'aggression' and 'command' which made her followers 'the terror of the surrounding country', provides a further example of the subtlety with which her image could be used, as well as the complexity of gendered rhetoric in contemporary discourse.[49] Despite the overt use of feminine signifiers to conceptualise, portray and identify Rebecca, 'she' could still be seen to represent or possess an actively aspirational form of masculinity.

Rebecca as the 'unruly woman'

The identities so far discussed tended to show Rebecca in a neutral or irreverent, if not overtly admiring light, but press commentators could also present her using archetypes which were meant to marshal popular indignation, outrage or condemnation. Her femininity could be used rhetorically to intensify the shock-value of her 'lawlessness' and 'daring', which transgressed the boundaries of expected female behaviour outside the licence afforded by carnival and festival. This characterisation could then become a means to present the movement as irrational and unruly, requiring a check by masculine military or political force.

This trend is especially evident in the *Quarterly Review*'s retrospective on the movement, published in June 1844. The article begins by establishing that 'Rebecca' was not an abstract mythological leader but a multitude of individuals drawn from the ranks of 'the plodding and unpoetical Welsh farmer', Rebecca as a male leader 'mounted and disguised, like his bodyguard, in female attire'.[50] However, as the article tracks Rebeccaism's increasingly lawless and violent progress, this insistence on the masculine pronoun fades from view in favour of a focus on Rebecca as abstract and definitively female, embodying disorderly and subversive characteristics calculated to provoke an authoritative response, and demonstrating the need for strong and conclusive intervention by outside, implicitly masculine agencies. Noting the movement's 'rapid and unbroken success', and the lack of judicial repercussions, the *Quarterly Review* describes its consequences in language that switches to a proliferation of feminine pronouns:

> the daughters of Rebecca grew and multiplied, till, flushed with success and the consciousness of their strength . . . the heroine of the tollgates set herself up as the general reformer and rectifier of all the social ills that affected the community . . . [Rebecca] now stepped forward as the mediatrix in questions of private right, and even the delicate subject of rent and tenures was not too sacred for her interference.[51]

This 'interference' is recounted as though it is the shocking work of an actual, and female, individual, even though this is the guise in which the article had previously denied that Rebecca existed. The article then uses this feminine persona to further stress the socially and politically disordered nature of conditions under Rebecca's rule, by observing that at public meetings held to discuss grievances, 'Rebecca herself' was 'probably not seldom a leading spokes*man*' (emphasis in original).[52] In fact, although women attended such meetings, they are not reported as speaking or taking up positions of authority – indeed, the document of grievances produced by Llandefylog farmers explicitly banned the presence of women at meetings.[53] The article's emphasis on a female figure as 'spokes*man*' suggests an attempt to present Rebeccaism symbolically as the unsettling spectacle of a world turned upside down. Over the next few pages, this anxiety escalates into an excitable condemnation of Rebeccaism as something 'overawing the law, invading the most sacred rights of property and person, issuing its behests with despotic effrontery, and enforcing them by the detestable agents of terror, incendiarism, and bloodshed'. As Rebecca becomes more solidly female in this representation, so her actions are presented as more reprehensible and more clearly necessitating an intervention by agencies characterised as masculine, rationally redressing feminine impudence and misrule:

> Rebecca, who had laughed at justices' warrants, and scattered special constables like chaff before the wind, suddenly found herself confronted with the War-Office, and 'the Great Captain of the age' at its head.[54]

Here the spectre of unchecked feminine 'despotism' is informed by an assertion of women's capacity for visceral violence, disorder and irrationality, contrasted with the rational and cerebral masculinity symbolised by 'the law' and property rights. Much contemporary discussion on Rebecca is similarly influenced by the association of women with violent disorder and the assertion of feminine power as symptomatic of unhealthy and threatening inversion. This could enable the construction of a sexually-charged narrative which pitted Rebecca, as the female embodiment of subversion and rebellion, against a male military and political establishment seeking to reassert patriarchal and constitutional authority.

Press references could portray Rebecca as more feminine when in disarray, as in the attack on Carmarthen workhouse or the clash between protesters and constabulary at Pontarddulais toll gate, or when particularly violent or flagrant attacks placed Rebecca's actions overtly and unsympathetically in the wrong. In these cases, 'her' irrationality and impudence were played up in order to stress the disordered nature of affairs ('misrule') and so to heighten the need for masculine military and political intervention and the restoration of established authority. Reports of Rebeccaite activities frequently emphasised the intensely physical nature of assaults on constables, bailiffs and tollkeepers as though they were actual assaults by women on men, thereby heightening their sensationalist and reprehensible quality. The *Cambrian*'s report that two bailiffs in Anglesey were dragged from their beds and driven from a house of which they had taken possession, 'pinched and pushed and even ridden by the wanton daughters of Rebecca', concluded that such events damage 'the honour of north Wales'.[55] The *Welshman* lamented the indignity of having Rebecca 'riding rampant over us', and other editorials and reports seethed with references to her as 'this refractory dame', 'insolent', 'impudent' and 'the Witch of Witches'.[56] Such depictions of Rebeccaism as unsettling and dangerous gained their rhetorical force by implicitly equating the movement with unchecked female sexuality, 'wanton' and 'rampant'.

The violent expulsion of Rebeccaite protesters from Carmarthen workhouse in June 1843 caused the *Carmarthen Journal* to print a jubilant editorial in which the sense of authoritative and sexual equilibrium restored is palpable, and in which Rebecca appears as unequivocally female:

> Assuming arms in the face of day, she (Rebecca) has forcibly resisted the officers of the law in the execution of their duty, and at last has arrived to a height of audacity which would lead one to suspect that no law existed in the land; but we trust that she has at last received a check, which will put a period to her insolence, and compel her to throw off the mask which she has for so long worn with impunity, and once more restore the majesty of the law within the disturbed districts of the Principality.[57]

Responses to the Carmarthen riot did little immediately to quell Rebeccaism, however, and at a public meeting the following September, Stephen Evans lodged a similar appeal against Rebecca's 'audacity' and 'insolence', couching it in terms of restraining female independence:

> As for Rebecca . . . he would very much like to see her, for he would himself tell her, that rather than wandering about at night in the manner she had lately done, he would maintain her for a night or two in his own house to prevent her doing mischief. He would advise all assembled to do the same thing if they saw her.[58]

A letter to Col. Powell in October 1843 resolved in a similarly res-
olute tone that the military 'must not allow Rebecca to show off
any more of her frolicks'.[59] In each of the above instances, Rebecca
takes on the guise of what Natalie Zemon Davis characterises as
the disorderly 'unruly woman', whose agency and independence,
outside the licensed bounds of carnival and festival, poses a threat
to authority at the level of family, society and government.[60] Presenting Rebecca as wholly female allowed the threat posed by the
movement which she represented to be construed in established
and immediately recognisable terms. Moreover, by using these
terms to insist that, in the words of the *Quarterly Review*, 'all men
perceived that a decided effort had become necessary to repress
disorders which tended to the dissolution of society', Rebecca's
opponents were able to issue calls for support, and to justify their
own position, based on references to order and rationality in which
aligning oneself with these masculine attributes was paramount.[61]

This survey of the various public images of women onto which
the specific image of Rebecca was projected demonstrates the
multivalent and contested nature of gendered identities in these
arenas. In many cases these images were not mutually exclusive;
the writer of the doggerel verse 'On the Rebecca Riots in Wales
(Adapted to Modern Times)' presents her in a rapidly shifting succession of roles, from 'Amazon' to charmer of 'love-sick youth', to
sharp-tongued 'Scold', to hard-to-please 'Old Lady', to 'Genteel'
commander of lackeys.[62] Rebecca's impact on public consciousness
should be sought as much within a discourse which enabled the
appropriation or subversion of a range of pre-existing symbols and
stereotypes, as in direct popular representations. While commentators were able to call up a tradition of female agency or heroism
to describe Rebecca and her actions, her detractors were able to
raise the disquieting spectre of feminine irrationality, disorder and
impudence. Rebecca could be imbued with masculine characteristics of 'daring' and 'valour' in order to emphasise the lack of such
qualities in her opponents, but it was equally possible for her femininity to be negatively constructed and set against the masculine
rationality and order of established authority.

'A very creditable portion of Welsh history'?
Rebeccaism's Aftermath and
Longer-Term Political and Cultural Impact

Four years after the conclusion of Rebecca's best-known phase of
activity, the economist Nassau William Senior recorded his trav-
els through Wales with a party which included Thomas Frankland
Lewis, chair of the 1844 Commission of Inquiry. One August evening, Lewis gave his fellow travellers a 'eulogium on the Rebecca
rioters' which pronounced them 'a very creditable portion of
Welsh history'.[1] This judgement stands in contrast to the panicked
or condemnatory official responses to Rebecca which abounded at
the time of the riots. The ways in which Rebecca was resolved into
official and popular memory, and the motivations behind these
processes, form the subject of this chapter. The previous chapter
explored Rebecca's use as a multivalent symbol, demonstrating
the range of political purposes which her identity was adapted to
serve. In the years following the disturbances, mentions of Rebecca
in press, popular and political representations displayed a similar
variety of narratives into which the movement's causes, objectives and methods, and the government's response to them, could
be integrated.

Subsequent official and popular references to the movement can
be shown to concentrate on a narrower set of causes and events
than existed at the time. This is most apparent in the 1844 Commission of Inquiry; a consideration of the form and content of
the commission demonstrates its reduction of Rebeccaite grievances to that of opposition to toll gates, thus excluding an array
of other expressed objections, and the reasons of political expe-
diency behind this reduction. The use of Rebeccaism in political
rhetoric as a foil to unrest in Ireland utilised a similar technique,
concentrating on presenting the events in Wales as a narrative of

beneficial government intervention. Finally, as the nineteenth century progressed, Rebecca's image was evoked in press editorials and letters which attempted publicly to disparage or defend the Welsh character. Debates over the nature of Rebeccaism treated the movement as symptomatic of the Welsh 'national character' and its inherent respectability or lawlessness, particularly when these qualities were linked with adherence to the Welsh language and to Nonconformism.

Rebeccaism in popular and political memory

The impression of Rebeccaism which persists most strongly in mentions after 1844 is, perhaps inevitably, that of its being defined by male cross-dressing. In addition to the several nineteenth-century examples noted in previous chapters, this aspect forms the basis of references made throughout the twentieth century: a 1956 review of Williams's work on the riots notes that 'Their central feature was the destruction at night of tollgates by bands of men, usually wearing women's clothes and having blackened faces'. In 1962, a piece of choral music commissioned by Oxford University Press took as its lyrics a poem on Rebecca. *The Times*, explaining the subject matter, dismissed the rioters as 'armed men dressed in women's clothes'.[2] In May 1964, a commemorative pageant was held in Pembrokeshire's Precelly Mountains involving descendants of the original rioters, who took part 'with blackened faces and disguised in women's clothes'. In Gareth Elwyn Jones's 1984 history of modern Wales, 'Rebecca and her daughters' are summarised as 'men dressed in women's clothing'.[3] As has been argued throughout this book, the adoption of female clothing was only part of the repertoire used by participants; the above examples demonstrate how remembrance of Rebeccaism tends to be content with concentrating on its most visible and obvious characteristics.

Along with this narrow definition of the movement's form, *post-facto* references similarly limit their exploration of its content to the issue of attacks on toll gates. The idea of the riots as motivated solely by conflict with toll gates is a persuasive one, but its demonstrable inadequacy as an explanation is shown by both contemporary reports of Rebeccaism and in evidence presented to – though not prioritised by – the 1844 Commission of Inquiry. These sources reveal a wider range of grievances among participants, notably land reform, poverty, social tension and the payment of Church tithes, than is acknowledged after the event.[4] It is the emphasis on toll gates which has made the deepest impression in subsequent references. Two letters to *The Times* in 1846 and 1857 come from readers objecting respectively to the high number of tolls encountered during a single journey across London and to a proposed toll bar at Chelsea Bridge. Both writers display an awareness of Rebeccaism as a precedent in this matter, the first in his possibly tongue-in-cheek conclusion: 'If the Metropolitan Highway Trust Commissioners do not put their gates in better order, we must send for a deputation from Wales,' and the second more earnestly in his warning that 'if care were not taken, there would be excited in the metropolis as violent a feeling against these toll-bars as had been manifested in the Rebecca riots of south Wales some years ago'.[5] In later references to the riots, this aspect remains central: the Carmarthen printer and publisher William Spurrell's 'Notes on the 'Becca Riots', written in 1872, also locates the riots' origin in the establishment of turnpike trusts, whose effect 'was not unnaturally felt to be a grievance'.[6] An 1878 letter from the Radnorshire magistrate John Lloyd defined the riots' purpose as the destruction of turnpike gates.[7] In a letter of 1888, Edwin Chadwick reduced the multitudinous resistance movement to 'in fact riots against paying sixpence in a toll'.[8]

In his 1895 memoir, the Anglo-American artist and radical W. J. Linton describes 'the "Rebecca Movement"' as 'the one successful uprising in England since the Great Rebellion', in which 'farming people . . . masked and otherwise disguised, mostly as women, passed at night through the county, smashing the toll gates . . . The movement was successful: the tolls were not reimposed'.[9] A 1929 *Times* article on turnpikes recounts 'the story of the Rebecca riots in south Wales a hundred years ago or more' – a picturesque but inaccurate chronology, suggestive of the fairy-tale quality the events are by now assuming – in which 'the Welsh arose in their indignation and destroyed them by the score at night . . . until authority was compelled to submit to the popular will'.[10] This subtle turn towards a more heroic rendering of the movement is continued in a 1935 article on road improvements, which states that county road boards were established as a direct

result of the Rebecca riots, and in the 1964 commemorative pageant at which a tablet was unveiled 'to mark the destruction of
the tollgate at Efailwen by the hosts of Rebecca in May 1839,
which led to the freeing of the turnpikes'. Finally, Derek Draisey's 2010 account states that by 1844 Rebecca 'had achieved her
aim', to wit, the removal of gates, toll reductions and the curbing
of arbitrary Trust powers. The movement is warmly described as
'truly a people's protest, one that has become firmly established
as an important part of Welsh history'.[11]

The above references demonstrate that, although many details
of the riots may have faded from public memory, that which most
strongly persists is their focus on toll gates and their success in
opposing them. This is explained in part by the importance placed
on this aspect in contemporary and subsequent political discourse. In parliamentary debate after 1844, Rebeccaism figured
most highly in relation to events in Ireland, where, throughout
the nineteenth century, a range of grievances including poverty,
high rents and land consolidation, as well as the crop failure and
subsequent famine of 1845–51, had provoked widespread agrarian unrest and political agitation.[12] Debates on the appropriate
political response to Ireland sometimes referenced Rebeccaism,
usually presenting it as a precedent for non-coercive state intervention. In doing so, commentators accepted and affirmed the
government's insistence that the riots had been concerned solely
with toll gates, and ratified its preoccupation with its own
response to them – firstly establishing a Commission of Inquiry
and subsequently rationalising the administration of toll gates
through the 1844 Turnpike Act.

The impression of Rebeccaism as motivated by a single grievance, which was then promptly addressed by government
intervention, appears in several speeches on Ireland after 1844.
The points emphasised are that, in the Welsh case, 'nothing in the
way of coercion was done . . . a commission of enquiry was sent,
and when it found out what the grievance was, it was redressed,
and the riots ceased'.[13] Two months later, the House of Commons
was reminded that 'a special commission was found sufficient to
prevent [the riots'] recurrence, and that was what ought to have
been tried in Ireland'.[14] The insistence on this interpretation of
Rebeccaism became a rhetorical device lending weight to both
proactive and defensive arguments in the Irish debate. The above

accounts called for the implementation of a commission in Ireland, on the grounds that this had settled matters in Wales. Conversely, in 1847 an Irish MP contrasted the lack of military and judicial measures against Welsh rioters with the use of military force in Ireland, and called upon the government 'to extend to Ireland the same measure of justice as to Welshmen'.[15] In a later response to Irish agitation, the Earl of Dunraven observed a greater breadth of motivation to the unrest, which set it apart from Rebeccaism and meant it could not be addressed by the same means, since in the Welsh instance 'the objects of the rioters were well understood, and, their ends having been attained, the riots ceased. Nothing was easier'.[16] In each case, the salient point is the government's success in subduing single-issue unrest in Wales through non-coercive arbitration. The expounding of this narrative reaches its apex in Peel's speech of April 1849:

> Three or four years since we found all the southern counties of Wales in a state of insurrection on account of the turnpike tolls within those districts. The Rebecca riots must be familiar to many of those whom I address. The Queen's troops were resisted: it became necessary to apply a remedy. We proposed to Parliament to send down a commission to inquire into these tolls; we found the necessity of extinguishing them, and placing them on a new footing . . . We offered to the parties that simple arbitration, leaving them to go to law if they pleased. There was a general disposition to acquiesce in our proposal, on account of the saving of expense; the turnpike tolls have been abolished in Wales; peace has been restored.[17]

By the time of Peel's speech, enough time may be judged to have elapsed for political authority to produce a definitive construction of events, which could then be used as a case study against which to measure events in Ireland and advocate responses to them. Peel's account both exaggerates the extent of the riots and simplifies their solution, besides ignoring the complex variety of grievances which underpinned them and the fact that protest and disorder under the auspices of Rebecca persisted long after 1844.[18] The prevalence of this particular version of events can be attributed less to its historical accuracy and more to its convenience as a rhetorical device which could reinforce a narrative of appropriate and beneficial government action.

The 1844 Commission of Inquiry and its reinterpreting of Rebeccaism

The government and media's rendering of Rebeccaism as a single-issue anti-toll gate campaign is prefigured in the 1844 Commission of Inquiry. The inclusion of evidence in the commissioners' report was determined by the ease with which it could be fitted into a predetermined narrative, in which the concern with providing legislative remedies was paramount and grievances were priori-tised accordingly.

The royal commission as a form of investigatory body grew increasingly frequent and refined in the early nineteenth century, with more than one hundred set up between 1832 and 1846. Their proliferation reflects the extension of the Victorian administrative state and its growing intervention in areas including public health, education, law enforcement, factory operation and poor relief.[19] The majority of government commissions adhered to a pattern established by the 1832 Poor Law inquiry, which saw a central board of three commissioners devising questionnaires and overseeing operations from London while delegating itinerant sub-commissioners to collect information over a designated geo-graphical area. Each commissioner then produced an initial report, bringing together 'relevant' evidence from individual testimonies, before a final First Report by all commissioners consolidated the evidence to produce 'a digest of the whole matter returned'.[20]

In most respects, the Rebecca commission followed this estab-lished pattern. It was chaired by Thomas Frankland Lewis, who owned land on the Radnorshire borders and had previously chaired the Poor Law Commission before resigning in 1838. His fellow commissioners – Robert Henry Clive, MP for South Shrop-shire and second son of the Earl of Powis, and William Cripps, a barrister and MP for Cirencester – likewise fit the pattern of 'rising professional men' assigned responsibility for previous com-missions.[21] The major divergence was that the three appointed commissioners, rather than conducting operations from London, spent seven weeks touring the major centres of south Wales, not limiting themselves solely to places disturbed by rioting. Beginning on 24 October with eleven days spent at Carmarthen, they then moved on to spend shorter periods at Haverfordwest, Narberth, Newcastle Emlyn, Cardigan, Aberystwyth, Rhayader, Presteigne, Brecon, Llandeilo, Llanelli, Swansea, Bridgend and Cardiff, before finishing at Merthyr Tydfil on 13 December. They also delegated several parties to investigate the affairs of turnpike trusts in each area; when the commissioners moved on to a different locality, the minutes of evidence usually open with a prolonged and detailed report on this from the relevant subcommittee.[22] The submission of evidence was invited through newspaper advertisements and publicly circulated handbills, with interpreters employed where necessary. Over ten thousand questions were asked and the information obtained amounted to over four hundred pages.

The evidence taken by the commissioners, and their subsequent report and recommendations, form a body of evidence containing valuable insight into contemporary social conditions which has been used to varying degrees by historians. Howell considers its value to be limited, since 'only the local gentry and magistrates' provided its evidence.[23] This was also the basis of contemporary criticism by the *Times* correspondent, Thomas Campbell Foster.[24] However, Williams notes that, while the commission 'listened to anyone who chose to appear before it' and so could hardly avoid accepting submissions from gentry and magistrates, this did not preclude there being several 'humble men' among its witnesses, including at least one man alleged to have played Rebecca.[25] Jones notes the praise afforded the commission for gathering evidence 'from a wide selection of people' and deems it more satisfactory than previous investigations made in the area.[26]

The commission's findings, published in March 1844, began with a general discussion of dissatisfaction with the behaviour of the turnpike trusts, before a detailed examination of the affairs of each, which recorded mismanagement, and occasional abuse, but no deliberate attempt to defraud. It criticised the frequency and amount of payments demanded and in some cases the conduct of toll collectors. After 'long and careful deliberation', the commission recommended that trusts in each county be consolidated and boards created to take over road management in each shire.[27] The publication of the commission's final report was followed in May by the Home Secretary's announcement that the government's legislative response was already at an advanced stage. The Turnpike Consolidation Act was passed in August 1844 and closely followed the commission's recommendations. A further commission, again chaired by Frankland Lewis, transferred the work of the trusts to new county roads boards. David Williams suggests that the report's moderate nature made it uncontroversial and discouraged any widespread discussion of it.[28] In Parliament, the consolidation of the trusts was generally welcomed and satisfaction expressed that the Welsh grievances had been aired and examined.[29]

The commissioners' compilation of evidence reflects the growing contemporary emphasis on the economic, bureaucratic and administrative. Statistical tables, statutes and Acts of Parliament are all drawn upon in the First Report and Appendix, and this statistical preoccupation is sustained in the commission's examination of various turnpike trust officials. The repeated use of the word 'mismanagement' in reference to the operations of the trusts, for instance, illustrates the commission's bureaucratic understanding of the problems they uncover. This outlook is also apparent in the focus on quantifiable, material effects in the discussions of the Poor Law, tithes and magistrates' fees which are brought to the forefront in the First Report. The passages discussing popular discontent at the tithe commutation are based around tables showing the proportional increase in tithes for each county, with a fuller exposition of the figures provided in an Appendix.[30] The commission exhibits the increase in tithes as a cause for concern by way of these material statements, rather than by any reference to the subjective accounts of personal hardship offered in witness statements. An Appendix contains tables showing the salaries of medical officers, establishment charges and expenditure by Poor Law unions, and other data relating to the issues discussed. This further demonstrates the commission's preoccupation with establishing concrete and tangible evidence of error, wrongdoing or hardship, as opposed to witnesses' less tangible assertions of 'injustice'.[31]

A further notable aspect of the commission's report is the extent to which it marginalises the figure which lent the riots a name and public persona. As a figurehead, Rebecca is strangely absent from the commissioners' summation of evidence, despite her occasional prominence in the minutes. Although Rebecca and the concept of 'Rebeccaism' receive no mention in the First Report, witness statements demonstrate the term's assimilation into local vocabulary. William Chambers, a Llanelli trustee, reports that his trust's gates were 'Rebeccaized first of all, and then removed by order of the trustees', and at Swansea Thomas Penrice reports

that his 'parishioners are very much discontented . . . and in fact
I am almost afraid we shall have Rebeccaism there'. Despite this,
Rebecca remains a spectral presence in the commission, not for-
mally acknowledged by the commissioners themselves. The Rev.
Eleazar Evans presents the commission with two Rebecca letters
and describes her campaign of 'terror' against his curate's efforts
to establish a Church of England schoolroom in a parish 'of 800
or 1000 people that are not near the established church'.[32] Such
concerns do not make their way into the First Report, which is
concerned with stating problems and possible solutions, rather
than examining the process by which these problems were brought
to light. The abstract concept of Rebecca, and mentions of her in
the text, are glossed over in favour of framing grievances within a
practical and constitutional context.

   The demographics of those giving evidence, which are disputed
in historiographical accounts, can be clarified to some extent by
reference to the minutes of evidence. The stated occupations of
witnesses, including carriers and hauliers as well as tenant farmers, support David Williams's assertion that the commissioners
interviewed 'humble men' as well as local gentry and magistrates. However, a number of factors qualify this. Variations exist
in the commissioners' methods of examining witnesses, whereby
turnpike trust members and local officials were initially asked to
confirm details of their identity and occupations, before being
asked to confirm or elaborate on information already obtained
by the commissioners. This suggests that while the attendance of
officials and local authority figures was anticipated, the arrival of
those further down the social scale, being a less expected affair,
required them more actively to assert their presence and opinions.
The attendance of farmers and labourers to express their grievances, by contrast, appears to have been a collective affair, with
several names recorded together at a single appearance and the
majority of evidence given by one or more nominated spokesmen,
often figures of community status such as a Dissenting minister.[33] A
number of groups of farmers identify themselves as representative
of a larger collective, having been delegated to present the views,
often in written form, gathered at previous public meetings. Williams records that meetings of this type were held around a week
in advance of the commission's arrival in Llandowror, Haverfordwest, Narberth, Begelly and Pembroke, often reconvening later for

their delegates to report back.[34] One of the implications of this is that, while gentry, magistrates and trustees are assumed to speak in their individual capacity, the testimony of ordinary witnesses is often indicative of a wider collective or community opinion.

Statements by witnesses were presented in a question-and-answer format, which to some extent allows their responses to be heard outside the constraints of any controlling narrative. Sophie Hamilton, in her critique of other royal commissions of the time, makes the point that commissioners presided over all statements, chose the subjects for discussion and directed the course of the interviews.[35] This is not invariably the case in the Rebecca commission, where several interviews begin with open-ended questions including 'What do you wish to say to the commissioners?', 'What complaint have you to make?' and 'Can you give the commissioners any information...?'[36] However, the submission of evidence was also subject to more subtle influence and direction. Witnesses, regardless of status, were often instructed to speak only as regards a particular issue – usually turnpike trusts, magistrates' fees or the Poor Law – with a resultant loss of their opportunity to offer any holistic analysis of the causes of their discontent, as several witnesses attempt to do when left to speak undirected. In the case of farmers and labourers, their testimony was occasionally given under the direction of an authority figure. A Carmarthen magistrate who attended with a group of farmers introduced them by stating: 'They have got several grievances, but there are two subjects only [turnpike tolls and the fees of magistrates' clerks] that I wish them to touch upon'.[37] The farmers' testimony is thus predetermined and the rest of their 'several grievances' go unheard.

The process of compiling the First Report allowed the commissioners to omit or retain aspects of testimony at their discretion and, through this, to determine which factors were seen as sufficiently problematic to merit addressing. The criteria for inclusion within the First Report are acknowledged in its final stages, where the commissioners state that the matters outlined are those considered relevant to the disturbances, and those which are peculiar to Wales, although others may be mentioned in the evidence. This statement of intent is further refined in its subsequent dismissal of 'many of the evils which ... actually depress the community and retard its advancement', since they 'are not such as come within the reach of legislative remedy'.[38] In fact, in the commissioners' search for ways to pacify the disturbed districts, the gates assume the same symbolic importance that they held for the rioters themselves. The First Report locates the inception of the south Welsh problem at the 1842 disturbance at St Clears, following the erection of four new gates by the Whitland Trust:

> The country people thinking it wrong that the trustees should take tolls where they had incurred no expenditure, assembled 'in the midst of summer, at about six o'clock in the afternoon, and those gates were pulled down amidst all sorts of noise and disturbance and great jollity, and were destroyed without the interference of anybody'.[39]

The evidence quoted above is that of the acting magistrate for Pembroke, Lancelot Baugh Allen, who is further quoted as stating that 'there can be no doubt...that with the erection of those gates originated the disturbance'.[40] This appears a selective reading of the information provided, given that other witnesses deny that toll gates were the fundamental cause of the riots and that witness statements mention several other causes of hardship or concern, with toll gates singled out for attack as the most prominent symbol of a far broader but less tangible dissatisfaction. The First Report itself noted that the 1836 Tithe Commutation Act was second only to turnpikes as a cause of discontent, recording a 7 per cent increase in tithes and recommending that landlords grant their tenants some form of redress. The administration of the Poor Law Amendment Act was also strongly criticised, principally on account of the high salaries of the officers and the operation of the bastardy clauses. Other major named causes of discontent were the administration of justice by local magistrates and the amount of fees paid to their clerks. The report also acknowledged the negative effects of progressive increases in the county rate, consecutive severe winters and poor harvests, and reductions in the prices paid to farmers for sheep, cattle and butter.[41] Although the commission recognised flaws in the judicial system – notably magistrates' ignorance of Welsh and their infrequent attendance at petty sessions – it did not recommend establishing a stipendiary magistracy. Instead, the government's response in general and the commission in particular revolved around the attempt to assuage wider discontent by focusing on the need for practical changes to the administration of toll gates. Recognition of this both highlights discrepancies in emphasis between the First Report and the minutes of evidence and helps to explain them.

The First Report's preoccupation with proposing legislative solutions demonstrates the essentially practical nature which determined the limits of its analysis. In its preliminary stages, the commission was charged with inquiring into 'the present state of the laws, as administered in south Wales, which regulate the maintenance and repair of Turnpike-roads, highways and bridges'.[42] This initial pinpointing of turnpike trusts as a major issue is then followed by a detailed investigation of the affairs of local trusts in each area visited by the commission. The latter part of the clause outlining the commission's duty – 'and also into the circumstances which have led to recent acts of violence and outrage in certain districts of that country' – implicitly renders secondary these other problems which the commission might uncover. Within this narrative, investigating the operations of turnpike trusts became central to the collection of evidence and examination of witnesses, and the discontent expressed with turnpike tolls was emphasised above other grievances. These impressions were mobilised and sustained in subsequent parliamentary discourse to justify a particular course of legislative action. The government acted according to the commission's recommendations in consolidating the trusts and establishing road boards, but, as the above discussion demonstrates, this did not necessarily represent the expressed values and priorities of those interviewed. While criticism of the workings of the trusts is of course not undue, its centrality to the commission, and the alacrity with which remedial parliamentary legislation was introduced after the publication of its findings, suggests a preoccupation with providing a tangible response to the riots and a consequent decision to prioritise one particular aspect of their causes which could then be remedied on a national stage. The commission was, in this sense, a self-fulfilling prophecy.

Rebecca and the rise of a Welsh national dress

Despite press reports which spoke with grudging admiration, and ballads and poetry with more open approval, of her daring, strength and growing sphere of influence, there is surprisingly little evidence of attempts to depict Rebecca as a popular heroine in contemporary visual, rather than written, sources.[43] Significantly, some of those that did appear display the influence of a dominant contemporary image of Wales: the institution of Welsh national dress and its female wearer.

Within Wales itself, the early nineteenth century saw the promotion by a literary and artistic elite of reinvented images of the Welsh ancient past and present. The predominant image of Wales had remained that of 'Poor Taff', the poverty-stricken, hot-tempered and garrulous Welshman comically obsessed with his ancient lineage, up until the era of the Napoleonic Wars. At this point, formerly hostile caricatures of both Wales and Scotland underwent transition as the focus on a united defence of Britain, based on its constituent countries' common bonds of Protestantism and opposition to Catholic France, took precedence in popular culture. This loosening of the grip of older images, along with the flourishing of pictorial satire in the years 1760–1820 and the emergence of 'John Bull', who was frequently accompanied by complementary stereotypes of Wales and Scotland, supplied a fertile ground for the growth of alternative portraits of the Welsh nation.[44] The earlier less than flattering depictions of Wales also gave way in the early nineteenth century under the upsurge of Romantic interest in idealised popular culture, dress and customs among the Celtic nations. Devices such as Iolo Morganwg's revival of the Gorsedd of Bards, and the design and promotion of a standardised national costume by the Welsh heiress and arts patron Augusta Hall, Lady Llanover, formed a mutually beneficial relationship with the emerging Welsh tourist industry.[45]

Hall's prize-winning essay, submitted to the 1834 Eisteddfod, on 'Advantages Resulting from the Preservation of the Welsh Language and National Costume of Wales', was instrumental in the promotion throughout the 1830s and 1840s of the idea of a Welsh national dress, and in the consequent shift of the dominant symbolic image of Wales from male to female.[46] The outfits in Hall's 1834 *Book of Welsh Costumes* were based on the more archaic elements of female rural and occupational dress, tailored to incorporate the local manufactures of specific regions. Hall's basic template involved a flannel petticoat, apron and shawl, with a tall hat of black felt or velvet. While not necessarily representative, authentic or popular, versions of the dress were adopted and promoted by Hall's landowning and artistic circle, foisted upon their female servants and exhibited at balls, dinners and Eisteddfods. The boom in mass tourism occasioned by the expansion of the railway network into Wales throughout the 1830s and 1840s reinforced the idea of particular costume as a conscious expression of authentic Welshness, as artists and publishers mass-produced lithographs and prints showing 'typical' Welsh scenes which invariably included women in Welsh dress. The early nineteenth century consequently saw the promotion of images of Wales which may have borne little or no relation to the realities of contemporary Welsh life, but which contained instantly and widely recognised visual symbols: the mountainous landscape, the harp, the leek, the spinning-wheel, the market-day or Eisteddfod scene and, above all, the female figure in 'traditional' Welsh dress.[47] This image was by default female, and by further specification was elderly and rural.

The extent to which the concept of Welsh national dress took hold in the 1830s and 1840s, and, more significantly, its potential for use in political caricature, may be glimpsed in its infiltration of the work subsequently produced by cartoonists and satirists, particularly within Wales. C. J. Grant's 1842 satirical cartoon on the baptism of the new Prince of Wales was a transitional image, which included 'Poor Taff' in a pantheon of Welsh stereotypes but also employed dancing milkmaids wearing the tall black hats promoted by Lady Llanover.[48] Prys Morgan observes how this image of Welsh womanhood became 'very soon accepted as the symbol par excellence of the Welsh, a kind of Welsh Marianne or John Bull'.[49]

At the height of Rebeccaism in June 1843, the *Illustrated London News* carried an artist's impression of 'Rebecca Rioters, or 'Beccas'. This illustration showed Rebecca participants as recognisably male but wearing female dress which included the same stereotypical tall black hats – despite the absence of mentions of such headgear in press and court reports. The illustration thereby drew on the highest-profile symbols of Welsh national identity in order to locate and fix its subject, adding a larger dimension to Rebecca's public image by suggesting her as a representative of Wales as a whole rather than specifically of its south-western tenant farmers. The idea of Rebecca, prevalent in contemporary press reports and popular consciousness, as a dispenser of popular justice and opponent of unjust authority, provided a symbol of female agency more conducive to popular acceptance and support than the passive and objectified fashion-plates promoted by Lady Llanover. This absorption of Rebecca's image into other contemporary high-profile images of national identity, perhaps facilitated by the prominence of feminine signifiers within her representation and performance, indicates a further step in Rebecca's journey into abstract characterisation. It also demonstrates the use of her image for popular representation in a manner that transcended its initial objectives.

The use of Rebeccaism in debates on the Welsh character

This section looks at the use made of Rebeccaism in debates on the nature of the Welsh character and its portrayal as intrinsically lawless, disorderly and, especially, as corrupted by its lack of adherence to English language and religion. Commentaries on the political history of Wales generally agree that the country did not develop a 'recognisably modern' political life until the 1860s, electoral politics having hitherto been the preserve of various factions of the landowning elite.[50] As the nineteenth century progressed, however, the political prominence of Wales increased, not only in the view of external observers but also in its internal political life. For Matthew Cragoe, the catalyst for this development was the growth of a distinctively Welsh politics, at the core of which was the awareness of Wales as a self-conscious and separate nation.[51]

The 1847 report by the Commission of Inquiry into the State of Education in Wales has been proposed as a crisis point in the development of Welsh national consciousness. The work of English commissioners, the 'Blue Books' attacked the country's levels of morality, religiosity, sobriety and cleanliness as well as its standards of education. Cragoe views the 1847 commission as having sparked off a 'new and defiant national identity', which facilitated the growth of a distinctively Welsh politics, through the discussions which followed the outcry over its negative depiction of Wales. Prys Morgan sees the commissioners' insistence on state intervention 'to help the common people learn English' as having disturbed 'a hornet's nest'.[52] The extensive debates and counter-arguments marshalled in defence of the Welsh national character were expressed in literary and visual popular culture and facilitated by the spread of a Welsh weekly press after 1820.[53]

These defensive arguments drew to a large extent on claims for the positive moral influence of the two aspects of Welsh life most criticised by the education commission – Nonconformism and the Welsh language – and defined the nascent idea of Welsh national identity by adherence to these two pillars.[54] R. Merfyn Jones sees a distinctly Welsh political identity developing along these lines from the mid-nineteenth century, associated with Liberal and Nonconformist tenets and present especially after the 1867 franchise reforms and the election of Henry Richard as MP for the Merthyr boroughs.[55] Helped by parliamentary reform and the secret ballot in particular, by the late nineteenth century Welsh politics had become dominated by the Liberal Party and its espousal of legislation influenced by deference to linguistic and denominational issues.[56]

The 1844 Commission of Inquiry foreshadowed the links between a self-conscious Welsh identity and its central tenets of Nonconformism and the Welsh language, in its concerns over the linguistic and religious gulf between Wales and England. A certain paternalist sympathy is apparent in the commissioners' conceptualisation of Welsh farmers as 'frugal, cautious', and in need of regulatory rescue and protection from the machinations of lawless turnpike trusts.[57] However, the First Report ends by veering from this sympathetic approach towards a more overtly didactic and hostile slant, in its identification of linguistic and religious factors which differentiate Wales from England and its call for their eradication. Although choosing to exclude from the First Report several grievances mentioned by witnesses, because they were deemed beyond the scope of legislation, the commissioners nevertheless concluded by stressing what they themselves saw as problematic factors endemic to south Wales. They do not, however, propose specific solutions, since to do so would likewise 'exceed . . . the province of our duty'.[58] The First Report goes on to specify these problems as ignorance of the English language and the prevalence of chapel-based worship:

> the ignorance of the English language which pervades so large a portion of the country [is] a serious impediment to the removal of those evils which most require correction. [It presents obstacles] to the efficient working of many laws and institutions . . . the operations of the Established Church and to the administration of justice. As an impediment

to social intercourse it excludes a large portion of the community from the career of advancement or change of occupation, and it prevents the development of their minds.[59]

The First Report also expresses 'serious concern and regret that so large a proportion of the lower and middle classes are seceders from [the Church of England]':

Of the very serious evils now adverted to, a large class is still in active operation, and the consequences are apparent in that widespread alienation from the doctrines and discipline of the Established Church, which is so prominent a feature in many districts of the country.[60]

The indictment of the Welsh language and Nonconformism as 'evils which ... depress the community and retard its advancement' is justified first by their 'general bearing on the sentiments and feelings of the people' and only latterly by reference to 'the indirect ... influence which may be traced to [them] in connection with those disturbances which were the immediate object of our enquiry'. Despite having denied any 'general spirit of dissatisfaction, or organized hostility to the laws' on the report's first page, the commission nevertheless creates a departing impression of cultural and spiritual malaise attributable to the secession of the disturbed districts from the institutions that symbolise English authority.

The importance of language and religion in the background to Rebeccaism is strongly implied in witness statements. Two Anglican clergymen assert that the disturbances were linked with the attempts of Nonconformist agitators to stir up resistance to the Established Church.[61] In the first of these cases, the Rev. Eleazar Evans produced threatening letters sent to him and written 'in very bad Welch', hinting at the appeal to local and ethnic solidarity which characterised the later stages of the movement. This concern also figures in the statement of Thomas Penrice, a trust surveyor, who links the increased likelihood of Rebeccaism in his locality to the fact that the trustees 'are all English people'.[62] The Pembroke magistrate, Lancelot Baugh Allen, also describes the initial discontent over the Whitland Trust gates as exacerbated by the trustees' English origin.[63] In this context, Nonconformism and the Welsh language do indeed appear as subversive elements feeding into, if not initiating a significant part of the unrest, despite the commission's ultimate reduction of its resolvable causes to that of toll gates. Furthermore, the commission's advocacy of Anglicanism and English speaking is a function of the mentality – of which the commission is representative – which sees association with English as key to enhancing or impeding understanding and social progress. Throughout the First Report, the concept of the Welsh language as a barrier to any 'career of advancement' is contrasted with English as 'the language of advancement and promotion', bringing to the surface the submerged view of Welsh as regressive and disempowering.[64] The commission may represent a step in the process identified by Ieuan Gwynedd Jones whereby the transition to modern political economy tended to reinforce the prestige value of English and to lower the esteem of Welsh among the classes most sensitive to the possibilities of social change and mobility.[65] The *Hereford Times* in its comments on Rhayader displayed a similar perception of Welsh as a barrier to parliamentary or constitutional engagement:

> Separated from the rest of the kingdom to some extent by their language, [the Welsh] are inarticulate when measures that affect their real or supposed interests are pending. They wait to oppose them till they are already enacted.[66]

This is compounded by the First Report's reference to English as 'the language in which [the law] is written', with the implicit result that 'an imperfect knowledge of its provisions . . . must necessarily prevail' among monoglot Welsh-speakers.[67] Here knowledge of the English language is conflated with the validity of written law and the ability to gain its protection and to articulate appeals to it. The commission's insistence on the necessity of English may therefore be perceived more sympathetically – although no less imperialistically – as an attempt to empower the Welsh to defend themselves against the turnpike trusts by use of a weapon more legitimate in the commission's eyes than the unconstitutional destruction of toll gates.

The perception of Rebeccaism as rooted both in the inherent lawlessness of the Welsh, and in the Welsh language and Nonconformism, made its way into official and popular rhetoric during and after the events. In press letters and editorials following the

riots, debates over the nature and objectives of Rebeccaism contained implicit judgements on the character of the Welsh. As
further explored in this book's Epilogue, Rebeccaism's fading
from Carmarthenshire after 1844 was followed by sporadic disturbances in mid- to late nineteenth-century Radnorshire against
the privatisation of salmon weirs, which revived the ritual and
symbolic motifs of earlier Rebeccaism. Within and outside Wales,
commentary on the Radnorshire unrest invoked this specific manifestation of Rebecca as a symbol of the Welsh character in general.
In 1879, an outraged editorial in the *Daily Telegraph* declared:

> Rebecca is an ominous name with Wales and the Welsh… thirty-six
> years have passed since 'Rebecca' started into active life, and became
> synonymous not only with popular discontent, but with lawlessness
> that did not stop short even of murder…. 'Rebecca' has ever since been
> a name of reproach to Wales, and something more. It has been the ral-
> lying-cry of discontent, representative of the 'ultimate argument' of a
> people too impatient or too ignorant to redress their grievances by con-
> stitutional means.[68]

In the same month, the *Hereford Times* considered the disturbances to prove that:

> [while] Welshmen are not more addicted to crime than Englishmen . . .
> it must be admitted their views to the title of laws to be obeyed because
> they are the law are in a more rudimentary stage than the views of
> their fellow-citizens east of the Wye and Severn. The working classes in
> Wales still act from time to time as if open force were the only weapon
> against a law they consider unjust.[69]

In 1910, a letter to the *Times* accused Lloyd George of inciting an
increase in salmon poaching in Wales through his speech opposing the creation of private salmon weirs.[70] The letter alluded to
events in Radnorshire in its reference to locals invading salmon
reserves under 'the cry of Rebecca', and implied the existence of a
fundamental disorderly streak in the Welsh. A subsequent correspondent, perceiving this as an insulting wholesale 'charge against
the Welsh people', denied having seen 'any reference to any such
incidents', but more particularly asserted his own contrasting picture of Rebecca:

S. Salar is quite mistaken in associating the 'Rebecca' with poaching. The Rebecca 'riots' took place more than sixty years ago, and had to do with toll gates, many of which the 'rioters' destroyed. Very few of the gates were re-established.[71]

Here Rebeccaism is again presented as a single-minded mission which successfully achieved its goal. The second writer's wish to detach it from any taint of 'acts of lawlessness' is evident in the cloaking of 'riots' and 'rioters' inside inverted commas, implicitly calling these terms into question, as much as in the explicit denial of Rebecca's association with poaching. Similarly, a letter to *The Times* in April 1944 begins by stating that the riots 'secured for south Wales in 1844, and for the rest of England and Wales in 1862, the public control of turnpike roads'.[72] This continues to portray the riots as a progressive success story, but the architects of progress are now the rioters themselves rather than the government. Welsh correspondents and commentators who wrote to correct or challenge what they regarded as misconceptions of the movement were both demonstrating conflicting ideas of what Rebecca represented and underlining Rebecca's function in enabling the Welsh to represent themselves on a national stage.

Conclusion

By studying the symbol, ritual and costume used by and associated with participants in Rebeccaism, we can see where gaps exist in established knowledge of the movement. Such a focus also makes apparent Rebecca's development over the course of the nineteenth century into a celebrity, stock character, and symbol of popular authority and resistance. Conceptualising the riots' figurehead as an abstract character, based on a commonly acknowledged set of stylised identifiers, allowed 'Rebecca's' identity to be performed by individuals within and outside the arena of protest, and to function in popular and official rhetoric as a multivalent figure serving a variety of constituencies and agendas. In time, the development of a 'myth' of Rebecca enabled her image to transcend the movement's original objectives and serve as a popular motif divested of any specific moral code or political ideology.

The re-examination of Rebeccaite cross-dressing demonstrates that the movement's use of costume was more complex than previously recognised. A preoccupation with viewing protesters simply as 'men dressed as women' fails to explain the integral role in Rebeccaite dress of masculine as well as feminine signifiers – notably false beards, swords and work clothes – which indicate that the figure of Rebecca involved more than straightforward disguise or female imitation. Exploring the ways in which individual male participants experienced their use of costume draws out further unexamined facets of the movement. Although Rebecca was conceptualised in the popular imagination and in press representations as an abstract female figure, this did not extend to the public perception of her individual male actors and supporters, who retained or returned to an essential 'male' identity despite the 'femininity' involved in their participation in protest. A disjuncture is apparent between references to the abstract feminine identities which men assumed in protest, and the use of descriptive masculine pronouns for protesters in court and the press, suggesting that the adoption of feminine guise by male Rebeccaites was acknowledged as a temporary and stylised performance. In addition, the act of performing Rebecca could supply an alternative or expanded presentation of masculinity, which could confer prestige and community status on those who adopted it. Paradoxically, the assumption of female guise could therefore be a strengthening and enabling act for male protesters. However, this 'feminine' guise derived its fundamental strength from being deliberately combined with clashing 'masculine' signifiers to identify the wearer as the character 'Rebecca'. This clarifies the use of feminine garments as neither disguise nor attempts by male protesters to pass as women, although it may have contained incidental or peripheral elements of both.

Individuals who performed 'Rebecca' were able to adopt an abstract persona, highly theatrical and often comic, alluding to contemporary elements of carnival and festival, in which their audience and followers were complicit. They were also able to maintain the detachment between the role they played in protest and their everyday self, in a way that left their essential identity uncompromised. As a trope of inversion, ritual cross-dressing derives its power from the contrast between gender identities in any given cultural context and the ability to deconstruct these contrasts. The use of signifiers emphatically associated with either 'masculine' or 'feminine' suggests that contemporary views of gender were informed by such a deconstruction, in which a sexual binary had to be recognised in order for protesters to transgress or blur its boundaries effectively. However, this transgression appears to have been viewed as a purely temporary and practical measure in order to produce a liminal state in which particular activities could be carried out – not a process which was considered to permanently compromise an individual's gender identity.

The disjuncture between the everyday identities of individual protesters and the performed identity of Rebecca establishes 'Rebecca' as an abstract character, whose identity could be performed by any individual through the adoption of a commonly recognised set of signifiers. Chapter 7 explores how this abstract character, once developed, could be further abstracted from particular acts of protest and used in wider public discourse by supporters and opponents. Press portrayals of Rebecca brought into play aspects of allegory and performance which allowed the subversion or local adaptation of other highly visible images of Victorian femininity. Although as an abstract figure she was usually gendered as female, 'masculine' and 'feminine' qualities were blended in Rebecca's public image in a way reflective of the mixture of signifiers present in Rebeccaite costume. The attribution to Rebecca of 'masculine' qualities tended to be positive by her supporters and grudgingly admiring by her detractors, elevating her above her opponents by virtue of a public display of superior courage, strength and valour. This gendered rhetoric enabled the lampooning of Peel and other political opponents through likening to, or unfavourable contrast with, Rebecca's 'old woman', as well as the comic devalorising of figures in local authority whose besting by Rebecca implied their comparative lack of 'masculine' attributes.

While Rebecca could be portrayed with 'masculine' characteristics in order to underline the lack of these in her national and local opponents, these same attributes were downplayed or absent when 'she' suffered setbacks or defeat. The presentation of Rebecca in press reports and editorials may bear traces of the shift in contemporary attitudes to sexuality following the introduction of the New Poor Law, which encouraged the disapproving view of female agency and independence as threatening and disorderly. This anxiety is apparent in the characterisation of Rebecca as the 'unruly woman', whose gender was emphasised in presentations of 'her' unlicensed lawlessness, aggression and independence in order to accentuate its shocking and threatening nature. In the same way, appeals for and approval of military and political intervention could be constructed as an implicitly justified response to 'her' provocative disobedience and misrule, and as the much-needed restoration of established authority. The identification of Rebecca as female was an intrinsic part of demonstrating both this provocation and this need.

The 1844 Commission of Inquiry into Rebeccaism, which was situated at a formative point in the development of the Victorian state's engagement with and investigation into the lives of individuals, demonstrates some of the adjustments involved on both sides. The transmission of grievances from 'humble men' to the political elite necessitated their translation into a format appropriate for their intended audience. The compilation of the First Report entailed the assimilation of protesters' grievances through the interviewing of witnesses, the processing of this evidence into the written format of the report, and the report's eventual addressing in Parliament. This process shows how the government equipped itself to engage with and understand protesters who expressed themselves and legitimised their actions outside the official structures of power by references to popular authority and tradition, transforming their grievances into a form in which they could be visibly and effectively resolved within a framework of political economy and parliamentary legislation. Recognition of this didactic technique explains the emphasis placed on certain aspects of the movement over others – in this case, the focus on toll gates as a primary grievance, in order to exaggerate the success of legislative remedy.

Despite the changing representations of 'Rebecca' and Rebeccaism, the movement endured as a reference point in popular and political consciousness, partly because of the highly symbolic and performative nature of Rebeccaite activity. The flexible nature of symbols, their power of communication and the ease with which they can be appropriated, are especially apparent when considering the multiplicity of guises attributed to Rebecca and her followers in the press and popular imagination, and when following the steady reduction of the movement in official and popular discourse to an essential understanding based around the adoption of feminine dress as the movement's form and the opposition to toll gates as its content. The persistence of these symbolic and ritual details reflects not only their prominence within Rebeccaite activity but also their importance in the construction of official and popular narratives. Tracing the progress of Rebecca not only displays 'her' capacity to function as a multivalent symbol onto which an array of national and local preoccupations was projected, but also indicates the social, cultural and political concerns behind these various portrayals.

Epilogue. 'The rallying-cry of discontent': Repurposing Rebecca

It is a mistake to consider the pranks of the Rebeccaites in a serious light, or to regard the movement as a rebellion requiring oppression. It is as harmless a demonstration as Guy Fawkes, and is only a playful manifestation of enthusiasm which will very soon cease if not encouraged by public recognition. You should not poke a fire unless you want it to blaze.

(LETTER FROM 'SCRUTINEER'
TO THE *HEREFORD TIMES*, 8 JANUARY 1879)

After 1844, Rebecca's most documented reappearance took place in Radnorshire, where the long-established right of the public to fish for salmon in the weirs of the upper Wye was being increasingly threatened by the creation of privately owned salmon reserves. These events began in 1856, just over a decade after the end of Rebeccaism in Carmarthenshire. Although peaking in the 1860s and 1870s, they continued up to the twentieth century. In 1867–8, and again in the winters of 1877 and 1879, 'a black lot', armed and disguised with blackened faces, made raids on salmon weirs at Rhayader, Llandrindod and Penybont. These protests were described in the local press as 'the revival and reappearance of the terrifying Rebecca and her daughters'.[1] Drawing on the enduring impression of Rebecca as a justified outlaw and anti-hero(ine), *The Times* declared: 'Rhayader has proclaimed war against private property in salmon, as Robin Hood did against royal property in Sherwood stags, and Rob Roy did against Lowland purses and broadcloth'.[2] Beyond the fishery laws, Rebecca's activities in Radnorshire encompassed actions against evictions and enclosures, overpricing by shopkeepers and the depredations of landowners such as the Duke of Beaufort, who through commercial night-netting operations were taking thousands of fish each season from the Wye.

Despite its divergence in location from the events of 1839–44, the Radnorshire unrest evidently represented a continuation of protest inspired by Rebecca, and was carried out with the same emphasis on ritual and costume, and 'popularity and joke', which had characterised the movement in Carmarthenshire. The events saw the revival of Rebecca both as a visible leadership figure, being 'performed' by a participant in the parade which preceded an 1860 attack on a weir at Rhayader, and as an abstract concept lending popular sanction to otherwise illegal activities. At a meeting of magistrates at Presteigne in December 1879, the local clergyman, R. L. Venables, acknowledged: 'The very word "Rebecca" showed [the protests to be] connected with a feeling that prevailed all over Radnorshire more than 30 years ago . . . Then the grievance was the turnpike gates; now it was the river'.[3] The same meeting of magistrates heard a complaint from a Mr Green-Price that a salmon taken during the 'lawless proceedings' of a raid on the Wye had subsequently been 'exposed at the Christmas market in Rhayader labelled "Bred and fed by John Lloyd, of Huntingdon; butchered by Rebecca"'. In a similar vein, a salmon was found nailed to Rhayader market-hall 'with Rebecca's compliments' and the mocking note: 'Where were the river watchers when I was killed? Where were the police when I was hung here?'[4] The laughter of Green-Price's peers, recorded after his report of the former incident, suggests that it was imbued with the same subversive and comical spirit as earlier Rebeccaite activity, and had a similar regard for the power of symbolic display. Green-Price himself admitted that the incident formed 'a public exhibition of the power of Rebeccaism' – part of this power being to challenge authority by asserting an older, alternative authority deriving from popular custom. As in Carmarthenshire, high levels of community solidarity prevented judicial repercussions for the Radnorshire Rebeccaites.[5]

As late as 1898, a Cardiff newspaper reported 'a Rebecca Gang' in the Radnorshire village of Llanbister, who, 'attired in a variety of costumes, and, with faces sooty black', had ducked and flogged a local couple suspected of an unspecified 'breach of the laws of morality'.[6] This late instance of charivari-like activity being attributed to Rebecca recalls the assertion in 1843 that the movement had 'stepped into the place of the old-fashioned Ceffil-prens'. There exists, too, a photograph of masked salmon poachers which claims to show Radnorshire Rebeccaites on the river Edw in December 1932.[7] There is no doubt that Rebecca's name and iconography have endured both in popular memory and as a facilitator of newly minted protest. In 1973 the Irish-born journalist Paddy French founded 'a radical magazine for Wales', providing scrutiny of and challenge to corruption among establishment figures, for which he took the name *Rebecca*. Its circulation peaked at 17,000.[8] The 1970s also saw the forming of the Welsh arts collective known as the BECA group, in protest at the lack of official recognition or support in Wales for politicised art. The group's foundational performance at the 1977 National Eisteddfod recalled not only Rebeccaism's theatricality in protest, but also the outrage surrounding the Blue Books.[9] In millennial Pembrokeshire, an area in which the combination of bad weather, foot and mouth disease, and the impact of both on local tourism, had provoked a sense of crisis, protesters against genetically modified crops took the name Deffro Rebecca ('Wake up Rebecca') and wore 'traditional' Welsh dress to symbolise agrarian culture. An observer of their protest in the summer of 2001 recorded:

> Welsh flags, Welsh costumes and men dressed as Rebecca were all in evidence . . . In general it was a very good-natured crowd and many of the older people referred back to other protests they had been involved in during the 1960s and 1970s.[10]

Over a decade later, on St David's Day in 2014, singing clubs from Chepstow, Usk and the Forest of Dean wore shawls, bonnets and coal-blackened faces to highlight the price of tolls across the Severn Bridge and their economic impact on local communities. An accompanying crowd sported leeks and daffodils and played drums, tambourines and kazoos, in what was intended as, again, a 'light-hearted and entertaining' protest.[11] The notably upbeat and irreverent nature of contemporary references to Rebecca by protest groups seems to stem from the enduring, if simplistic, impression of the movement as a cheerfully triumphant success story, and perhaps also from the comical and fun associations carried by its instantly recognisable motifs of parading and costume – particularly the pantomime connotations of performative cross-dressing by male protesters. (It is difficult to imagine the Scotch Cattle, with their grim hypermasculinity and uncompromising guerrilla tactics, inspiring 'light-hearted and entertaining' popular demonstrations in the modern era.)

The evolution and expansion of the meaning of 'Rebecca' in protest over the past century and a half illustrates the way in which the movement's repertoire was, and remains, able to transcend its original frame of reference. Since their inception in 1840s Carmarthenshire, the name and image of Rebecca have become fluid symbols, capable of inspiring and facilitating popular action far removed from the use to which they were initially put. In July 1843 a writer to the *Welshman*, reporting the demolition of toll gates at Scleddy and Fishguard Hill, speculated that the events in fact 'had no connexion with "Becca", but were a kind of "*Becca fach*"'. Over the next hundred and fifty years, these subsequent 'little Rebeccas', with their variety of targets and modes of operation, were linked only by their use of the original's name or symbols to express opposition. The evolving use of 'Rebecca' after 1844 constitutes, to recall Nicolas Rogers's description of the subversive referencing of Jacobitism, 'an idiom of defiance . . . a mobile script [which was] deployed in a variety of contexts and could generate multiple meanings'. In contemporary parlance, this evolution fits the modern definition of a 'meme' – described at its most basic as 'a unit for carrying cultural ideas, symbols, or practices that can be transmitted from one mind to another through writing, speech, gestures, rituals, or other imitable phenomena with a mimicked theme'.[12]

Over a century and a half after Rebecca's first appearance, 2011 was a year encompassing unrest on an international scale. In what the *Financial Times* dubbed a 'year of global indignation', the 'Arab Spring' protests convulsed Tunisia, Egypt, Libya, Bahrain, Syria and Yemen, and coincided and overlapped with anti-austerity protests in Spain and Greece, riots in London and the international advent of Occupy, described as a 'movement-cum-meme'.[13] These protests' underlying reasons were not uniform or consistent, but the discontent of participants coalesced around their perception of growing economic hardship and inequality, of political authorities in thrall to corporate or private financial interests, and of local, national and global institutions which were increasingly closed off to directly democratic accountability or influence. Although comparisons were drawn with other turbulent years, including 1848, 1968 and 1989, the protests of 2011 were notable for their global reach, their collective basis and their instinctively extra-parliamentary nature – protesters overwhelmingly did not appeal to party political or constitutional channels of redress, but rejected them with greater or lesser degrees of distrust, disillusion or disgust.

At the close of the year, *Time* magazine acknowledged this 'global wave of dissent' by choosing 'The Protestor' as its Person of the Year. This symbolic figure appeared on the magazine's cover masked with a woollen hat and scarf, with only the eyes meeting those of the reader. Effectively anonymised, they were therefore able to represent a varied and multivalent constituency. Pollyanna Ruiz notes that in the image:

> the usually identifying features of the human face are concealed, the individual's gender, race and age remain deliberately undetermined . . . the protestor's masked face speaks for all those who perceive themselves to have been excluded from the process of democracy.[14]

The image and concept of the anonymous protester had of course been present in twenty-first-century public consciousness prior to its illumination by such a beacon of the mainstream as *Time*. Rebeccaism's leadership by 'sinister personifications' rather than 'known men' was among the components which saw it categorised as a 'primitive rebellion', and other authorities have stated that the disturbances 'must have been the last in any advanced western country in which the participants felt the need to personify their cause'.[15] And yet contemporary protest continues to make use of many techniques of the past, and is increasingly favouring what might be seen by some as 'sinister personifications' of the general causes that unite its anonymous, leaderless movements. Most notably, following the 2005 film adaptation of the dystopian comic-book series *V for Vendetta*,[16] a variety of protest groups and individuals have made mimetic use of the stylised Guy Fawkes mask designed by David Lloyd for the series's vigilante protagonist.[17] Initially cropping up on internet discussion forums, the mask became a recognised symbol of the online collective Anonymous, but it also appeared extensively within the Occupy movement and other protests against political, judicial, corporate and financial institutions.[18] The group Anonymous is itself multifaceted, leaderless and adaptable to a variety of causes. Since its inception in the mid-2000s, its membership has carried out a wide range of protests, whistleblowings and pranks against international targets. As an analyst of the collective observed in 2012:

> what Anonymous has become, in reality, is a culture, one with its own distinctive iconography (the Fawkes masks, the headless man in the business suit), its own self-referential memes, its own coarse sense of humor ... Like a plastic Fawkes mask, Anonymous is an identity that anyone can put on, whenever they want to join up with the invisible online horde.[19]

The same emphasis on collective strength through individual identification with a symbolic figure enabled a servant of Thomas Frankland Lewis, discussing the events retrospectively in 1848, to remark that 'we are all of us Rebeccas'.[20]

Membership of Anonymous is not exclusively dependent on the display of this symbol, and the symbol itself has transcended its association with both Anonymous and *V for Vendetta*. Like the frock, bonnet, false beard and horsehair wig worn by Rebeccaites, the stylised Guy Fawkes mask has become an all-purpose 'idiom of defiance'. Broadly speaking, it can be used to signify one's passive or active participation in a populist, loosely collective response to local, national or global authority which is perceived as corrupt, oppressive, negligent or failing. The mask has been worn in the UK to highlight the fraudulent claiming of expenses by MPs, in India to protest against government censorship of the internet, by members of the Polish parliament to express opposition to the Anti-Counterfeiting Trade Agreement, and by anti-government protesters in countries including Thailand, Turkey, Brazil, Egypt, Australia and Venezuela. Following its appearance in 'Arab Spring'-inspired protests in Bahrain and Saudi Arabia, governments there attempted to ban the mask's importation, referring to it as 'revolution-mask' and describing it as a symbol of 'rebels and revenge'.[21] The rapid spread and adaptation of this particular iconography, and the panic and suspicion it can invoke in authorities, may call to mind the excitable analysis in a *Carmarthen Journal* editorial of 1843:

> We are everywhere asked, Who is Rebecca? We answer, Rebecca is an impersonality – a mere political abstraction, or if she has any corporeal

form or essence, we say that she is AN EMBODIMENT OF THE PRINCIPLES OF REVOLUTION.[22]

In this context, too, the 1844 description of Rebecca in *Blackwood's Magazine* as 'no more than a living figure to give effect to the drama, as boys dress up an effigy and parade it as the Guy Fawkes' appears spectacularly far-sighted.[23] 'Idioms of defiance' such as these are able to unite single-issue campaigns and movements, giving them a broad umbrella – a brand – under which to operate and by which to communicate their common oppositions. The late twentieth-century turn in Western democracies away from mass interest and involvement in traditional party politics, leading to a proliferation of discrete single-issue campaigns, is increasingly giving way to an environment in which 'previously separate campaign strands have coalesced into a shared multiplicity of differing positions', with 'protest coalition movements attempting to articulate polyvocal dissent', characterised by ideological flexibility and multiplicity.[24] Contemporary anti-capitalist movements have tended to define themselves by slogans like 'one no, many yeses', emphasising and articulating their common ground while acknowledging their differences in contexts, solutions and preferred alternatives.

The global financial crisis of 2008 has inspired movements united by their common resentment of remote elites, economic and social dislocation, and the distance they perceive between themselves and sites and mechanisms of decision-making power. In Western Europe, while 2011 may have dramatically pulled back the curtain on the extent of popular discontent, the decades beforehand were spent setting the stage for it – not only through growing economic hardship in an increasingly post-industrial economy, but also through the accumulation of wealth by a 'superrich' elite, marginalising of workers' organisations, spread of precarious labour and diminishing of the welfare state. In addition, following the dissolution of the Soviet Union after 1991, the trend among Western political parties founded to represent the interests of organised labour has increasingly been to pursue a post-socialist direction which neglects their traditional working-class base of support. The resultant lack of any coherent electoral alternative to the socioeconomic status quo, and the narrowing of working-class access to roles as elected representatives or within political parties, has been widely referred to as a crisis of political representation. The political vacuum thus created has been filled, in part, by a resurgence of leaderless, anonymous, mimetic protest movements, in contrast to mass-membership political parties or trade unions seeking constitutional channels of redress.

The increasing abandonment of the organised demonstrations and constitutional petitioning which characterised nineteenth-century industrial society, and the unsettling of the distinction between protester and public which movements like Occupy represent, has, as Noam Chomsky observes, begun to shift the focus of contemporary protest away from the issue of demanding access to democratic channels and towards the current failures and flaws of the democratic process itself.[25] In doing so, those taking part in such movements have found themselves criticised as naïve idealists at best and irresponsible insurrectionaries at worst, in tones which recall the judgement of the *Daily Telegraph* in 1879 on, not Occupy, but Rebeccaism, as 'the rallying-cry of discontent, representative of the "ultimate argument" of a people too impatient or too ignorant to redress their grievances by constitutional means'.[26]

Contemporary movements against elite corruption, austerity and democratic deficits have much in common with pre-industrial ways of expressing opposition and agitating for change, like the 'Wilkes and Liberty' mobs whom James M. Jasper describes as 'part election campaign, part agitation for civil liberties, and part drunken festival'.[27] They echo the kind of Rebeccaite rhetoric which emphasised collective numbers and strength, gathering multiple grievances and sectors of the community under the 'children of Rebecca' umbrella much as Occupy's slogan of 'We are the 99% [of society, vs the elite 1%]' attempts to do. Viewing Rebeccaism as a flexible organisational method defined by the use of iconography and symbol, rather than as a concrete organisation or single-issue campaign, illuminates how its participants may have experienced their part in it. Conceiving of Rebeccaism as a broad movement, which allowed the expression of 'polyvocal dissent' towards disparate targets, lets us attempt an answer to the bafflement voiced in June 1843 by the *Carmarthen Journal*:

> *Rebel*ca [*sic*] would be a more proper designation for this refractory dame; for we defy any sane man to trace any necessary connection

between toll gates and work-houses to make them indiscriminate objects of hostility to the rural population of this country.[28]

Nor should the use by contemporary protest movements of past techniques seem baffling or anachronistic. Creative and spontaneous forms of protest other than the mass demonstration have played a consistent part in popular opposition throughout the nineteenth and twentieth centuries, and have frequently drawn on the mocking or subversive power of humour against a repressive state apparatus. The contemporary use of such techniques is appropriate to an altered post-industrial context in which protest increasingly takes place on a local or global rather than a national stage, and which therefore employs a symbolic repertoire through which protesters can transcend language barriers and communicate instantly through visual media. Their increasing use today demonstrates – returning us from the general to the specific – that the type of oral-visual repertoire employed by Rebeccaites to articulate broad popular opposition was and remains adaptable to multiple contexts. Although not tied to any enduring organisation or campaign, this repertoire has endured as a set of symbols available to those wishing to express popular opposition to one or many perceived injustices. For as long as such popular opposition is required, we will continue to find the likes of Rebecca resurgent.

Notes

Chapter 1

1 *The Times*, 5 August 1843; 'Rebecca: Anti-turnpike League', *Quarterly Review*, 74 (June 1844), no. 779, 123–54; 125. (All *Quarterly Review* citations come from this issue.)

2 Following the early account of Henry Tobit Evans, *Rebecca and her Daughters: Being a History of the Agrarian Disturbances in Wales Known as the 'Rebecca Riots'* (Cardiff, 1910), see the major works by David Williams, *The Rebecca Riots: A Study in Agrarian Discontent* (Cardiff, 1955) and David J. V. Jones, *Rebecca's Children: A Study of Rural Society, Crime and Protest* (Oxford, 1989). See also Pat Molloy, *And They Blessed Rebecca: An Account of the Welsh Tollgate Riots, 1839–1844* (Llandysul, 1983); David Egan, *People, Protest and Politics: Case Studies in Nineteenth-Century Wales* (Llandysul, 1987); and the overview by David Howell in Trevor Herbert and Gareth Elwyn Jones (eds), *People and Protest: Wales 1815–1880* (Cardiff, 1988), pp. 113–38.

3 See Elizabeth Amy Dillwyn, *The Rebecca Rioter: A Story of Killay Life* (London, 1880); Violet Jacob, *The Sheep Stealers* (London, 1902); and Alexander Cordell's relatively well-known *Hosts of Rebecca* (London, 1960). Alun Hoddinott's piece for chamber choir, as reported in *The Times*, 16 February 1962, sets to music a poem on the riots by Jon Manchip White.

4 See, for example, letters to *The Times*, 8 April 1846, 20 June 1857, 27 April 1888; articles in *The Times*, 16 September 1929, 10 December 1935; and the commemorative pageant recorded in the papers of E. T. Lewis, Pembrokeshire Record Office, D/ETL 84.

5 James M. Jasper, *Protest: A Cultural Introduction to Social Movements* (Cambridge, 2014), p. 6.

6 NLW, Ormathwaite FG 1.14, journal of John Walsh, p. 18; Minutes of Evidence to the 1844 Commission of Inquiry, pp. 125, 371.

7 *Welshman*, 17 February 1843.

8 *Swansea Journal*, 5 July 1843.

9 *Swansea Journal*, 26 July 1843.

10 *The Times*, 30 June 1843, 14 April 1944; Tobit Evans, *Rebecca and her Daughters*, pp. 9–10; Williams, *Rebecca Riots*, pp. 155, 189; Jones, *Rebecca's Children*, p. 206; Molloy, *And They Blessed Rebecca*, pp. 29, 342. An exegesis of the name itself as that of a fertility or earth goddess can be found in W. F. Albright, 'The Name Rebecca', *Journal of Biblical Literature*, 39/3–4 (1920), 165–6; 166.

11 Jones, *Rebecca's Children*, p. 256; Tobit Evans quoted in Jones, *Rebecca's Children*, p. vii.

12 Williams, *Rebecca Riots*, pp. 75, 255.

13 Howell, 'Rebecca riots', in Herbert and Jones (eds), *People and Protest*, pp. 113–38; p. 124.

14 See, for instance, Lowri Ann Rees, 'Paternalism and Rural Protest: The Rebecca Riots and the Landed Interest of South-West Wales', *Agricultural History Review*, 59/1 (2011), 36–60; Prys Morgan, 'Wild Wales: civilizing the Welsh from the sixteenth to the nineteenth centuries', in Peter Burke, Brian Harrison and Paul Slack (eds), *Civil Histories: Essays Presented to Sir Keith Thomas* (Oxford, 2000), pp. 265–83; p. 280; Ivor Wilks, *South Wales and the Rising of 1839: Class Struggle as Armed Struggle* (London, 1984), pp. 250–1.

15 Howell, 'Rebecca riots', p. 119; Jones, *Rebecca's Children*, pp. vi, 242; Williams, *Rebecca Riots*, p. 75.

16 Jasper, *Protest: A Cultural Introduction*, p. 6.

Chapter 2

1 Pat Molloy, *And They Blessed Rebecca: An Account of the Welsh Tollgate Riots, 1839–1844* (Llandysul, 1983), p. 20.

2 Ieuan Gwynedd Jones, *Mid Victorian Wales: The Observers and Observed* (Cardiff, 1992), p. 104; Ryland Wallace, *Organise! Organise! Organise! A Study of Reform Agitations in Wales 1840–1886* (Cardiff, 1991), p. 1; John Williams, *A Digest of Welsh Historical Statistics* (Cardiff, 1985), p. 81.

3 David J. V. Jones, *Rebecca's Children: A Study of Rural Society, Crime and Protest* (Oxford, 1989), pp. 21–7; Harold Carter, 'Urban and industrial

settlement in the modern period', in D. Huw Owen (ed.), *Settlement and Society in Wales* (Cardiff, 1989), pp. 269–96; David W. Howell, *The Rural Poor in Eighteenth-Century Wales* (Cardiff, 2000), pp. 13, 27.

4   See David Howell, *Patriarchs and Parasites: The Gentry of South-West Wales in the Eighteenth Century* (Cardiff, 1986); Howell, *Rural Poor*, pp. 10–11; Matthew Cragoe, *An Anglican Aristocracy: The Moral Economy of the Landed Estate in Carmarthenshire 1832–1895* (Oxford, 1996), pp. 9–27; Glyn Williams (ed.), *Crisis of Economy and Ideology: Essays on Welsh Society, 1840–1980* (London, 1983); J. E. Thomas, *Social Disorder in Britain 1750–1850: The Power of the Gentry, Radicalism and Religion in Wales* (London, 2011).

5   Gwyn A. Williams, *The Welsh in their History* (London, 1982), pp. 7–8, 76; Jones, *Rebecca's Children*, p. 21; Ieuan Gwynedd Jones, *Mid-Victorian Wales*, p. 107.

6   Jones, *Rebecca's Children*, p. 35; NLW, Nanteos Estate MS L1326, L1349, letter from Morgan Williams, 23 December 1844; Howell, 'Rebecca riots', in Trevor Herbert and Gareth Elwyn Jones (eds), *People and Protest: Wales 1815–1880* (Cardiff, 1988), pp. 113–38.

7   Peter D. G. Thomas, *Politics in Eighteenth-Century Wales* (Cardiff, 1998), pp. 3–8; Cragoe, *Anglican Aristocracy*, pp. 1–4, 111.

8   Frank O'Gorman, 'Campaign Rituals and Ceremonies: The Social Meaning of Elections in England 1780–1860', *Past & Present*, 135 (1992), 79–115; Matthew Cragoe, *Culture, Politics and National Identity in Wales 1832–1886* (Oxford, 2004), pp. 10, 206–40; Carmarthenshire Archives Service, Brigstocke MS 4, pp. 34–5.

9   R. Merfyn Jones, 'Beyond Identity? The Reconstruction of the Welsh', *Journal of British Studies*, 31/4 (1990), 330–57; 344; Trefor M. Owen, *Welsh Folk Customs* (Llandysul, 1987), pp. 17–18.

10   Quoted in Jones, *Rebecca's Children*, p. 41.

11   John R. Gillis, *For Better, for Worse: British Marriages, 1600 to the Present* (Oxford, 1985), pp. 153–9; NLW, Cefn Bryntalch MS 399.

12   Thomas, *Politics in Eighteenth-Century Wales*, p. 240.

13   See David Jones, 'Rural crime and protest in the Victorian era', in G. E. Mingay (ed.), *The Unquiet Countryside* (London, 1989), pp. 111–124; p. 113; Glyn Williams, 'On class and status groups in Welsh rural society', in Williams (ed.), *Crisis of Economy and Ideology*, pp. 134–46; Cragoe, *Anglican Aristocracy*, p. 94.

14   *The Times*, 27 September 1843; Jones, *Rebecca's Children*, pp. 95–9.

15   *The Times*, 2 April 1844; see also Thomas, *Social Disorder in Britain*, p. 211.

16   See Rees, 'Paternalism and Rural Protest'; Howell, 'Rebecca riots', pp. 115–16.

17   NLW, MS 21209C, letter of Thomas Cooke, 24 August 1843.

18   Howell, 'Rebecca riots', p. 122; *The Times*, 19 August 1843; NLW, MS 14590E, Letter 18; Williams, *Welsh in their History*, p. 75.

19   NLW, Cwrt Mawr MS 1201F, pp. 1–3.

20   Aled Jones, *Press, Politics and Society: A History of Journalism in Wales* (Cardiff, 1993), p. 2.

21   Cragoe, *Culture, Politics and National Identity*, pp. 208–10.

22   E. P. Thompson, 'The Moral Economy of the English Crowd in the Eighteenth Century', *Past & Present*, 50 (1971), reprinted in E. P. Thompson, *Customs in Common: Studies in Traditional Popular Culture* (New York, 1993), pp. 185–258. On agrarian extensions of this concept, see Adrian Randall and Andrew Charlesworth, 'The moral economy: riot, markets and social conflict', pp. 1–32, and Roger Wells, 'The moral economy of the English countryside', pp. 209–72; 250–2, both in Adrian Randall and Andrew Charlesworth (eds), *Moral Economy and Popular Protest: Crowds, Conflict and Authority* (London, 2000); Bob Bushaway, *By Rite: Custom, Ceremony and Community in England 1700–1880* (London, 1982); Mick Reed and Roger Wells (eds), *Class, Conflict and Protest in the English Countryside, 1700–1880* (London, 1990).

23   Thompson, *Customs*, p. 340.

24   Randall and Charlesworth, 'Moral economy', p. 10.

25   Rees 'Paternalism and Rural Protest, 36–60; 53–7.

26   TNA, HO 42/35.

27   On Welsh crime and protest, see Jones, 'The Welsh and crime', in Clive Emsley and James Walvin (eds), *Artisans, Peasants and Proletarians 1760–1860: Essays Presented to Gwyn A. Williams* (London, 1985), pp. 81–103; Gwyn A. Williams, 'Locating a Welsh working class: the frontier years', in David Smith (ed.), *A People and a Proletariat: Essays in the History of Wales 1780–1980* (London, 1980), pp. 16–46. On the 1816 strike, see Jones, *Before Rebecca*, pp. 69–85. On the Scotch Cattle see Jones, *Before Rebecca*, pp. 86–116; Wilks, *South Wales and the Rising*, pp. 79–87; Rhian E. Jones, 'An analysis of the significance of popular ritual, with reference to the "Scotch Cattle" movement in early nineteenth-century Wales' (M.St. dissertation, Oxford University, 2005). On the significance of Newport in studies of Chartism, Welsh radicalism and the Victorian period in general, see Wilks, *South Wales and the Rising*; David Williams, *John Frost: A Study in Chartism*

(Cardiff, 1939); David J. V. Jones, *The Last Rising: The Newport Insurrection of 1839* (Oxford, 1985). Historiographical opinion is divided on the intentions behind the march, with David Williams viewing it as a poorly planned and executed 'fiasco' which 'marked the eclipse of Chartism in south Wales'. He makes the further claim that Newport was a local affair with relatively little connection with Chartists outside the area, intended only as a 'monster demonstration' rather than any serious attempt at an armed popular uprising. Jones argues conversely that the Newport Chartists were in fact mobilised by hopes of a general national rising which overcame sectional and regional rivalries. Ivor Wilks goes furthest in claiming Newport as a manifestation of a 'new proletarian class consciousness' (Williams, *John Frost*, p. 149; Wilks, *South Wales and the Rising*, p. 235).

28 See Thompson, *Customs*, pp. 467–538.
29 David J. V. Jones, *Crime in Nineteenth-Century Wales* (Cardiff, 1992); Jones, 'Welsh and crime', pp. 81–103; Jones, 'Rural crime and protest', pp. 111–24; Frank Welsh, *The Four Nations: A History of the United Kingdom* (London, 2002), p. 242. On Carmarthen see Jones, *Before Rebecca*, pp. 117–32.
30 Jones, *Rebecca's Children*, pp. 24ff.; Howell, 'Rebecca riots', pp. 113–24.
31 NLW, Harpton Court MS 3 C/1733, letter of T. F. Lewis, April 1843.
32 NLW, Ormathwaite MS FG 1/14, journal of John Walsh 1843, pp. 40–5.
33 *Welshman*, 23 March 1843.
34 Commission of Inquiry for South Wales, Evidence, pp. 4–28; NLW, MS 11342, Alcwyn C. Evans 13, p. 189.
35 NLW, MS 11342, Alcwyn C. Evans 13, pp. 189–90.
36 *Carmarthen Journal*, 26 July 1839; Jones, *Rebecca's Children*, pp. 204–7.
37 Henry Tobit Evans, *Rebecca and her Daughters: Being a History of the Agrarian Disturbances in Wales Known as the 'Rebecca Riots'* (Cardiff, 1910), pp. 29–31; *Welshman*, 30 December 1842; *Carmarthen Journal*, 16 December 1842; Carmarthenshire Archives Service, Bryn Myrddin MS 73; Dynefor MS 159, address by George Rice Trevor.
38 *Welshman*, 23 June 1843.
39 The events of 19 June were widely reported. See accounts in *The Times*, 23, 24 June 1843; *Swansea Journal*, 21, 28 June 1843; and the *Carmarthen Journal*, *Cambrian* and *Welshman* of 23 June 1843.

See also NLW, MS 11342, Alcwyn C. Evans 13, pp. 197–200; David Williams, *The Rebecca Riots: A Study in Agrarian Discontent* (Cardiff, 1955), pp. 204–9; Jones, *Rebecca's Children*, pp. 218–21.

40 *The Times*, 27 June 1843. On Foster's background and subsequent career, see Williams, *Rebecca Riots*, pp. 210–11; Howell, 'Rebecca riots', pp. 134, 137.

41 *Quarterly* Review, 134–5.

42 *Swansea Journal*, 28 June 1843.

43 Williams, *Rebecca Riots*, p. 210; *Quarterly Review*, 31.

44 *The Times*, 10 July 1843.

45 *Welshman*, 5 May 1843.

46 Howell, 'Rebecca riots', p. 119; *The Times*, 27 July 1843.

47 *The Times*, 5 September 1843.

48 NLW, MS 11342, Alcwyn C. Evans, 13 October 1843; *Cambrian*, 30 December 1843.

49 *The Times*, 25 September, 14 October 1843.

50 NLW, Ormathwaite FG 1.14, journal of John Walsh, p. 18.

51 Howell, 'Rebecca riots', pp. 123–4.

52 West Glamorgan Archives, RISW DL49, 'Notes connected with the Rebecca riots in the year 1843'.

53 Jones, *Rebecca's Children*, pp. 308–9.

54 Williams, *Rebecca Riots*, pp. 246–58; Howell, 'Rebecca riots', pp. 123–4.

55 Commission of Inquiry for South Wales, Minutes of Evidence, pp. 254, 295.

56 Jones notes that preparations for the march on Newport were finalised in the Scotch Cattle territory of Blackwood, and that 'certainly the keenest supporters of Frost, Williams and Jones came from the Scotch Cattle areas' (Jones, *The Last Rising*, pp. 138–9; Jones, *Before Rebecca*, pp. 110–12, 193). On the fascinating endurance of the Scotch Cattle in name and technique in south Welsh clandestine protest, see Wilks, *South Wales and the Rising*, pp. 74–5, 88 n. 7; Hywel Francis and Dai Smith, *The Fed: A History of the South Wales Miners in the Twentieth Century* (Cardiff, 1980), pp. 62–3.

57 NLW, Bute Estate records, L88/258, letter from Charles Napier, 11 September 1843.

58 TNA, HO 45/453, letter from Col. Love to HO, 21 November 1843.

59 Graham Seal provides an overview in 'Tradition and Agrarian Protest in Nineteenth-Century England and Wales', *Folklore*, 99/2 (1988), 146–69; 158–60. See also A. W. Smith, 'Some Folklore Elements in

Movements of Social Protest', *Folklore*, 77 (1966), 241–52; Thomas Pettitt, '"Here Comes I, Jack Straw": English Folk Drama and Social Revolt', *Folklore*, 95/1 (1984), 3–20; 8, 15–16. On Luddism, see Frank Darvall, *Popular Disturbances and Public Order in Regency England: Being an Account of the Luddite and Other Disorders in England during the Years 1811–1817 and of the Attitude and Activity of the Authorities* (London, 1969). On the Swing riots, see Eric Hobsbawm and George Rudé, *Captain Swing* (London, 1970); On the *Tarw Scotch*, see Jones, *Before Rebecca*, pp. 86–116.

60 Smith, 'Some Folklore Elements', 244.
61 Norman Simms, 'Ned Ludd's Mummer's Play', *Folklore*, 89 (1978), 166–78; 167.
62 D. C. G. Allan, 'The Rising in the West 1628–31', *Economic History Review*, 2nd series, 5/1 (1952–3), 76–85; 76.
63 NLW, MS 2843, letter of O. Morgan, 18 October 1843.
64 NLW, Harpton Court 3, 1733–6, 1757, C/1735, letter of Thomas Frankland Lewis, 14 November 1843.

Chapter 3

1 See Neil Evans, 'When Men and Mountains Meet: Historians' Explanations of the History of Wales, 1890–1970', *Welsh History Review*, 22/2 (2004), 222–51; 243.
2 Emrys Bowen, *Wales: A Study in Geography and History* (Cardiff, 1941).
3 David J. V. Jones, *Rebecca's Children: A Study of Rural Society, Crime and Protest* (Oxford, 1989), pp. 257, 320.
4 See Bronterre O'Brien's objections to Rebeccaism in the *Poor Man's Guardian*, nos. 10, 11 and 12, September 1843.
5 Sharon Howard, 'Riotous Community: Crowds, Politics and Society in Wales, c.1700–1840', *Welsh History Review*, 20/4 (2001), 656–86; 679.
6 Jones, *Rebecca's Children*, pp. 257–8.
7 Williams, 'The frontier years', in David Smith (ed.), *A People and a Proletariat: Essays in the History of Wales 1780–1980* (London, 1980), p. 41; see also Thomas, *Social Disorder in Britain*, pp. 61, 178.
8 Evans, 'Men and Mountains', 29. See E. P. Thompson, *The Making of the English Working Class* (London, 1963); E. J. Hobsbawm, *The Age of Revolution: Europe 1789–1848* (London, 1962); George Rudé, *Revolutionary Europe: 1783–1815* (London, 1964).

9   See, for instance, Hywel Francis, 'The secret world of the south Wales miner: the relevance of oral history', in Smith (ed.), *People and Proletariat*, pp. 166–81.

10 Glanmor Williams, *History in a Modern University* (Swansea, 1959).

11 Evans, 'Men and Mountains', 251, Dai Smith, Introduction, in Smith (ed.), *People and Proletariat*, p. 12.

12 Eric Hobsbawm, *Primitive Rebels: Studies in Archaic Forms of Social Movement in the Nineteenth and Twentieth Centuries* (Manchester, 1959).

13 Williams, 'The frontier years', in Smith (ed.), *People and Proletariat*, pp. 16–46; pp. 22–4, 27.

14 David Howell, *Land and People in Nineteenth-Century Wales* (London, 1978), p. 109.

15 Jones, *Rebecca's Children*, pp. 58, 371.

16 Paul O'Leary, 'Masculine Histories: Gender and the Social History of Modern Wales', *Welsh History Review*, 22/2 (2004), 242–77; 249–50, 255.

17 See Chris Williams, 'Problematizing Wales: an exploration in history and postcoloniality', in Jane Aaron and Chris Williams (eds), *Postcolonial Wales* (Cardiff, 2005), pp. 3–22.

18 Joan Wallach Scott, *Gender and the Politics of History* (New York, 1999), pp. 84, 88.

19 Deirdre Beddoe, 'Images of Welsh women', in Tony Curtis (ed.), *Wales, the Imagined Nation: Studies in Cultural and National Identity* (Bridgend, 1986), pp. 225–38; p. 229.

20 Angela V. John (ed.), *Our Mothers' Land: Chapters in Welsh Women's History, 1830–1939* (Cardiff, 1991), pages preceding introduction; Rosemary A. N. Jones, 'Women, community and collective action: the "Ceffyl pren" tradition', in John (ed.), *Our Mothers' Land*, pp. 17–42; p. 17; Seal, 'Tradition and Agrarian Protest', 161; David Williams, *The Rebecca Riots: A Study in Agrarian Discontent* (Cardiff, 1955), pp. 53–6.

21 Angela V. John, Introduction, in John (ed.), *Our Mothers' Land*, pp. 7–9. David Jones links this latter aspect to the communal nature of Rebecca protests and meetings – whole families were present at public demonstrations and women were 'enthusiastic spectators' even if rarely involved in smashing gates – and concludes that Rebecca's closeness to the *ceffyl pren* made it 'a channel for the moral force of females as well as for the physical force of males' (*Rebecca's Children*, p. 243). On the *ceffyl pren* more generally, see Chapters 4–6, *passim*.

22 O'Leary, 'Masculine Histories', 258, 161; on some aspects of gender in modern and early modern Wales, see Michael Roberts and Simone Clarke (eds), *Women and Gender in Early Modern Wales* (Cardiff, 2000); Jane Aaron (ed.), *Our Sisters' Land: The Changing Identities of Women in Wales* (Cardiff, 1994).

23 Smith, Introduction, in Smith (ed.), *People and Proletariat*, p. 13.

24 O'Leary, 'Masculine Histories', 258–9; Williams, 'Problematizing Wales', in Aaron and Williams (eds), *Postcolonial Wales*, p. 3. See also Andy Croll, 'Holding onto History: Modern Welsh Historians and the Challenge of Postmodernism', *Journal of Contemporary History*, 38/2 (2003), 323–32.

25 Evans, 'Men and Mountains', 248.

26 Malcolm Thomis and Jennifer Grimmett, *Women in Protest 1800–1850* (London, 1982), pp. 139–40.

27 Seal, 'Tradition and Agrarian Protest', 163–4; Howell, 'Rebecca riots', p. 123.

28 Fraser Easton, 'Gender's Two Bodies: Women Warriors, Female Husbands and Plebeian Life', *Past & Present*, 180 (2003), 131–74; David Cressy: 'Gender Trouble and Cross-Dressing in Early Modern England', *Journal of British Studies*, 35/4 (1996), 438–65; Beth H. Friedman-Romell, 'Breaking the Code: Toward a Reception Theory of Theatrical Cross-Dressing in Eighteenth-Century London', *Theatre Journal*, 47/4 (1995), 459–80. See also Natalie Zemon Davis, *Society and Culture in Early Modern France: Eight Essays* (London, 1975), pp. 131–6.

29 Robert Shoemaker and Mary Vincent, Introduction, in Robert Shoemaker and Mary Vincent (eds), *Gender and History in Western Europe* (London, 1998), pp. 1–20; p. 7.

30 Linda Colley, 'The Politics of Eighteenth-Century British History', *Journal of British Studies*, 25/4 (1986), 359–79; Frank O'Gorman, *Voters, Patrons and Parties: The Unreformed Electoral System of Hanoverian England* (Oxford, 1989), p. 246.

31 See Matthias Reiss, Introduction, in Reiss (ed.), *The Street as Stage: Protest Marches and Public Rallies since the Nineteenth Century* (Oxford, 2007), p. 5; Katrina Navickas, *Protest and the Politics of Space and Place, 1789–1848* (Manchester, forthcoming 2015).

32 Pollyanna Ruiz, *Articulating Dissent: Protest and the Public Sphere* (London, 2014), pp. 18–19.

33 Frank O'Gorman, 'Campaign Rituals and Ceremonies: The Social Meaning of Elections in England 1780–1860', *Past & Present*,

135 (1992), 88–91; Nicolas Rogers, *Crowds, Culture and Politics in Georgian Britain* (Oxford, 1998), pp. 176, 19; James Epstein, 'Understanding the Cap of Liberty: Symbolic Practice and Social Conflict in Early Nineteenth-Century England', *Past & Present*, 122 (1989), 75–118; James Vernon, *Politics and the People: A Study in English Political Culture c.1815–1867* (Cambridge, 1993).

34 Thompson, *Customs*, pp. 16–96.

35 Rogers, *Crowds, Culture and Politics*, pp. 122–51.

36 Frank O'Gorman, 'Campaign Rituals and Ceremonies: The Social Meaning of Elections in England 1780–1860', *Past & Present*, 135 (1992), 79–115; Paul A. Pickering, 'Class Without Words: Symbolic Communication in the Chartist Movement', *Past & Present*, 112 (1986), 144–62; Davis, *Society and Culture*, pp. 152–88.

37 The work of Lucien Febvre and Marc Bloch on early modern Europe, which also utilised aspects of geography and economics, drew particularly on anthropology for its potential to illuminate the study of belief systems, or *mentalités*. For the application of this methodological model to areas of history where similar conditions prevailed but for which direct evidence is less easily obtained, see Keith Thomas's 1971 study of witchcraft in early modern England, which drew on the work of earlier ethnographers, notably Evans-Pritchard; Lynn Hunt's study of the French Revolution, which echoed Geertz's assertion that the exercise of power always requires symbolic and ritual practice; and Mervyn James's study of the dramatic and mythological associations of Corpus Christi rites, influenced by the anthropological work of Victor Turner and its further exploration by Mary Douglas. John Tosh, *The Pursuit of History* (London, 1984), pp. 79–80, 185; T. G. Ashplant and Gerry Smyth, *Explorations in Cultural History* (London, 2001), pp. 20–7; Keith Thomas, *Religion and the Decline of Magic* (New York, 1971); Lynn Hunt, *Politics, Culture and Class in the French Revolution* (London, 1984), pp. 55–7; p. 60; Mervyn James, 'Ritual, Drama and Social Body in the Late Medieval English Town', *Past & Present*, 98 (1983), 3–29.

38 Clifford Geertz, *The Interpretation of Cultures* (London, 1975), p. 27; Clifford Geertz, 'Ideology as a cultural system', in David Apter (ed.), *Ideology and Discontent* (New York, 1964), p. 209 n. 9.

39 Davis, *Society and Culture*, pp. 97–188; Thompson, *Customs*, pp. 16–96, 467–538; John Stevenson, 'Social history', in L. J. Butler and Anthony Gorst (eds), *Modern British History: A Guide to Study and Research* (London, 1997), pp. 207–17; pp. 210–13.

40 Thompson, *Customs*, pp. 185–258; Robert Darnton, *The Great Cat Massacre and Other Episodes in French Cultural History* (London, 1984), pp. 75–104.
41 Dorothy Thompson, 'Chartism as a Historical Subject', *Bulletin of the Society for the Study of Labour History*, 20 (1970), 10–12.
42 Epstein, 'Cap of Liberty', 76.
43 Pickering, 'Class Without Words', 144.
44 James, 'Ritual, Drama and Social Body', 3–29; Richard Suggett, 'Festivals and Social Structure in Early Modern Wales', *Past & Present*, 152 (1996), 79–112; Paul O'Leary, *Claiming the Streets: Processions and Urban Culture in South Wales 1830–1880* (Cardiff, 2012).
45 Henry Tobit Evans, *Rebecca and her Daughters: Being a History of the Agrarian Disturbances in Wales Known as the 'Rebecca Riots'* (Cardiff, 1910), p. 13.
46 Tosh, *Pursuit of History*, pp. 185–6; Darnton, *Great Cat Massacre*, p. 78; T. G. Ashplant and Gerry Smyth, 'Schools, methods, disciplines, influences', in Ashplant and Smyth, *Cultural History*, p. 22; Geertz, *Interpretation of Cultures*, p. 435; Biersack, 'Local knowledge, local history: Geertz and beyond', in Lynn Hunt (ed.), *The New Cultural History* (Berkeley, 1989), pp. 72–96; p. 80; Shoemaker and Vincent, *Gender and History*, pp. 1–20; pp. 9ff.
47 Clifford Geertz, *Local Knowledge: Further Essays in Interpretative Anthropology* (London, 1993), p. 30.

Chapter 4

1 See David J. V. Jones, *Rebecca's Children: A Study of Rural Society, Crime and Protest* (Oxford, 1989), pp. 150–98; pp. 177, 181, 193; 371–4.
2 Barry Reay, *Popular Cultures in England, 1550–1750* (London and New York, 1998), p. 133.
3 E. P. Thompson, *Customs in Common: Studies in Traditional Popular Culture* (New York, 1993), pp. 16–96, 478.
4 *Cambrian*, 6 January 1844.
5 *Welshman*, 30 June 1843.
6 Trefor M. Owen, *Welsh Folk Customs* (Llandysul, 1987), pp. 175–81. On the use of urban space and processional activities to enforce social and political hegemony in 1840s Wales, see Paul O'Leary, *Claiming the Streets: Processions and Urban Culture in South Wales 1830–1880* (Cardiff, 2012), *passim*.

7 Matthew Cragoe, *Culture, Politics and National Identity in Wales 1832–1886* (Oxford, 2004), pp. 225–31.

8 *Hereford Times*, 17 November 1843.

9 *Swansea Journal*, 19 July 1843; NLW, MS 11342, Alcwyn C. Evans, p. 192.

10 David Williams, *The Rebecca Riots: A Study in Agrarian Discontent* (Cardiff, 1955), pp. 156–7. Although contemporaries, including the *Times* correspondent, occasionally hinted at a direct connection between Rebeccaism and the discontent fomented by local Baptist and Independent chapels, the condemnation and attempted expulsion of Rebeccaite members from Dissenting congregations makes this a difficult charge to sustain. See Jones, *Rebecca's Children*, pp. 332–4.

11 *Swansea Journal*, 7 June, 14 June 1843.

12 Carmarthenshire Archives Service, Brigstocke MS 4.

13 *Carmarthen Journal*, 23 June 1843.

14 O'Leary, *Claiming the Streets*, p. 24.

15 Lynn Davies, 'Aspects of Mining Folklore in Wales', *Folk Life*, 9 (1971), 79–106; 97; John R. Gillis, *For Better, for Worse: British Marriages, 1600 to the Present* (Oxford, 1985), p. 60.

16 Natalie Zemon Davis associates the use of water in ritual destruction with its role as 'a sacred means of purification'. It may have held further significance among rural peoples, with a cultural reference of cycles of death and renewal, as a universal symbol of rebirth and a force which is simultaneously destructive and life-giving, as Robert Kuhlken notes of the iconographic appeal of fire in rural incendiarism. Davis, *Society and Culture*, p. 179; Robert Kuhlken, 'Settin' the Woods on Fire: Rural Incendiarism as Protest', *Geographical Review*, 89/3 (1999), 343–63; 360; J. C. Cooper, *An Illustrated Encyclopaedia of Traditional Symbols* (London, 1978), pp. 188–9.

17 The concept of social protest as an evolution or mutation of charivari can also be applied, with some qualifications, to the operations of the Scotch Cattle. See Rhian E. Jones, 'Symbol, Ritual and Popular Protest in Early Nineteenth-Century Wales: The Scotch Cattle Rebranded', *Welsh History Review*, 26/1 (2012), 34–57.

18 Gillis, *For Better, for Worse*, p. 79.

19 Mikhail Bakhtin, *Rabelais and his World* (Ithaca, 1941); Davis, *Society and Culture*, pp. 97–123; Peter Burke, *Popular Culture in Early Modern Europe* (London, 1978); Pettitt, '"Here Comes I, Jack Straw"', 3–20; A. W. Smith, 'Some Folklore Elements in Movements of Social Protest' *Folklore*, 77 (1966), 241–52.

20 Owen, *Welsh Folk Customs*, pp. 80–99, p. 17.
21 Alcwyn C. Evans provides several examples in his chronology of events in NLW, MS 11342, Alcwyn C. Evans 13, pp. 195–230. See also NLW, MS 3/27399, p. 8; NLW, MS 21209C, letter of Thomas Cooke, 23 July 1843; *Cambrian*, 22 July 1843; *Welshman*, 10 March 1844; Jones, *Rebecca's Children*, p. 208. For an overview of the symbolic use and associations of the horse motif, see Cooper, *Traditional Symbols*, pp. 85–6.
22 *Welshman*, 14 March 1844.
23 NLW, MS 11342, Alcwyn C. Evans 13, pp. 197, 230; *Welshman*, 16 June 1843.
24 *Cambrian* 5 August, 3 September 1843; NLW, Spurrell MS A1987; NLW, MS 11342, Alcwyn C. Evans 13, pp. 201, 205; Carmarthenshire Archives Service, Bryn Myrddin MS 90, p. 16. The links between this image of Rebecca and popular social and cultural images of females on horseback are considered in Chapter 6.
25 Owen, *Welsh Folk Customs*, pp. 162–3.
26 *Welshman*, 15 September 1843.
27 Bryn Myrddin 73 (7A), address by E. C. Lloyd Hall, 20 June 1843.
28 *Welshman*, 23 June 1843.
29 Trefor Owen, 'West Glamorgan Customs', *Folk Life*, III (1965), 50–1; Gillis, *For Better, for Worse*, pp. 58–9.
30 See Chapter 5. On the motif of inversion and binary opposition in festival and beyond, see Barbara A. Babcock, *The Reversible World: Symbolic Inversion in Art and Society* (London, 1978), especially David Kunzle, 'World upside-down: the iconography of a European broadsheet type', pp. 39–94, Roger D. Abrahams and Richard Baumann, 'Ranges of festival behaviour', 193–208; Davis, *Society and Culture*, pp. 117–21; Rodney Needham (ed.), *Right and Left: Essays on Dual Symbolic Classification* (London, 1973).
31 The *Mari Lwyd* took place throughout Wales with some regional variations. Various attempts by historians and antiquarians have been made to explain the custom: Owen describes it as a pre-Christian horse ceremony associated with similar customs spread over many parts of the world, while Iorwerth C. Peate associates it with rituals of health and purification related to the worship of the Virgin Mary. Owen, *Welsh Folk Customs*, p. 50; Iorwerth C. Peate, *Tradition and Folk Life: A Welsh View* (London, 1972), p. 100.
32 Owen, *Welsh Folk Customs*, pp. 50, 93.

33 Williams, *Rebecca Riots*, pp. 53–6; Gareth Elwyn Jones, *Modern Wales: A Concise History* (Cambridge, 1984), pp. 52–3; Jones, *Rebecca's Children*, pp. 196–8; Howell, 'Rebecca riots', in Herbert and Jones, *People and Protest*, p. 122.

34 Reay, *Popular Cultures*, pp. 155–8; Thompson, *Customs*, p. 469. See E. Scourfield, 'References to "Y *Ceffyl pren*" ("The Wooden Horse") in South-West Wales', *Folklore*, 87/1 (1976), 60–2.

35 Owen, *Welsh Folk Customs*, p. 169.

36 TNA ASSI 72/1, deposition of David Griffiths, 27 May 1837.

37 NLW, D. G. Lloyd Hughes MS F/196.

38 Peate, *Folk Life*, p. 78; Owen, *Welsh Folk Customs*, p. 169; T. Gwynn Jones, *Welsh Folklore and Welsh Custom* (London, 1930), p. 191.

39 *Welshman*, 5 May 1843.

40 NLW, HO/45/642, letter of E. C. Lloyd Hall, 7 October 1843.

41 CRO TW 12, letter to George Rice Trevor, 1 October 1844.

42 Owen, *Welsh Folk Customs*, pp. 167–8.

43 Thomas, *Eighteenth-Century Wales*, pp. x–xi; Wallace, *Organise!*, pp. 3–4; Cragoe, *Anglican Aristocracy*, pp. 9–27.

44 R. U. Sayce, 'The One-Night House, and Its Distribution', *Folklore*, 53/3 (1942), 161–3.

45 Jones, *Rebecca's Children*, p. 53; Howell, *Rural Poor*, p. 201.

46 Kuhlken, 'Settin' the Woods on Fire', 344–5; Hobsbawm and Rudé, *Captain Swing*, p. 80.

47 Jones, *Before Rebecca*, pp. 48–50.

48 Jones, 'The Welsh and crime', in Emsley and Walvin (eds), *Artisans, Peasants and Proletarians*, p. 97.

49 Jones, *Rebecca's Children*, p. 52.

50 NLW, MS 11342, Alcwyn C. Evans 13, p. 211.

51 Commission of Inquiry (1844), Evidence, pp. 262, 259.

52 Hywel Francis, 'The Law, Oral Tradition and the Mining Community', *Journal of Law and Society*, 12/3 (1985), 267–71; 267. A similar privileging of tradition over constitutional law has been claimed by Andy Wood for English mining communities, whose sense of customary rights to common land was challenged over the eighteenth and nineteenth centuries by the new concept of entrepreneurial right. Andy Wood, 'Custom, identity and resistance: English free miners and their law c.1550–1800', in Paul Griffiths, Adam Fox and Steve Hindle (eds), *The Experience of Authority in Early Modern England* (London, 1996), pp. 249–85.

Chapter 5

1 Marc Baer, *Theatre and Disorder in Late Georgian London* (Oxford, 1992), pp. 193–4.
2 See E. P. Thompson, *Customs in Common: Studies in Traditional Popular Culture* (New York, 1993), pp. 16–96; John Brewer, 'The number 45: a Wilkite political symbol', in Stephen Baxter (ed.), *England's Rise to Greatness 1660–1763* (London, 1983); Katrina Navickas, '"That Sash Will Hang You": Political Clothing and Adornment in England, 1780–1840', *Journal of British Studies*, 49/3 (2010), 540–65; A. W. Smith, 'Some Folklore Elements in Movements of Social Protest', *Folklore*, 77 (1966), 241–52; Pettitt, '"Here Comes I, Jack Straw"', 3; Ingram, 'Ridings, rough music and mocking rhymes', in Barry Reay (ed.), *Popular Culture in Seventeenth Century England* (London, 1975), pp. 155–8, 166–97.
3 Malcolm Thomis and Jennifer Grimmett, *Women in Protest 1800–1850* (London, 1982), pp. 139–40. See anso Bushaway, *By Rite*; Smith, 'Some Folklore Elements', 244–5; Richard Wilson, '"Like the old Robin Hood": "As You Like It" and the Enclosure Riots', *Shakespeare Quarterly*, 43/1 (1992), 1–19; 10–11.
4 David J. V. Jones, *Rebecca's Children: A Study of Rural Society, Crime and Protest* (Oxford, 1989), pp. 208, 248: he notes Rebecca's frequent appearance on a white horse and compares it to 'the Holy One in Revelation, or a latter-day Captain Swing'.
5 David Howell, 'Rebecca riots', in Herbert and Jones (eds), *People and Protest*, pp. 122–3.
6 John Bohstedt, 'Gender, Household and Community Politics: Women in English Riots 1790–1820', *Past & Present*, 120 (1988), 88–122; John Bohstedt, *Riots and Community Politics in England and Wales, 1790–1810* (Cambridge, Mass., 1983); Thompson, *Customs*, pp. 305–36; Nicolas Rogers, *Crowds, Culture and Politics in Georgian Britain* (Oxford, 1998), pp. 229–34; John Stevenson, *Popular Disturbances in England, 1700–1832* (London, 1992), p. 125.
7 See Dorothy Thompson, 'Women and nineteenth-century radical politics: a lost dimension?', in Juliet Mitchell and Ann Oakley (eds), *The Rights and Wrongs of Women* (Harmondsworth, 1976), pp. 115–38; Thompson, *Customs*, pp. 234, 307; Olwen Hufton, 'Women in revolution 1789–1796', in Douglas Johnson (ed.), *French Society and the Revolution* (Cambridge, 1976), p. 157; Bohstedt, 'Community Politics', 90, 93; Bohstedt, *Riots and Community Politics*; Thompson, *Customs*, pp. 306–10; R. E. Quinault, review of John Bohstedt, *Riots*

and Community Politics in England and Wales, 1790–1810, English Historical Review, 102/403 (1987), 509.

8   Smith, 'Some Folklore Elements', 244–5; Kevin Binfield, 'Industrial gender: manly men and cross-dressers in the Luddite movement', in Elizabeth Dell and Jay Losey (eds), *Mapping Male Sexuality: Nineteenth-Century England* (London, 2000), pp. 29–48.

9   Natalie Zemon Davis, *Society and Culture in Early Modern France: Eight Essays* (London, 1965), pp. 127–30; Ingram, 'Ridings, rough music and mocking rhymes', in Reay (ed.), *Popular Cultures*, pp. 175–8; Davis, *Society and Culture*, pp. 97ff., 124ff.

10 Howell, 'Rebecca riots', p. 123; Rogers, *Crowds, Culture and Politics*, p. 224; Davis, *Society and Culture*, pp. 147–50.

11 *The Times*, 5 August 1843; *Carmarthen Journal*, 23 June 1843.

12 *Quarterly Review*, 123–54; 124–5. Rebecca's frequently grim sense of humour was evident in incidents such as that in which a bailiff acting for the undersheriff of Carmarthen, who had distrained upon the goods of a local farmer, was himself bound hand and foot and placed in Brechfa pound, and released in the morning only on payment of the customary fourpence for redeemed strays. See David Williams, *The Rebecca Riots: A Study in Agrarian Discontent* (Cardiff, 1955), p. 238.

13 Evidence of William Davies Phillips, *Cambrian*, 23 March 1844.

14 Evans was reported to have justified her actions by saying 'she had seen enough of the workhouse'. At her trial she 'assumed a bold appearance – and said she was glad she had not done sufficient to forfeit her life'. *Swansea Journal*, 5 July 1843; *Welshman*, 7 July 1843.

15 *Carmarthen Journal*, 23 June 1843; *Swansea Journal*, 19 July 1843.

16 *Welshman*, 16 June 1843, NLW, MS 11342, pp. 195, 191.

17 See, for instance, the report of the trial of Rebeccaites for riot at Carmarthen workhouse, *Cambrian*, 23 March 1844.

18 Williams, *Rebecca Riots*, pp. 188, 191, 199.

19 *The Examiner and London Review*, 3 August 1843; *Welshman*, 4 August 1843; 'Notes on a Tour of the Disturbed Districts in Wales', *Blackwood's Edinburgh Magazine*, 54/338 (December 1843), 766–71; 767; TNA HO 40/51, letters of J. M. Child and W. B. Swann, 14, 18, 21 June 1839; *Carmarthen Journal*, 26 July 1839.

20 See for example, *The Times*, retrospective article on Rebecca, 14 April 1944; Pembrokeshire Record Office, D/ETL/84, papers of E. T. Lewis detailing a commemorative pageant to mark the centenary of the destruction of Efailwen toll gate.

21 *Punch*, 1843; *Illustrated London News* print of 1843, in Jones, *Rebecca's Children*, pp. 122, 205; *L'Illustration* print, 1843, in Herbert and Jones (eds), *People and Protest*, p. 120.

22 Easton, 'Gender's Two Bodies', 132–3. See also Davis, *Society and Culture*, pp. 132–3.

23 *The Times*, 22 June, 30 June, 5 August 1843; Jones, *Rebecca's Children*, p. 248; Howell, 'Rebecca riots', p. 122.

24 *Hereford Times*, 11 November 1843.

25 *Swansea Journal*, 25 October 1843, evidence of Supt Peake; see also *Swansea Journal*, 13 December 1843, arrest of Jonathan Jones; *Cambrian*, 5 August 1843, trial of David Jones and others; Carmarthenshire Archives Service, Carmarthenshire Winter Assizes, 22 December 1843, trial of Thomas Lewis and Thomas Morgan.

26 *Swansea Journal*, 12 July 1843; *Welshman*, 16 June 1843; Molloy, *And They Blessed Rebecca*, pp. 136, 153–7.

27 *Swansea Journal*, 13 December 1843, 26 June 1843.

28 *The Times*, 7 February, 5 August 1843. Tobit Evans claims that participants commonly adopted the names of the women from whom their clothes were borrowed, presumably taking their cue from Thomas Rees, who is alleged to have done so at Efailwen in the role of the first recorded Rebecca. Henry Tobit Evans, *Rebecca and her Daughters: Being a History of the Agrarian Disturbances in Wales Known as the 'Rebecca Riots'* (Cardiff, 1910), pp. 9–10.

29 *Hereford Times*, 11 November 1843.

30 TNA ASSI 72/1; *Cambrian*, 3 September 1843.

31 David J. V. Jones, *Rebecca's Children: A Study of Rural Society, Crime and Protest* (Oxford, 1989), p. 248.

32 Jones, *Rebecca's Children*, p. 248; Molloy, *And They Blessed Rebecca*, p. 29. Conversely, Alun Ifan's children's book *Twm Carnabwth* (Llandysul, 1984) has a cover and illustrations showing Rebeccaites in bonnets and gowns, but also muscular and recognisably masculine, with obtrusive facial hair and sideburns.

33 *Cambrian*, 6 January, 16 March 1844; *Welshman*, 15 March 1844.

34 *Welshman*, 15 March 1844.

35 Douglas A. Reid, 'Interpreting the festival calendar: wakes and fairs as carnivals', in Robert Storch (ed.), *Popular Culture and Custom in Nineteenth Century England* (London, 1982), pp. 125–53.

36 Thompson, *Customs*, pp. 570–4; Jones, 'Women, community and collective action', p. 17; Seal, 'Tradition and Agrarian Protest', 161.

37 Ingram, 'Ridings, rough music', in Reay (ed.), *Popular Cultures*, pp. 175–8.

38 Alun Howkins and Linda Merricks, 'Wee Be Black as Hell: Ritual, Disguise and Rebellion', *Rural History*, 4/1 (1993), 41–54; 41, 46–9.

39 Frank W. Wadsworth, 'Rough music in The Duchess of Malfi: Webster's dance of madmen and the charivari tradition', in John J. MacAloon (ed.), *Rite, Drama, Festival, Spectacle: Rehearsals Toward a Theory of Cultural Performance* (Philadelphia, 1984), pp. 58–75; p. 64; Rebecca Solnit, *Wanderlust: A History of Walking* (London, 2002), p. 217; Victor Turner, *The Forest of Symbols: Aspects of Ndembu Ritual* (Ithaca, 1967), pp. 93–111.

40 Victor Turner, *The Ritual Process: Structure and Anti-Structure* (London, 1969), p. 108; Arnold van Gennep, *The Rites of Passage* (Chicago, 1960). See also Graham Cunningham, *Religion and Magic: Approaches and Theories* (Edinburgh, 1999), pp. 58–65; John Tosh (ed.), *Historians on History* (London, 2000), pp. 285–330.

41 Mary Douglas, *Purity and Danger* (London, 2002), pp. 114–16.

42 Davis, *Society and Culture*, pp. 136–48, 181.

43 Leonard R. Berlanstein, 'Breaches and Breeches: Cross-Dress Theatre and the Culture of Gender Ambiguity in Modern France', *Comparative Studies in Society and History*, 38/2 (1996), 338–69; 338; Christie Davis, 'Sexual Taboos and Social Boundaries', *The American Journal of Sociology*, 87/5 (1982), 1032–63; 1032.

44 Alan Brody, *The English Mummers and their Plays: Traces of Ancient Mystery* (Philadelphia, 1969), p. 5.

45 Davis 'Women on top', in James B. Collins and Karen L. Taylor, *Early Modern Europe: Issues and Interpretations* (Malden, Mass., 2006), pp. 398–411; p. 401.

46 See Evelyn Blackwood, 'Sexuality and Gender in Certain North American Tribes: The Case of Cross-Gender Females', *Signs*, 10/1 (Autumn 1984), 27–42; Harald Beyer Broch, '"Crazy Women are Performing in Sombali": A Possession–Trance Ritual on Bonerate, Indonesia', *Ethos*, 13/3 (1985), 262–82; 275–6.

47 See Ronald Hutton, *Shamans: Siberian Spirituality and the Western Imagination* (London, 2001); Cooper, *Traditional Symbols*, pp. 12, 176; Brian W. Rose, 'A Note on the Hobby Horse', *Folklore*, 66/3 (1955), 362–4; Arnold Bakè, 'Some Hobby-Horses in South India', *Journal of the International Folk Music Council*, 2 (1950), 43–5; Verrier Elwin, 'The Hobby-Horse and the Ecstatic Dance', *Folklore*, 53/4 (1942), 209–13; E. T. Kirby, 'The Origin of the Mummers' Play',

Notes

Journal of American Folklore, 84/333 (1971), 275–88; 276–7, 288; Violet Alford, *The Hobby-Horse and Other Animal Masks* (London, 1978), p. xix; M. Peacock, 'The Staffordshire Horn–Dance', *Folklore*, 8/1 (1897), 71.

48 Will Fisher, 'The Renaissance Beard: Masculinity in Early Modern England', *Renaissance Quarterly*, 54/1 (2001), 155–87; 177.

49 Anthony Synnott, 'Shame and Glory: A Sociology of Hair', *British Journal of Sociology*, 38/3 (1987), 381–413; 391.

50 *Swansea Journal*, 13 September 1843; Pembrokeshire Winter Sessions, December 19 1843; *Quarterly Review*, 129; Molloy, *And They Blessed Rebecca*, pp. 125–32.

51 NLW, MS 11342, Alcwyn C. Evans 13, p. 217.

52 NLW, MS 21209C, letters of Thomas Cooke, 23 July, 6 August 1843.

53 Wilson, '"Like the old Robin Hood"', p. 11.

54 David Mayer, *Harlequin in his Element: The English Pantomime 1806–1836* (Cambridge, Mass., 1969), p. 184; Roy Palmer (ed.), *A Touch on the Times: Songs of Social Change* (Harmondsworth, 1974), pp. 162–4.

55 Synnott, 'Shame and Glory', 384, Thomis and Grimmett, *Women in Protest*, p. 145.

56 NLW, Cwrt Mawr MS 1201F, pp. 2–3.

57 NLW, MS 11342, Alcwyn C. Evans 13, pp. 192–3; see also an account of the same incident in Tobit Evans, *Rebecca and her Daughters*, pp. 2–3.

58 Michael Roberts identifies the construction of masculinity among the Welsh elite as a conflict between the restraints of social leadership and military valour and pride, symbolised by the sword. John Tosh and Linda Colley identify arms bearing as a central attribute of manhood from feudal times. Although its importance began to decline after 1815, it remained symbolically significant. See Michael Roberts, 'More prone to be idle and riotous than the English? Attitudes to male behaviour in early modern Wales', in Roberts and Clarke (eds), *Women and Gender in Early Modern Wales* (Cardiff, 2000), pp. 259–90; John Tosh, *Manliness and Masculinities in Nineteenth-Century Britain* (Harlow, 2005), p. 65; Linda Colley, *Britons: Forging the Nation 1707–1837* (London, 1992), pp. 178, 193.

59 Anthony Fletcher, *Gender, Sex and Subordination in England 1500–1800* (New Haven, 1995), pp. xxii, 391.

60 Fisher, 'Renaissance Beard', 184–5; Marjorie Garber, *Vested Interests: Cross-Dressing and Cultural Anxiety* (London, 1992), p. 125.

61 Fisher, 'Renaissance Beard', 157.
62 Synnott, 'Shame and Glory', 392. This supports Fisher's critique of Thomas Laqueur's assertion that genital markers of sexual difference have historically been central to conceptions of gender identity. See Thomas Laqueur, *Making Sex: Body and Gender from the Greeks to Freud* (London, 1990), p. 141; Fisher, 'Renaissance Beard', 184–5; Jean E. Howard, 'Cross-Dressing, the Theatre, and Gender Struggle in Early Modern England', *Shakespeare Quarterly*, 39 (1988), 418–40.
63 *The Times*, 5 August, 22 June 1843.
64 *The Times*, 29 June 1843; *Welshman*, 10 June, 13 July 1843; *Cambrian* 17 June, 1 September 1843; *Swansea Journal* 29 November, 23 December 1843.
65 *Welshman*, 10 June 1843.
66 *Swansea Journal*, 16 August 1843.
67 *Cambrian*, 21 January 1843; *Welshman*, 5 May, 16 June 1843.
68 *Swansea Journal*, 13 September 1843.
69 *Swansea Journal*, 5 August 1843.
70 *Welshman*, 17 March 1843.
71 *Swansea Journal*, 26 June 1843.
72 *Welshman*, 6 January 1843; NLW, MS21209 C, letter from Thomas Cooke, 23 July 1843.
73 NLW, MS 11342, Alcwyn C. Evans, p. 195.
74 *Carmarthen Journal*, 14 July 1843; *The Times*, 28 October 1843.
75 *Farmers' Journal*, 23 February 1846, evidence of Rev. Edward Francis Arden. See also *The Times*, 16–19 February 1846.
76 *Hereford Times*, 18 November 1843.
77 NLW, MS 11342, Alcwyn C. Evans 13, p. 197.
78 Mayer, *Harlequin in his Element*, pp. 178–81.
79 Amelia Rauser, 'Hair, Authenticity, and the Self-Made Macaroni', *Eighteenth-Century Studies*, 38/1 (2004), 101–17; 101–5, 114; Marcia Pointon, *Hanging the Head* (London, 1993), pp. 114–23.
80 Peter Bailey, 'Conspiracies of Meaning: Music-Hall and the Knowingness of Popular Culture', *Past & Present*, 144 (1994), 138–70.
81 *Cambrian*, 16 August 1843; Molloy, *And They Blessed Rebecca*, pp. 125–32.
82 *Welshman*, 5 September 1843.
83 *Swansea Journal*, 2 August 1843.
84 *The Times*, 23 September 1843; *Welshman* 18, 25 August, 30 December 1843.
85 Molloy, *And They Blessed Rebecca*, p. 199.

Chapter 6

1   Malcolm Thomis and Jennifer Grimmett, *Women in Protest 1800–1850* (London, 1982), pp. 138–40; Natalie Zemon Davis, *Society and Culture in Early Modern France: Eight Essays* (London, 1965), pp. 146–7; Nicolas Rogers, *Crowds, Culture and Politics in Georgian Britain* (Oxford, 1998), pp. 216, 226.

2   Epstein, 'Cap of Liberty', p. 116.

3   Ieuan Gwynedd Jones, *Mid-Victorian Wales: The Observers and Observed* (Cardiff, 1992), p. 107.

4   David J. V. Jones, *Rebecca's Children: A Study of Rural Society, Crime and Protest* (Oxford, 1989), pp. 39–40.

5   John R. Gillis, *For Better, for Worse: British Marriages, 1600 to the Present* (Oxford, 1985), p. 121; Thomis and Grimmett, *Women in Protest*, p. 20.

6   NLW, MS 13199D, J. M. Howell broadsides collection. As previously noted, Rebeccaites at Pontarddulais toll gate assumed voices which made them resemble 'a host of old market-women'. *Cambrian*, 3 September 1843.

7   Jones, 'Women, community and collective action', p. 17; Jones, *Rebecca's Children*, pp. 7–8; Trefor M. Owen, *Welsh Folk Customs* (Llandysul, 1987), p. 127.

8   NLW, Cwrt Mawr MS 1201F, p. 7.

9   *Bygones*, 2/3 (1893), 108.

10 Gillis, *For Better, for Worse*, p. 199.

11 F. S. Price, *History of Llansawel, Carmarthenshire* (1898), pp. 34–5; Owen, *Welsh Folk Customs*, p. 163.

12 *Welshman*, 15 September 1843.

13 Jones, *Rebecca's Children*, p. 248.

14 See Ann Hyland, *The Horse in the Ancient World* (Westport, Conn., 2003); *The Mabinogion*, trans. Gwyn Jones and Thomas Jones (London, 1949), pp. 8–10.

15 NLW, MS 4857D, Lloyd of Caerwys miscellanea.

16 Peter Lord, *Words with Pictures: Welsh Images and Images of Wales in the Popular Press, 1640–1860* (Aberystwyth, 1995), pp. 136–7.

17 *Quarterly Review*, 123–54; *Welshman*, 15 September 1843.

18 NLW, MS 819C (*A Wedding in Wales*, comic opera); NLW, MS 23303B (Wynnstay Theatre papers).

19 NLW, MS 21820F.

20 H. H. Vaughan, *Welsh Proverbs with English Translations* (London 1889), pp. 171–2, 316; British Library, papers of: J. H. S. (John Henry Scourfield), 1808–76, p. 10.

21 J. H. Davies, *A Bibliography of Welsh Ballads Printed in the Eighteenth Century* (London, 1911); Ernest Rhys, *Welsh Ballads, and Other Poems* (London, 1898); George Henry Borrow, *Welsh Poems and Ballads* (London, 1915). On images of powerful or belligerent women in English popular ballads, see Anna Clark, *The Struggle for the Breeches: Gender and the Making of the British Working Class* (London, 1995), pp. 69, 82, 165–8.

22 John Knott, *Popular Opposition to the 1834 Poor Law* (London, 1986), pp. 83, 256, 270.

23 Anthony Fletcher, *Gender, Sex and Subordination in England 1500–1800* (New Haven, 1995), pp. 274–9.

24 See Hannah Barker and Elaine Chalus (eds), *Women's History: Britain 1700–1850: An Introduction* (London, 2005), pp. 4–6; Kathryn Gleadle, *British Women in the Nineteenth Century* (Basingstoke, 2001), pp. 1–4, 24–47; Martha Vicinus (ed.), *Suffer and Be Still: Women in the Victorian Age* (London, 1980).

25 Natalie Zemon Davis, 'Women on top', in James B. Collins and Karen L. Taylor (eds), *Early Modern Europe: Issues and Interpretations* (Malden, Mass., 2006), pp. 398–400.

26 Fletcher, *Sex and Subordination*, p. 377; Davis, 'Women On Top', pp. 398–411.

27 Davis, 'Women on top', pp. 398–400; Ellen Ross and Rayna Rapp, 'Sex and Society: A Research Note from Social History and Anthropology', *Comparative Studies in Society and History*, 23/1 (1981), 51–72; 65; Clark, *Struggle for the Breeches*, pp. 47, 190–4, 208.

28 Catherine Hall, 'The tale of Samuel and Jemima: gender and working-class culture in nineteenth-century England', in Harvey J. Kaye and Keith McClelland (eds), *E. P. Thompson: Critical Perspectives* (Oxford, 1990), pp. 78–102; pp. 84, 98; U. R. Q. Henriques, 'Bastardy and the New Poor Law', *Past & Present*, 37 (1967), 103–29; 105–9.

29 Poor Law Commissioners Report (1834), pp. 94–5; Henriques, 'New Poor Law', 105–9.

30 Henriques, 'New Poor Law', 129; Knott, *Popular Opposition*, p. 27.

31 Gillis, *For Better, for Worse*, pp. 109ff.; Joan Perkin, *Women and Marriage in Nineteenth-Century England* (London, 1989), pp. 182–4.

32 Commission of Inquiry into the State of Education in Wales (1847), xxvii (iii), pp. 57ff.; Jones, *Mid-Victorian Wales*, pp. 103–65.

33 Commission of Inquiry into the State of Education in Wales, pp. 58–60; Jones, *Mid Victorian Wales*, p. 143; Beddoe, 'Welsh women', p. 234.

34 See Howell, *Rural Poor*, p. 146; Roger L. Brown, 'Clandestine Marriage in Wales', *Trans. Cymru* (1982), 74–5; R. B. Outhwaite, *Clandestine Marriage in England 1500–1850* (London, 1995), pp. 139–40.

35 E. W. Jones, 'Medical Glimpses of Early Nineteenth-Century Cardiganshire', *NLW Journal*, XIV (1965–6), 260–75; Howell, *Rural Poor*, pp. 146–8; Commission of Inquiry (1847), pp. 56, 60; Commission of Inquiry, First Report, Evidence of Capt. J. M. Child, p. 81.

36 David Williams, *The Rebecca Riots: A Study in Agrarian Discontent* (Cardiff, 1955), p. 240.

37 Gillis, *For Better, for Worse*, p. 198.

38 M. Baker, *Folklore and Customs of Love and Marriage* (Aylesbury, 1974), p. 37.

39 Jones, *Rebecca's Children*, p. 221; Williams, *Digest of Welsh Historical Statistics*, p. 56; G. R. Quaife, *Wanton Wenches and Wayward Wives: Peasants and Illicit Sex in Early Seventeenth Century England* (London, 1979); Commission of Inquiry (1844), Evidence, p. 30.

40 Commission of Inquiry (1844), Evidence, pp. 30. 64.

41 Ibid., pp. 28–31, 119; Evidence of Rev. R. B. Jones, Narberth, pp. 3, 6, 5. Evidence of Mr. Greenish, pp. 213, 66. Evidence of Rev. Henry Davies and others, Narberth, p. 203. See also *The Times*, 29 March 1844; NLW, Harpton Court MS 3 C/1733, letter of Thomas Frankland Lewis, 5 October 1843; Clark, *Struggle for the Breeches*, pp. 190–4; Henriques, 'New Poor Law',118–21.

42 Russell Davies, 'Voices from the void: social crisis, social problems and the individual in south-west Wales, c. 1876–1920', in Geraint Jenkins and J. Beverley Smith (eds), *Politics and Society, 1840–1922: Essays in Honour of Ieuan Gwynedd Jones* (Cardiff, 1988), pp. 81–93; p. 87.

43 See John Glyde, 'Localities of crime in Suffolk', *Journal of the Royal Statistical Society of London*, 19/1 (1856), 102–6; Knott, *Popular Opposition*, pp. 75, 83; David Jones, 'Rural crime and protest', pp. 111–24; pp. 118–19; TNA, MH12/1581, letter of Edmund Head, 27 March 1837; Alun Eirug Davies, 'The New Poor Law in a Rural Area 1834–1850s', *Ceredigion*, 8/3 (1978), 245–90.

44 See, for instance, 13 January 1837.

45 *Welshman*, 23 June 1843.

46 *Welshman*, 3 February 1843; TNA, HO 73/54.

47 *Can Newydd, sef Hanes Bywyd Becca a'i Merched*, by Levi Gibbon, Cwmfelin. A ballad containing twenty-five stanzas, translated in Lord, *Words with Pictures*, p. 137. Another translation appears in V. Eirwen Davies, *Helynt y 'Beca* (1961), p. 43.

48 *Welshman*, 23 August 1843, cutting in CRO Bryn Myrddin 90.

49 *Cambrian*, 23 December 1843; Williams, *Rebecca Riots*, p. 236.

50 *Swansea Journal*, 16 August.

51 See Peter Fryer, *Staying Power: The History of Black People in Britain* (London, 1984); Norma Myers, *Reconstructing the Black Past: Blacks in Britain 1780–1830* (London, 1996).

52 C. L. Innes, *A History of Black and Asian Writing in Britain, 1700–2000* (Cambridge, 2002), p. 12; Sukhdev Sandhu, 'The First Black Britons', at *http://www.bbc.co.uk/history/british/empire_seapower/black_britons_01.shtml*, retrieved March 2015.

53 Elizabeth Amy Dillwyn, *The Rebecca Rioter: A Story of Killay Life* (London, 1880), *passim*; Molloy, *And They Blessed Rebecca*, p. 153; Jessica Gerard, 'Lady Bountiful: Women of the Landed Classes and Rural Philanthropy', *Victorian Studies*, 30/2 (1987), 183–211; 187.

54 PP 1846, xxiv (i), p. 362.

Chapter 7

1 Catherine Hall, 'The tale of Samuel and Jemima: gender and working-class culture in nineteenth-century England', in Harvey J. Kaye and Keith McClelland (eds), *E. P. Thompson: Critical Perspectives* (Oxford, 1990), p. 90.

2 Nicolas Rogers, *Crowds, Culture and Politics in Georgian Britain* (Oxford, 1998), pp. 185, 212–21; Frank O'Gorman, 'Campaign Rituals and Ceremonies: The Social Meaning of Elections in England 1780–1860', *Past & Present*, 135 (1992), p. 86.

3 Rogers, *Crowds, Culture and Politics*, pp. 242–3; Epstein, 'Cap of Liberty', 75–118.

4 Natalie Zemon Davis, *Society and Culture in Early Modern France: Eight Essays* (London, 1965), pp. 124–5; Rogers, *Crowds, Culture and Politics*, pp. 216, 226.

5 James Vernon, *Politics and the People: A Study in English Political Culture c.1815–1867* (Cambridge, 1993), *Politics and the People*, pp. 251ff.

6 *Cambrian*, 23 June 1843.

7   *Quarterly Review*, 130. Contemporary and posthumous rumours persisted that the individual 'mastermind' behind Rebecca was Hugh Williams, a radical lawyer from Carmarthen who was active in the spread of Welsh Chartism, but there is little serious suggestion that he or any other one person consistently played Rebecca. See the letters of Edward Davies to the *Welsh Gazette* in the course of a newspaper controversy to prove 'the claim of Mr Hugh Williams to the leadership of the Rebecca riots', NLW, MS 2114C. Pat Molloy comprehensively dismisses the idea of Williams as Rebecca's *éminence grise*: Molloy, *And They Blessed Rebecca*, pp. 335–40.

8   'A Tour of the Disturbed Districts', 767.

9   *Welshman*, 28 July 1843; *Carmarthen Journal*, 23 June 1843.

10 Rogers, *Crowds, Culture and Politics*, pp. 50–4.

11 *Welshman*, 25 August, 17 November 1843; *Swansea Journal*, 4 October 1843.

12 *Cambrian*, 12 May 1843.

13 *Swansea Journal*, 4 October 1843.

14 Carmarthenshire Archive Service, Bryn Myrddin MS 90, p. 34.

15 See Susan Pedersen, 'Hannah More Meets Simple Simon: Tracts, Chapbooks and Popular Culture in Eighteenth-Century England', *Journal of British Studies*, 25/1 (1986), 84–113.

16 *Swansea Journal*, 12 July 1843; *Carmarthen Journal*, 12 May 1843; *Cambrian*, 10 June, 22 July 1843.

17 *Cambrian*, 1 July 1843; *Hereford Times*, 11 November 1843.

18 NLW, MS 11342, Alcwyn C. Evans 13, pp. 191–2.

19 *Hereford Times*, 23 December 1843.

20 NLW, MS 11342, Alcwyn C. Evans 13, p. 222.

21 Ibid., p. 230.

22 *Cambrian*, 10 June 1843.

23 *Hereford Times*, 2 September 1843.

24 See John Davies, 'Victoria and Victorian Wales', in Jenkins and Smith (eds), *Politics and Society in Wales*, pp. 7–28; pp. 13–17.

25 *Welshman*, 28 July, 1 September, 15 September 1843; 'A Tour of the Disturbed Districts', 767; *Hereford Times*, 18 November 1843.

26 NLW, Cwrt Mawr MS 1201F, p. 13; Carmarthenshire Archives Service, Brigstocke MS 4, pp. 34–5.

27 Amy Dillwyn, *The Rebecca Rioter*, p. xviii.

28 *Welshman*, 28 July 1843.

29 David Mayer, *Harlequin in his Element: The English Pantomime 1806–1836* (Cambridge, Mass., 1969), pp. 199–201, 238.

30 Sara Hudston, *Victorian Theatricals: From Menageries to Melodrama* (London, 2000), p. 3.

31 Carmarthenshire Archives Service, Brigstocke MS 4, pp. 34–5; NLW, Cwrt Mawr MS 1201F, p. 13. For other instances of broadsides employing theatrical tropes, see Mayer, *Harlequin in his Element*, p. 11.

32 NLW, Cwrt Mawr MS 1201F, p. 13.

33 Shannon L. Rogers, 'From Wasteland to Wonderland: Wales in the Imagination of the English Traveller, 1720–1895', *North American Journal of Welsh Studies*, 2/2 (2002), 15–26; Morgan, 'Wild Wales', pp. 265–84; Prys Morgan, 'Early Victorian Wales and its crisis of identity,' in Laurence Brockliss and David Eastwood (eds), *A Union of Multiple Identities: The British Isles, c.1750–c.1850* (Manchester, 1997), pp. 93–109.

34 Ralph Samuel and Paul Thompson (eds), *The Myths We Live By* (London, 1990), p. 17.

35 *Quarterly Review*, 125. The Volscian heroine is presumably Queen Camilla, the warrior virgin described in the *Aeneid*. Madge Wildfire appears in Sir Walter Scott, *The Heart of Midlothian* (1818), driven mad by seduction and the loss of her child.

36 *Welshman*, 15 September 1843. Compare Shakespeare, *Romeo and Juliet*, Act I, Scene iv. Mab's origins are uncertain; Shakespeare may have borrowed her name from a Celtic goddess, the Irish Medb or her Welsh counterpart Mabb, both 'heroic characters': W. P. Reeves, 'Shakespeare's Queen Mab', *Modern Language Notes*, 17/1 (1902), 10–14. A connection is also possible with Shelley's *Queen Mab: A Philosophical Poem* (1812–13), popular in contemporary radical circles, in which the fairy Queen Mab shows the mortal maiden Ianthe the past, present, and future states of the human world.

37 NLW, MS 11342, Alcwyn C. Evans 13, pp. 191–2.

38 *Carmarthen Journal*, 23 June 1843; *Quarterly Review*, 128; *Cambrian*, 14 April 1843.

39 *Welshman*, 8 September 1843.

40 NLW, MS 11342, Alcwyn C. Evans 13, pp. 191–2.

41 See Kathryn Gleadle, 'Charlotte Elizabeth Tonna and the Mobilization of Tory Women in Early Victorian England', *Historical Journal*, 50/1 (2007), 97–117; 110.

42 Anthony Fletcher, *Gender, Sex and Subordination in England 1500–1800* (New Haven, 1995), p. 386.

43 Ellen Ross and Rayna Rapp, 'Sex and Society: A Research Note from Social History and Anthropology', *Comparative Studies in Society and History*, 23/1 (1981), 65.
44 *Welshman*, 15 September 1843.
45 *Welshman*, 4 August 1843.
46 *Welshman*, 8 September 1843.
47 *Welshman*, 3 February 1843; *Cambrian*, 22 March 1843.
48 NLW, MS 11342, Alcwyn C. Evans 13, pp. 207, 210.
49 *Welshman*, 6 January 1843; *Cambrian*, 14 April, 5 May 1843; *Swansea Journal*, 21 January, 23 August 1843.
50 *Quarterly Review*, 129.
51 Ibid., 132–3.
52 Ibid., 132.
53 PP 1844, xvi (ii), pp. 110–12.
54 *Quarterly Review*, 139.
55 *Cambrian*, 30 December 1843.
56 *Welshman*, 5 May, 14 July 1843; *Carmarthen Journal*, 23 June 1843.
57 *Carmarthen Journal*, 23 June 1843.
58 *Welshman*, 5 September 1843.
59 NLW, Nanteos MS L1307, letter of 22 October 1843.
60 Davis, *Society and Culture*, p. 129.
61 *Quarterly Review*,139.
62 British Library, papers of: J. H. S. (John Henry Scourfield), 1808–76, p. 10.

Chapter 8

1 NLW, Nassau Senior 1: A12, journals of Nassau Senior, 1848–63, pp. 22–3.
2 *The Times*, 15 March 1956, 16 February 1962.
3 Pembrokeshire Record Office, D/ETL/84; Gareth Elwyn Jones, *Modern Wales: A Concise History* (Cambridge, 1984), p. 231.
4 *The Times*, 13 July, 11 September 1843.
5 *The Times*, 8 April 1846, 20 June 1857.
6 NLW, Spurrell MS A1987/10.
7 TNA, HO 144/28/69990, letter of John Lloyd, 7 December 1878.
8 *The Times*, 27 April 1888.

9   W. J. Linton, *Memories* (London, 1895), pp. 89–91. Linton was a friend of Hugh Williams, the Kidwelly lawyer considered by some to have been an animating spirit of Rebeccaism. Linton also created a widely known engraving of Rebeccaites attacking a toll gate which was published in an 1843 edition of the *Illustrated London News* (see pp. 128–9).

10 *The Times*, 16 September 1929.

11 *The Times*, 10 December 1935; Pembrokeshire Record Office, D/ETL/84; Derek Draisey, *The Rebecca Riots Within Ten Miles of Swansea* (Swansea, 2010), p. 49.

12 See S. Clark and J. S. Donnelly (eds), *Irish Peasants: Violence and Unrest, 1740–1914* (Manchester, 1983); Peter Gray, *Famine, Land and Politics: British Government and Irish Society, 1843–50* (Dublin, 1999).

13 Hansard, 3rd series, 1846, lxxxv, 703; *The Times*, 18 April, 1846.

14 Hansard, 3rd series, 1846, lxxxvii, 486; *The Times*, 16 June 1846.

15 Hansard, 3rd series, 1847, lv, 983.

16 Hansard, 3rd series, 1881, cclvii, 845.

17 Hansard, 3rd series, 1849, civ, 910–11; *The Times*, 27 April 1849.

18 Jones, *Rebecca's Children: A Study of Rural Society, Crime and Protest* (Oxford, 1989), pp. 373–5.

19 H. G. Williams, 'Nation-State vs National Identity: State and Inspectorate in Mid-Victorian Wales', *History of Education Quarterly*, 20/2 (2000), 145–68; 150; Oliver Macdonagh, *Early Victorian Government 1830–1870* (London, 1977); William C. Lubenow, *The Politics of Government Growth: Early Victorian Attitudes Towards State Intervention, 1833–1848* (Newton Abbot, 1971).

20 Sophie Hamilton, 'Images of femininity in the royal commissions of the 1830s and 1840s', in Eileen Yeo (ed.), *Radical Femininity: Women's Self-Representation in the Public Sphere* (Manchester, 1998), pp. 79–105; p. 80.

21 Ibid., p. 79. On Lewis, see the *Dictionary of National Biography*, vol. 33 (1893), pp. 197–8 (Thomas Frankland Lewis, 1780–1855).

22 See, for instance, PP 1844, xvi (ii), Saturday 18 November, at Narberth; Monday 20 November at Newcastle Emlyn; Saturday 9 December at Bridgend.

23 David Howell, 'Rebecca riots', in Trevor Herbert and Gareth Elwyn Jones (eds), *People and Protest: Wales 1815–1880* (Cardiff, 1988), p. 279.

24 See, for instance, *The Times*, 23 November 1843.

25 David Williams, *The Rebecca Riots: A Study in Agrarian Discontent* (Cardiff, 1955), p. 280.

26 Jones, *Rebecca's Children*, p. 347.

27 Commission of Inquiry, First Report, pp. 5–26.

28 Williams, *Rebecca Riots*, p. 281.

29 Hansard, 3rd series, 1844, lxxiii, 1567ff.; *The Times*, 29 March 1844.

30 Commission of Inquiry, First Report, pp. 27ff.

31 Commission of Inquiry, Evidence, p. 111.

32 Ibid., pp. 125, 371, 254.

33 See, for instance, Commission of Inquiry, Evidence, pp. 150–2, 200–4, 262–4.

34 Williams, *Rebecca Riots*, p. 278.

35 Hamilton, 'Images of femininity', p. 81.

36 Commission of Inquiry, Evidence, pp. 85, 125, 136.

37 Ibid., p. 131.

38 Ibid., p. 36.

39 Commission of Inquiry, First Report, p. 3.

40 Commission of Inquiry, Evidence, pp. 33–8.

41 Commission of Inquiry, First Report, pp. 26–36; see also Williams, *Rebecca Riots*, p. 280; Howell, 'Rebecca riots', p. 116.

42 Commission of Inquiry, preliminary address, p. iii.

43 Malcolm Jones, review of Lord, *Words with Pictures*, *Folklore*, 110 (1999), 115–116; 116.

44 Peter Lord, *Words with Pictures: Welsh Images and Images of Wales in the Popular Press, 1640–1860* (Aberystwyth, 1995), pp. 117, 34–73; Morgan, 'Wild Wales', p. 270; Linda Colley, 'Whose Nation? Class and National Consciousness in Britain 1750–1830', *Past & Present*, 113 (1986), 97–117; Tamara L. Hunt, *Defining John Bull: Political Caricature and National Identity in Late Georgian England* (Aldershot, 2003); Gwyn A. Williams, 'Romanticism in Wales', in Roy Porter and Mikulas Teich (eds), *Romanticism in National Context* (Cambridge, 1988), pp. 9–37; 11–12; Morgan, 'Early Victorian Wales', pp. 93–109.

45 Christine Stevens, 'Welsh Costume and the Influence of Lady Llanover' (2005), at *http://www.llgc.org.uk/fileadmin/fileadmin/docs_gwefan/amdanom_ni/cyfeillion/darlithoedd/cyfn_dar_CStevens_000916S.pdf*, retrieved March 2015; Beddoe, 'Welsh women', p. 232.

46 Lord, *Words with Pictures*, pp. 130–5; Stevens, 'Welsh costume', pp. 7–9. Beddoe notes how the donning of national dress objectified the wearer through its ornamental and impractical nature, rendering her fit only for the passive demonstration of nationhood despite the costume's basis in occupational dress. Beddoe, 'Welsh women', p. 233;

Juliette Wood, 'Perceptions of the Past in Welsh Folklore Studies', *Folklore*, 108 (1997), 93–102; 93.

47 Stevens, 'Welsh costume', pp. 9–10; Lord, *Words with Pictures*, p. 117.

48 Reprinted in Lord, *Words with Pictures*, p. 143.

49 Prys Morgan, 'Keeping the legends alive', in Tony Curtis (ed.), *Wales, the Imagined Nation: Studies in Cultural and National Identity* (Bridgend, 1986), p. 33.

50 Matthew Cragoe, *Culture, Politics and National Identity in Wales 1832–1886* (Oxford, 2004), p. 7; Thomas, *Eighteenth-Century Wales*, pp. 3–8.

51 Cragoe, *Culture, Politics and National Identity*, pp. 16, 38.

52 Ieuan Gwynedd Jones, *Mid-Victorian Wales: The Observers and Observed* (Cardiff, 1992), pp. 103–65; Cragoe, *Culture, Politics and National Identity*, pp. 16, 38–40; Morgan, 'Early Victorian Wales', p. 99.

53 Jones, *Mid-Victorian Wales*, pp. 103–65.

54 Cragoe, *Culture, Politics and National Identity*, pp. 40–1.

55 Jones, 'Beyond Identity?', 335.

56 Ieuan Gwynedd Jones, 'Parliament and people in mid-nineteenth-century Wales', in Herbert and Jones (eds), *People and Protest*, pp. 39–72.

57 Williams, *Rebecca Riots*, p. 280; Commission of Inquiry, First Report, p. 2.

58 Commission of Inquiry, First Report, p. 37.

59 Ibid., p. 36.

60 Ibid., p. 37.

61 Ibid., pp. 254–7, 295–6.

62 Ibid., p. 371.

63 Ibid., pp. 33–8.

64 Ibid., p. 36.

65 Ieuan Gwynedd Jones, 'Language and community in nineteenth-century Wales', in Smith (ed.), *People and Proletariat*, pp. 47–71; p. 52

66 *Hereford Times*, 8 January 1879.

67 Commission of Inquiry, First Report, p. 2.

68 NLW, Pencelley MS 690, pp. 14–16: cutting from *Daily Telegraph*, 6 January 1879.

69 NLW, Pencelley MS 690, p. 24: cutting from *Hereford Times*, 8 January 1879.

70 *The Times*, 26 December 1910, letter of S. Salar.

71 *The Times*, 29 December 1910, letter of John Morgan.

72 *The Times*, 14 April 1944.

Epilogue

1 See *The Rebecca Riots in Radnorshire, Extracted from the Hereford Times, from an Occasional Correspondent* (Hereford, 1879); *Hereford Times*, 8 January 1879; David Jones, 'The Second Rebecca Riots: A Study of Poaching on the River Wye', *Llafur*, 2/1 (1976), 32–56. The Radnorshire events are referred to as 'the later Rebecca' by Henry Tobit Evans, and are included in Keith Parker, *Parties, Polls and Riots: Politics in Nineteenth Century Radnorshire* (Hereford, 2009).

2 Cutting in NLW, Pencelley 690, p. 24.

3 NLW, Llysdinam MS 1/B1558, p. 13.

4 W. C. Maddox, *History of the Radnorshire Constabulary* (Llandrindod Wells, 1959); Pamela Horn, *Pleasures and Pastimes in Victorian Britain* (Stroud and New York, 1999), p. 119.

5 *The Times*, 4 January 1879; NLW, Llysdinam 1, B1558, letter from Richard Venables, 12 December 1880.

6 'A Midnight Drama', *Evening Express*, 14 January 1898.

7 *http://tredelyn.blogspot.co.uk/2010/10/when–governments–fear–people–there–is.html*, retrieved December 2014.

8 Closed in 1982, the magazine was relaunched in 2010 in the form of the 'investigative website' Rebecca Television, and still survives today. See *http://news.bbc.co.uk/2/hi/uk_news/wales/8662156.stm*, retrieved February 2015.

9 Sara Rhoslyn Moore, 'Wales, the Artist and Society: The Legacy of BECA', in *Wales Arts Review* 2/4 (2013), at *http://www.walesartsreview.org/wales-the-artist-and-society-the-legacy-of-beca/*, retrieved March 2015.

10 Martin Waterhouse, 'A new Rebecca? G. M. crop protests', in 'On the edge: peripheral communities and marginal anthropology' (Ph.D. thesis, University of Glamorgan, 2002), at *http://dspace1.isd.glam.ac.uk/dspace/bitstream/10265/462/1/397886.pdf*, 16, 19–20.

11 *The Gloucester Citizen*, 25 February 2014.

12 Gordon Graham, *Genes: A Philosophical Inquiry* (New York, 2002), p. 196; *https://en.wikipedia.org/wiki/Meme*, retrieved December 2014.

13 See, among a huge amount of reportage and analysis, Paul Mason, *Why It's Kicking Off Everywhere: The New Global Revolutions* (London, 2012); *http://www.theguardian.com/world/2011/nov/15/global–protests–2011–change–the–world*, retrieved December 2014; Gianpaolo Baiocchi and Ernesto Ganuza, 'No Parties, No Banners: The Spanish Experiment with Direct Democracy' at *http://www.*

bostonreview.net/world/no-parties-no-banners-gianpaolo-baiocchi-ernesto-ganuza, retrieved March 2015.

14 Ruiz, *Articulating Dissent*, p. 51.

15 J. P. D. Dunbabin, 'The "Revolt of the Field": The Agricultural Labourers' Movement in the 1870s', *Past & Present*, 26 (1963), 68–97; 74; Adrian Cook, review of David J. V. Jones, *Rebecca's Children*, *Economic History Review* 43/4 (1990), 73–4.

16 David Lloyd and Alan Moore, *V for Vendetta* (London, 1990; first published March 1982).

17 See 'The Man Behind the Mask: Q&A with David Lloyd, "V For Vendetta" Artist and Creator of the Guy Fawkes Mask Embraced by Anonymous and Protestors Worldwide', 11 June 2013, at *http://www.ibtimes.com/man-behind-mask-qa-david-lloyd-v-vendetta-artist-creator-guy-fawkes-mask-embraced-anonymous-1302381*, retrieved 21 December 2014.

18 See Monica Nickelsburg, 'A Brief History of the Guy Fawkes Mask', *The Week*, 3 July 2013, at *http://theweek.com/article/index/245685/a-brief-history-of-the-guy-fawkes-mask*, retrieved 26 December 2014.

19 See Quinn Norton, 'How Anonymous Picks Targets, Launches Attacks, and Takes Powerful Organizations Down', *Wired Magazine*, 3 July 2012.

20 NLW, 1942102, 1949090, 1977061, papers of Nassau William Senior (1790–1864), 1848–63, pp. 22–3.

21 See Euclides Montes, 'The V for Vendetta Mask: A Political Sign of the Times', *The Guardian*, 9 December 2011 ('Not only does wearing a Guy Fawkes mask at demonstrations give protesters anonymity, it's an instant symbol of rebellion'); 'Anti-protest: Bahrain Bans Import of Plastic Guy Fawkes Masks', *The Independent*, 23 February 2013; 'Saudi Religious Police Confiscate Guy Fawkes Masks ahead of National Day', *Al Arabiya*, 22 September 2013.

22 *Carmarthen Journal*, 23 June 1843.

23 'A Tour of the Disturbed Districts', 767.

24 Ruiz, *Articulating Dissent*, pp. 180–1.

25 Noam Chomsky, *Occupy*, Occupied Media Pamphlet Series (London, 2012).

26 NLW, Pencelley MS 690, pp. 14–16: cutting from *Daily Telegraph*, 6 January 1879.

27 James M. Jasper, *Protest: A Cultural Introduction to Social Movements* (Cambridge, 2014), p. 16.

28 *Carmarthen Journal*, 23 June 1843.

Bibliography

Manuscript and Archival Sources

British Library

Music Coll. D.836.f.(11.), Hen faledi cymreig. Old Welsh Ballads (1946).
Music Coll. H.141.(2.), Mrs. J. R. Planché's vaudeville of "The Welsh Girl" (1834).
011651.l.3, Ernest Rhys, Welsh Ballads, and other poems (1898).
11595.h.3, George Henry Borrow, Welsh poems and ballads (1915).
YK.1996.b.1174, Peter Lord, Biography of Hugh Hughes (1995).
YC.1991.a.262, Hugh Hughes: 1790–1863: Exhibition catalogue (1990).

Carmarthenshire Archives Service, Parc Myrddin, Carmarthen

Brigstocke MSS 1, 4.
Bryn Myrddin MSS 73, 90.
Dynefor MSS 159.
TW MSS 12.

National Archives (cited as TNA)

Assize rolls 72/1: North and South Wales Circuit, South Wales Division: Criminal Depositions (cited as ASSI).
Home Office papers (cited as HO).

National Library of Wales, Aberystwyth (cited as NLW)

NLW GENERAL MSS
819C, A Wedding in Wales, comic opera.
959C, Short Sketches of the Eminent Men of Cardiganshire, by Daniel Williams, 1874.
2114C, Letters of Edward Davies, Machynlleth.

2982E, Letters to William Davies, Scoveston, MP for the county of Pembroke, or to solicitors associated with him, 1823–95.

3294E, Miscellaneous letters, including two original 'Rebecca' letters; papers relating to William Davies, Froodvale, Carmarthenshire.

4848C, Reviews of Swansea theatre, 1880.

4857D, Lloyd family of Caerwys miscellanea.

7176D, Letters to William 'Nefydd' Roberts from David Morris, 27 June 1857.

11342, Cuttings book and memoirs of Alcwyn C. Evans 13.

13199D, Broadsides, J. M. Howell Collection.

13756–7, Notebook containing transcribed folksongs.

13855–6, Notebooks of ballads and poetry by Wallis Jones Williams, 1835, 1839–1845.

14005E, A Rebecca letter dated 20 May 1847.

14536E, Letters and reports giving information on Rebecca, 1843.

14590E, The Carmarthenshire Antiquary – A File of 'Rebecca' Papers.

18943B, 'Anonymous Narrative of a Tour Through Wales, by an English Gentleman', early eighteenth century.

21209C, Letters of Thomas H. Cooke, Middleton Hall.

22699E, Correspondence relating to, and claims for, rewards offered for information leading to the conviction of Rebecca rioters, the majority from George Rice Trevor to William Chambers Jnr, Llanelli; copies of the calendar of prisoners to be tried at the Carmarthenshire Spring Assizes, 1844; and proclamations relating to the riots.

23303B, Wynnstay Theatre papers.

Other MSS

Brythonydd MS 15648.

Bute Estate records.

Cefn Bryntalch MS 399.

Cwrt Mawr MS 747C, 1201F.

D. G. Lloyd Hughes MS F196.

D. Rhys Phillips MS 2.

Dolaucothi correspondence 3.

EX MS 1328–1338.

Grace Williams MS H32.

Harpton Court MS 1/2419–4046, 3/1733–57.

J. Glyn Davies MS 2.

Lloyd Verney MS 153.

Llysdinam MS 1 and 2.

Nanteos Estate records L1264–1392.

Nassau Senior MS 1.

Nevill MS 4.

Ormathwaite MS FG 1/14.

Pencelley MS 690.
Spurrell MS 10.
Vivian MS B360.
Williams and Williams MS 3/27399.

Pembrokeshire Record Office, The Castle, Haverfordwest

DETL 84, Papers of E. T. Lewis.
HDX 343/1, Apologia of John Hughes, David Jones and John Hugh, transported for riot at Pontarddulais toll gate.

West Glamorgan Archives, County Hall, Swansea

RISW DL49, Notebook of James Meadow Taylor, 'Notes connected with the Rebecca Riots in the year 1843'.

Printed Primary Sources

Parliamentary Proceedings

PP 1844, xvi (ii), Report of the Commissioners of Evidence for South Wales, with minutes of evidence, appendix and maps.
PP 1847, xxiv, Commission of Inquiry into the State of Education in Wales.
Hansard, 3rd series, 1843–9, 1881.

Contemporary Periodicals

Blackwood's Edinburgh Magazine, 1843.
Cambrian, 1839–45.
Carmarthen Journal, 1834–45.
Farmer's Journal, February 1846.
Hereford Times, 1839–45, 1879.
The Times, 1839–46, 1857, 1879, 1888, 1919, 1929, 1935, 1944, 1962.
Poor Man's Guardian and Leeds Advertiser, nos. 10, 11, 12, September 1843.
Quarterly Review, 74/779 (June 1844).
Swansea Journal, 1839–45.
Welshman, 1839–45.

Bodleian Library

The Rebecca Riots in Radnorshire, extracted from the Hereford Times, from an occasional correspondent (Hereford, 1879).

Printed Secondary Works

Articles

Albright, W. F., 'The Name Rebecca', *Journal of Biblical Literature*, 39/3–4 (1920), 165–6.

Alexander, Sally, 'Men's Fears and Women's Work: Responses to Unemployment in London Between the Wars', *Gender and History*, 12/2 (2000), 401–25.

Baké, Arnold, 'Some Hobby-Horses in South India', *Journal of the International Folk Music Council*, 2 (1950), 43–5.

Bailey, Peter, 'Conspiracies of Meaning: Music-Hall and the Knowingness of Popular Culture', *Past and Present*, 144 (1994), 138–70.

Bascom, William, 'The Forms of Folklore: Prose Narratives', *Journal of American Folklore*, 78 (1965), 3–20.

Berlanstein, Leonard R., 'Breaches and Breeches: Cross-Dress Theatre and the Culture of Gender Ambiguity in Modern France', *Comparative Studies in Society and History*, 38/2 (1996), 338–69.

Binns, J. W., 'Women or Transvestites on the Elizabethan Stage? An Oxford Controversy', *Sixteenth Century Journal*, 5/2 (1974), 95–120.

Blackwood, Evelyn, 'Sexuality and Gender in Certain North American Tribes: The Case of Cross-Gender Females', *Signs*, 10/1 (1984), 27–42.

Bohstedt, John, 'Gender, Household and Community Politics: Women in English Riots 1790–1820', *Past & Present*, 120 (1988), 88–122.

Booth, Michael R., 'A Defence of Nineteenth-Century English Drama', *Educational Theatre Journal*, 26/1 (1974), 5–13.

Brett, Peter, 'Political Dinners in Early Nineteenth-Century Britain: Platform, Meeting–Place and Battleground', *History*, 81 (1996), 527–52.

Broch, Harald Beyer, '"Crazy Women are Performing in Sombali": A Possession–Trance Ritual on Bonerate, Indonesia', *Ethos*, 13/3 (1985), 262–82.

Brown, Roger L., 'Clandestine Marriage in Wales', *Trans. Cymru* (1982), 74–5.

Carrigan, Tim, Bob Cornell and John Lee, 'Towards a New Sociology of Masculinity', *Theory and Society*, 14/5 (1985), 551–604.

Clark, Stuart, 'Inversion, Misrule and the Meaning of Witchcraft', *Past & Present*, 87 (1980), 98–127.

Coles, Anthony James, 'The Moral Economy of the Crowd: Some Twentieth–Century Food Riots', *Journal of British Studies*, 18/1 (1978), 157–76.

Colley, Linda, 'The Politics of Eighteenth-Century British History', *Journal of British Studies*, 25/4 (1986), 359–79.

Colley, Linda, 'Whose Nation? Class and National Consciousness in Britain 1750–1830', *Past & Present*, 113 (1986), 97–117.

Connell, R. W., 'The Big Picture: Masculinities in Recent World History', *Theory and Society*, 22/5 (1993), 597–623.

Cressy, David, 'Gender Trouble and Cross-Dressing in Early Modern England', *Journal of British Studies*, 35/4 (1996), 438–65.

Croll, Andy, 'Holding onto History: Modern Welsh Historians and the Challenge of Postmodernism', *Journal of Contemporary History*, 38/2 (2003), 323–32.

Davies, A. E., 'The New Poor Law in a Rural Area, 1834–1850', *Ceredigion*, 8 (1978), 245–90.

Davies, Lynn, 'Aspects of Mining Folklore in Wales', *Folk Life*, 9 (1971), 79–106.

Davis, Christie, 'Sexual Taboos and Social Boundaries', *American Journal of Sociology*, 87/5 (1982), 1032–63.

Downer, Alan S., 'Players and Painted Stage: Nineteenth-Century Acting', *PMLAT* 61/2 (1946), 522–76.

Dundes, Alan, 'Binary Opposition in Myth: The Propp/Lévi–Strauss Debate in Retrospect', *Western Folklore*, 56/1 (1997), 39–50.

Easton, Fraser, 'Gender's Two Bodies: Women Warriors, Female Husbands and Plebeian Life', *Past & Present*, 180 (2003), 131–74.

Elwin, Verrier, 'The Hobby-Horse and the Ecstatic Dance', *Folklore*, 53/4 (1942), 209–13.

Epstein, James, 'Understanding the Cap of Liberty: Symbolic Practice and Social Conflict in Early Nineteenth-Century England', *Past & Present*, 122 (1989), 75–118.

Evans, Neil, 'When Men and Mountains Meet: Historians' Explanations of the History of Wales, 1890–1970', *Welsh History Review*, 22/2 (2004), 222–51.

Fisher, Will, 'The Renaissance Beard: Masculinity in Early Modern England', *Renaissance Quarterly*, 54/1 (2001), 155–87.

Francis, Hywel, 'The Law, Oral Tradition and the Mining Community', *Journal of Law and Society*, 12/3 (1985), 267–71.

Friedman-Rommell, Beth H., 'BreakingToward a Reception Theory of Theatrical Cross-Dressing in Eighteenth-Century London', *Theatre Journal*, 47/4 (1995), 459–80.

Fulton, Robert, and Steven W. Anderson, 'The Amerindian Man–Woman: Gender, Liminality, and Cultural Continuity', *Current Anthropology*, 33/5 (1992), 603–10.

Gerard, Jessica, 'Lady Bountiful: Women of the Landed Classes and Rural Philanthropy', *Victorian Studies*, 30/2 (1987), 183–21.

Gleadle, Kathryn, 'Charlotte Elizabeth Tonna and the Mobilization of Tory Women in Early Victorian England', *Historical Journal*, 50/1 (2007), 97–117.

Green, Thomas A, 'Towards a Definition of Folk Drama', *Journal of American Folklore*, 91/36 (1978) 843–50.

Hawkesworth, Mary, 'Confounding Gender', *Signs*, 22/3 (1997), 649–85.

Henriques, U. R. Q., 'Bastardy and the New Poor Law', *Past & Present*, 37 (1967), 103–29.

Howard, Jean E., 'Cross-Dressing, the Theatre, and Gender Struggle in Early Modern England', *Shakespeare Quarterly*, 39 (1988), 418–40.

Howard, Sharon, 'Riotous Community: Crowds, Politics and Society in Wales, c.1700–1840', *Welsh History Review*, 20/4 (2001), 656–86.

Howkins, Alun, and Linda Merricks, 'Wee Be Black as Hell: Ritual, Disguise and Rebellion', *Rural History*, 4/1 (1993), 41–54.

James, Mervyn, 'Ritual, Drama and Social Body in the Late Medieval English Town', *Past & Present*, 98 1983, 3–29.

Jones, Amelia, '"Clothes Make the Man": The Male Artist as a Performative Function', *Oxford Art Journal*, 18/2 (1995), 18–32.

Jones, David J. V., 'Law Enforcement and Popular Disturbances in Wales, 1793–1835', *Journal of Modern History*, 42/4 (1970), 496–523.

Jones, David, J. V., 'The Second Rebecca Riots: Salmon Poaching in Radnorshire and Breconshire', *Llafur*, II (1976), 32–56.

Jones, E. W., 'Medical Glimpses of Early Nineteenth-Century Cardiganshire', *National Library of Wales Journal*, XIV (1965–6), 260–75.

Jones, Malcolm, review of Peter Lord, *Words with Pictures*, *Folklore*, 110. (1999), 115–16.

Jones, Phillip D., 'The Bristol Bridge Riot and its Antecedents: Eighteenth-Century Perceptions of the Crowd', *Journal of British Studies*, XIX (1980), 78.

Jones, R. Merfyn, 'Beyond Identity? The Reconstruction of the Welsh', *Journal of British Studies*, 31/4 (1990) 330–57.

Jones, Rhian E., 'Symbol, Ritual and Popular Protest in Early Nineteenth-Century Wales: The Scotch Cattle Rebranded', *Welsh History Review*, 26/1 (2012), 34–57.

King, S. A., and J. Stewart, 'The History of the Poor Law in Wales: Under-Researched, Full of Potential', *Archives*, 36 (2001), 134–48.

Krieder, Jodie, '"Degraded and Benighted": Gendered Constructions of Wales in the Empire', *North American Journal of Welsh Studies*, 2/1 (2002), 1–12.

Kuhlken, Robert, 'Settin' the Woods on Fire: Rural Incendiarism as Protest', *Geographical Review*, 89/3 (1999), 343–63.

Lévi-Strauss, Claude, 'The Structural Study of Myth', *Journal of American Folklore*, 68/270 (October–December 1955), 428–44.

Lieber, Michael, and John W. Murphy, review of Erica Bourguignon (ed.), *Religion, Altered States of Consciousness, and Social Change*, *Journal for the Scientific Study of Religion*, 14/1 (1975), 79–83.

Mosko, Mark S., 'The Canonical Formula of Myth and Non-Myth', *American Ethnologist*, 18 126–51.

Navickas, Katrina, '"That Sash Will Hang You": Political Clothing and Adornment in England, 1780–1840', *Journal of British Studies*, 49/3 (2010), 540–65.

Newall, Venetia, 'Folklore and Male Homosexuality', *Folklore*, 97/2 (1986), 123–47.

O'Gorman, Frank, 'Campaign Rituals and Ceremonies: The Social Meaning of Elections in England 1780–1860', *Past & Present*, 135 (1992), 79–115.

O'Leary, Paul, 'Masculine Histories: Gender and the Social History of Modern Wales', *Welsh History Review*, 22/2 (2004), 242–77.

Owen, Trefor, 'West Glamorgan Customs', *Folk Life*, III (1965), 50–1.

Peacock, M., 'The Staffordshire Horn–Dance', *Folklore*, 8/1 (1897), 71.

Pedersen, Susan, 'Hannah More Meets Simple Simon: Tracts, Chapbooks and Popular Culture in Eighteenth-Century England', *Journal of British Studies*, 25/1 (1986), 84–113.

Pettitt, Thomas, 'English Folk-Drama in the Eighteenth Century: A Defense of the Revesby Sword Play', *Comparative Drama*, XV (1981), 3–29.

Pettitt, Thomas, '"Here Comes I, Jack Straw": English Folk Drama and Social Revolt', *Folklore*, 95/1 (1984), 3–20.

Pickering, Paul A., 'Class Without Words: Symbolic Communication in the Chartist Movement', *Past & Present*, 112 (1986), 144–62.

Rauser, Amelia, 'Hair, Authenticity, and the Self-Made Macaroni', *Eighteenth-Century Studies*, 38/1 (2004), 101–17.

Rees, Lowri Ann, 'Paternalism and Rural Protest: The Rebecca Riots and the Landed Interest of South-West Wales', *Agricultural History Review*, 59/1 (2011), 36–60.

Reeves, W. P., 'Shakespeare's Queen Mab', *Modern Language Notes*, 17/1 (1902), 10–14.

Rogers, Shannon L., 'Wasteland to Wonderland: Wales in the Imagination of the English Traveller, 1720–1895', *North American Journal of Welsh Studies*, 2/2 (2002), 15–26.

Rose, Brian W., 'A Note on the Hobby Horse', *Folklore*, 66/3 (1955), 362–4.

Ross, Ellen, and Rayna Rapp, 'Sex and Society: A Research Note from Social History and Anthropology', *Comparative Studies in Society and History*, 23/1 (1981), 51–72.

Sayce, R. U., 'The One–Night House, and Its Distribution', *Folklore*, 53/3. (1942), 161–3.

Scourfield, E., 'References to "Y *Ceffyl pren*" ("The Wooden Horse") in South-West Wales', *Folklore*, 87/1 (1976), 60–2.

Seal, Graham, 'Tradition and Agrarian Protest in Nineteenth-Century England and Wales', *Folklore* 99/2 (1988), 146–69.

Simms, Norman, 'Ned Ludd's Mummers' Play', *Folklore*, 89 (1978), 166–78.

Smith, A. W., 'Some Folklore Elements in Movements of Social Protest' *Folklore*, 77 (1966), 241–52.

Steinberg, Marc W., 'The Remaking of the English Working Class?', *Theory and Society*, 20/2 (1991), 173–97.

Stoller, Paul, 'Beatitudes, Beasts, and Anthropological Burdens: Three Studies of Shamanism, Trance and Possession', *Medical Anthropology Newsletter*, 13/4 (1982), 6–10.

Suggett, Richard, 'Festivals and Social Structure in Early Modern Wales', *Past & Present*, 152 (August 1996), 79–112.

Swidler, Ann, 'Geertz's Ambiguous Legacy', *Contemporary Sociology*, 25/3 (1996), 299–302.

Synnott, Anthony, 'Shame and Glory: A Sociology of Hair', *British Journal of Sociology*, 38/3 (1987), 381–413.

Thompson, Dorothy, 'Chartism as a Historical Subject', *Bulletin of the Society for the Study of Labour History*, XX (1970), 11.

Thompson, E. P., 'Rough Music Reconsidered', *Folklore*, 103/1 (1992), 3–23.

Underdown, David, 'The Chalk and the Cheese: Contrasts among the English Clubmen', *Past & Present*, 85 (1979), 25–48.

Walker, Simon, 'Rumour, Sedition and Popular Protest in the Reign of Henry VI', *Past & Present*, 166 (2000), 31–65.

Walzer, M., 'On the Role of Symbolism in Political Thought', *Political Science Quarterly*, 82 (1967), 191–204.

Williams, H. G., 'Nation-State vs National Identity: State and Inspectorate in Mid-Victorian Wales', *History of Education Quarterly*, 20/2 (2000), 145–68.

Wilson, Richard, '"Like the old Robin Hood": "As You Like It" and the Enclosure Riots', *Shakespeare Quarterly*, 43/1 (1992), 1–19.

Wood, Juliette, 'Perceptions of the Past in Welsh Folklore Studies', *Folklore*, 108 (1997), 93–102.

Books

Aaron, Jane (ed.), *Our Sisters' Land: The Changing Identities of Women in Wales* (Cardiff, 1994).

Aaron, Jane, and Chris Williams (eds), *Postcolonial Wales* (Cardiff, 1995).

Alford, Violet, *The Hobby Horse and Other Animal Masks* (London, 1978).

Apter, David (ed.), *Ideology and Discontent* (New York, 1964).

Archer, John, *Social Unrest and Popular Protest in England 1780–1840* (Cambridge, 2000).

Ashplant, T. G., and Gerry Smyth (eds), *Explorations in Cultural History* (London, 2001).

Babcock, Barbara A. (ed.), *The Reversible World: Symbolic Inversion in Art and Society* (London, 1978).

Baer, Marc, *Theatre and Disorder in Late Georgian London* (Oxford, 1992).

Bailey, Peter, *Popular Culture and Performance in the Victorian City* (Cambridge, 1998).

Baker, M., *Folklore and Customs of Love and Marriage* (Aylesbury, 1974).

Barker, Hannah, and Elaine Chalus (eds), *Gender in Eighteenth-Century England: Role, Representations, and Responsibilities* (New York, 1997).

Barker, Hannah and Elaine Chalus (eds), *Women's History: Britain 1700–1850: An Introduction* (London, 2005).

Baxter, Deirdre, *Out of the Shadows: A History of Women in Twentieth-century Wales* (Cardiff, 2001).

Baxter, Stephen (ed.), *England's Rise to Greatness 1660–1763* (London, 1983).

Bocock, Robert, *Ritual in Industrial Society: A Sociological Analysis of Ritualism in Modern England* (London, 1974).

Bohstedt, John, *Riots and Community Politics in England and Wales, 1790–1810* (London, 1983).

Borrow, George, *Wild Wales* (Ruthin, 1862).

Bourguignon, Erika (ed.), *Religion, Altered States of Consciousness, and Social Change* (Ohio, 1973).

Bowen, Emrys, *Wales: Study in Geography and History* (Cardiff, 1941).

Broadbent, R. J., *A History of Pantomime* (London, 1901).

Brockliss, Laurence, and David Eastwood (eds), *A Union of Multiple Identities: The British Isles, c.1750–c.1850* (Manchester, 1997).

Brody, Alan, *The English Mummers and their Plays: Traces of Ancient Mystery* (Philadelphia, 1969).

Bulfinch, Thomas, *The Age of Chivalry* (New York, 1913).

Burke, Peter, *Popular Culture in Early Modern Europe* (London, 1978).

Burke, Peter, Brian Harrison and Paul Slack (eds), *Civil Histories: Essays Presented to Sir Keith Thomas* (Oxford, 2000).

Bushaway, Bob, *By Rite: Custom, Ceremony and Community in England 1700–1880* (London, 1982).

Butler, Judith, *Gender Trouble: Feminism and the Subversion of Identity* (New York and London, 1990).

Butler, L. J., and Anthony Gorst, *Modern British History: A Guide to Study and Research* (London, 1997).

Calhoun, Craig, *The Question of Class Struggle: Social Foundations of Popular Radicalism during the Industrial Revolution* (Oxford, 1982).

Cawte, E. C., *English Ritual Drama* (London, 1967).

Charlesworth, Andrew, *An Atlas of Rural Protest in Britain 1548–1900* (London, 1983).

Chartier, Roger, *Cultural History: Between Practices and Representations* (Cambridge, 1988).

Chomsky, Noam, *Occupy* (Occupied Media Pamphlet Series) (London, 2012).

Clark, Anna, *Struggle for the Breeches: Gender and the Making of the British Working Class* (London, 1995).

Clark, S., and J. S. Donnelly (eds), *Irish Peasants: Violence and Unrest, 1740–1914* (Manchester, 1983).

Colley, Linda, *Britons: Forging the Nation 1707–1837* (London, 1992).

Collins, James B., and Karen L. Taylor (eds), *Early Modern Europe: Issues and Interpretations* (Malden, Mass., 2006).

Cooper, J. C., *An Illustrated Encyclopedia of Traditional Symbols* (London, 1978).

Cordell, Alexander, *Hosts of Rebecca* (London, 1960).

Cragoe, Matthew, *An Anglican Aristocracy: The Moral Economy of the Landed Estate in Carmarthenshire 1832–1895* (Oxford, 1996).

Cragoe, Matthew, *Culture, Politics and National Identity in Wales 1832–1886* (Oxford, 2004).

Cunningham, Graham, *Religion and Magic: Approaches and Theories* (Edinburgh, 1999).

Curtis, Tony (ed.), *Wales, the Imagined Nation: Studies in Cultural and National Identity* (Bridgend, 1986).

Darnton, Robert, *The Great Cat Massacre and Other Episodes in French Cultural History* (London, 1984).

Davies, J. H., *A Bibliography of Welsh Ballads Printed in the Eighteenth Century* (London, 1911).

Davies, Owen, *Witchcraft, Magic and Culture 1736–1951* (Manchester, 1999).

Davies, V. Eirwen, *Helynt y 'Beca* (Cardiff, 1961).

Davis, Natalie Zemon, *Society and Culture in Early Modern France: Eight Essays* (London, 1965).

Dell, Elizabeth, and Jay Losey (eds), *Mapping Male Sexuality: Nineteenth-Century England* (London, 2000).

Dillwyn, Elizabeth Amy, *The Rebecca Rioter: A Story of Killay Life* (Dinas Powis, 1880).

Dolgin, J. L. et al., *Symbolic Anthropology: A Reader in the Study of Symbols and Meanings* (New York, 1977).

Douglas, Mary, *Purity and Danger* (London, 2002).

Draisey, Derek, *The Rebecca Riots Within Ten Miles of Swansea* (Swansea, 2010).

Dundes, Alan, *The Study of Folklore* (Englewood Cliffs, 1965).

Egan, David, *People, Protest and Politics: Case Studies in Nineteenth-Century Wales* (Llandysul, 1987).

Emsley, Clive, and James Walvin (eds), *Artisans, Peasants and Proletarians 1760–1860: Essays Presented to Gwyn A. Williams* (London, 1985).

Epstein, James, *Radical Expression: Political Language, Ritual and Symbol in England 1790–1850* (Oxford, 1994).

Epstein, James, and Dorothy Thompson (eds), *The Chartist Experience: Studies in Working Class Radicalism and Culture, 1830–1860* (London, 1982).

Etheridge, Ken, *Welsh Costume in the Eighteenth and Nineteenth Century* (Swansea, 1977).

Fentress, James, and Chris Wickham (eds), *Social Memory* (Oxford, 1992).

Fletcher, Anthony, *Gender, Sex and Subordination in England 1500–1800* (New Haven, 1995).

Francis, Hywel, and Dai Smith, *The Fed: A History of the South Wales Miners in the Twentieth Century* (Cardiff, 1980).

Frow, Gerald, *Oh Yes It Is! A History of Pantomime* (London, 1985).

Fryer, Peter, *Staying Power: The History of Black People in Britain* (London, 1984).

Garber, Marjorie, *Vested Interests: Cross-Dressing and Cultural Anxiety* (London, 1992).

Geary, Dick, *European Labour Protest 1848–1939* (London, 1981).

Geertz, Clifford, *Local Knowledge: Further Essays in Interpretive Anthropology* (New York, 2000).

Geertz, Clifford, *The Interpretation of Cultures* (London, 1975).

Gillis, John R., *For Better, for Worse: British Marriages, 1600 to the Present* (Oxford, 1985).

Gleadle, Kathryn, *British Women in the Nineteenth Century* (Basingstoke, 2001).

Gray, Peter, *Famine, Land and Politics: British Government and Irish Society, 1843–50* (Dublin, 1999).

Griffiths, Paul, Adam Fox and Steve Hindle (eds), *The Experience of Authority in Early Modern England* (London, 1996).

Herbert, Trevor, and Gareth Elwyn Jones (eds), *People and Protest: Wales 1815–1880* (Cardiff, 1988).

Hobsbawm, Eric J., *Age of Revolution: 1789–1848* (Cleveland, 1962).

Hobsbawm, Eric J., *Primitive Rebels: Studies in Archaic Forms of Social Movement in the Nineteenth and Twentieth Centuries* (Manchester, 1959).

Hobsbawm, Eric J., and George Rudé, *Captain Swing: A Social History of the Great English Agricultural Uprising of 1830* (London, 1970).

Horn, Pamela, *Pleasures and Pastimes in Victorian Britain* (Stroud and New York, 1999).

Howell, David W., *Land and People in Nineteenth-Century Wales* (London, 1978).

Howell, David W., *Patriarchs and Parasites: the gentry of South-West Wales in the Eighteenth Century* (Cardiff, 1986).

Howell, David W., *The Rural Poor in Eighteenth-Century Wales* (Cardiff, 2000).

Hudston, Sara, *Victorian Theatricals: From Menageries to Melodrama* (London, 2000).

Hunt, Lynn, *The New Cultural History* (London, 1989).

Hunt, Lynn, *Politics, Culture and Class in the French Revolution* (Cambridge, 1984).

Hunt, Tamara L., *Defining John Bull: Political Caricature and National Identity in Late Georgian England* (Aldershot, 2003).

Hutton, Ronald, *Shamans: Siberian Spirituality and the Western Imagination* (London, 2001).

Hutton, Ronald, *Stations of the Sun: A History of the Ritual yYear in Britain* (Oxford, 1996)

Hyland, Ann, *The Horse in the Ancient World* (Westport, Conn., 2003).

Ifan, Alun, *Twm Carnabwth* (Llandysul, 1984).

Innes, C. L., *A History of Black and Asian Writing in Britain, 1700–2000* (Cambridge, 2002).

Jasper, James M., *Protest: A Cultural Introduction to Social Movements* (Cambridge, 2014).

Jacob, Violet, *The Sheep-Stealers* (London, 1902).

Jenkins, Geraint H. (ed.), *Language and Community in the Nineteenth Century* (Cardiff, 1998).

Jenkins, Geraint H., and J. Beverly Smith (eds), *Politics and Society in Wales 1840–1922: Essays in Honour of Ieuan Gwynedd Jones* (Cardiff, 1988).

John, Angela V. (ed.), *Our Mothers' Land: Chapters in Welsh Women's History, 1830–1939* (Cardiff, 1991).

Johnson, Douglas (ed.), *French Society and the Revolution* (London, 1976).

Jones, Aled, *Press, Politics and Society: A History of Journalism in Wales* (Cardiff, 1993).

Jones, David J. V., *Before Rebecca: Popular Protests in Wales 1793–1835* (London, 1973).

Jones, David J. V., *Crime in Nineteenth-Century Wales* (Cardiff, 1992).

Jones, David J. V., *The Last Rising: The Newport Insurrection of 1839* (Oxford, 1985).

Jones, David J. V., *Rebecca's Children: A Study of Rural Society, Crime and Protest* (Oxford, 1989).

Jones, Emrys (ed.), *The Welsh in London 1500–2000* (Cardiff, 2001).

Jones, Gareth Elwyn, *Modern Wales: A Concise History* (Cambridge, 1984).

Jones, Gwyn, and Thomas Jones (trans.), *The Mabinogion* (London, 1949).

Jones, Ieuan Gwynedd, *Communities: Essays in the Social History of Victorian Wales* (Llandysul, 1987).

Jones, Ieuan Gwynedd, *Mid-Victorian Wales: The Observers and the Observed* (Cardiff, 1992).

Jones, T. Gwynn, *Welsh Folklore and Welsh Custom* (London, 1930).

Kaye, Harvey J. and Keith McClelland (eds), *E. P. Thompson: Critical Perspectives* (Oxford, 1990).

Knott, John, *Popular Opposition to the 1834 Poor Law* (London, c.1986).

Landes, Joan B., *Visualizing the Nation: Gender, Representation and Revolution in Eighteenth-Century France* (London, 2001).

Laqueur, Thomas, *Making Sex: Body and Gender from the Greeks to Freud* (London, 1990).

Leach, Robert, *Victorian Melodrama* (London, 1978).

Linton, W. J., *Memories* (London, 1895).

Lord, Peter, *Words with Pictures: Welsh Images and Images of Wales in the Popular Press, 1640–1860* (Aberystwyth, 1995).

Lubenow, William C., *The Politics of Government Growth: Early Victorian Attitudes Towards State Intervention, 1833–1848* (Newton Abbott, 1971).

MacAloon, John J., *Rite, Drama, Festival, Spectacle: Rehearsals Toward a Theory of Cultural Performance* (Philadelphia, 1984).

Macdonagh, Oliver, *Early Victorian Government 1830–1870* (London, 1977).

Maddox, W. C., *History of the Radnorshire Constabulary* (Llandrindod Wells, 1959).

Mason, Paul, *Why It's Kicking Off Everywhere: The New Global Revolutions* (London, 2012).

Mayer, David, *Harlequin in his Element; The English Pantomime, 1806–1836* (Cambridge, Mass., 1969).

Mingay, G. A. (ed.), *The Unquiet Countryside* (London, 1989).

Mitchell, Juliet, and Ann Oakley (eds), *The Rights and Wrongs of Women* (Harmondsworth, 1976).

Molloy, Pat, *And they Blessed Rebecca: An Account of the Welsh Tollgate Riots, 1839–1844* (Llandysul, 1983).

Myers, Norma, *Reconstructing the Black Past: Blacks in Britain 1780–1830* (London, 1996).

Navickas, Katrina, *Protest and the Politics of Space and Place, 1789–1848* (Manchester, forthcoming 2015).

Needham, Rodney (ed.), *Right and Left: Essays on Dual Symbolic Classification* (London, 1973).

O'Gorman, Frank, *Voters, Patrons and Parties: The Unreformed Electoral System of Hanoverian England* (Oxford, 1989).

O'Leary, Paul, *Claiming the Streets: Processions and Urban Culture in South Wales 1830–1880* (Cardiff, 2012).

Outhwaite, R. B., *Clandestine Marriage in England 1500–1850* (London, 1995).

Owen, D. Huw, *Settlement and Society in Wales* (Cardiff, 1989).

Owen, Trefor M., *Welsh Folk Customs* (Llandysul, 1987).

Palmer, Roy (ed.), *A Touch on the Times: Songs of Social Change* (Harmondsworth, 1974).

Peate, Iorwerth C., *Tradition and Folk Life: A Welsh View* (London, 1972).

Pointon, Marcia, *Hanging the Head* (London, 1993).

Porter, Roy, and Mikulas Teich (eds), *Romanticism in National Context* (Cambridge, 1988).

Price, F. S., *History of Llansawel, Carmarthenshire* (Swansea, 1898).

Propp, Vladimir, *Theory and History of Folklore* (Minneapolis, 1984).

Quaife, G. R., *Wanton Wenches and Wayward Wives: Peasants and Illicit Sex in Early Seventeenth Century England* (London, 1979).

Randall, A., and Andrew Charlesworth (eds), *Moral Economy and Popular Protest: Crowds, Conflict and Authority* (London, 2000).

Reay, Barry (ed.), *Popular Culture in Seventeenth Century England* (London, 1975).

Reay, Barry, *Popular Cultures in England 1550–1750* (London and New York, 1998).

Reed, Mick and Roger Wells (eds), *Class, Conflict and Protest in the English Countryside* (London, 1990).

Reiss, Matthias, *The Street as Stage: Protest Marches and Public Rallies since the Nineteenth Century* (Oxford, 2007).

Richards, Henry, *Letters and Essays on Wales* (London, 1866).

Roberts, Michael and Simone Clarke (eds), *Women and Gender in Early Modern Wales* (Cardiff, 2000).

Rogers, Helen, *Women and the People: Authority, Authorship and the Radical Tradition in Nineteenth-Century England* (Aldershot, 2000).

Rogers, Nicolas, *Crowds, Culture and Politics in Georgian Britain* (Oxford, 1998).

Rowell, George, *The Victorian theatre, 1792–1914: A Survey* (London, 1956).

Rudé, George, *The Crowd in History* (London, 1964).

Rudé, George, *Revolutionary Europe 1783–1815* (London, 1964).

Ruiz, Pollyanna, *Articulating Dissent: Protest and the Public Sphere* (London, 2014).

Samuel, Raphael and Paul Thompson, *The Myths We Live By* (London, 1990).

Scholz, Suzanne, *Body Narratives: Writing the Nation and Fashioning the Subject in Early Modern England* (London, 2000).

Scott, Joan W., *Gender and the Politics of History* (New York, 1988).

Shepherd, Alexandra, *Meanings of Manhood in Early Modern England* (Oxford, 2003).

Shoemaker, Robert, and Mary Vincent (eds), *Gender and History in Western Europe* (London, 1998).

Smith, David (ed.), *A People and a Proletariat: Essays in the History of Wales 1780–1980* (London, 1980).

Solnit, Rebecca, *Wanderlust: A History of Walking* (London, 2002).

Stedman-Jones, Gareth, *Languages of Class: Studies in English Working-Class History 1832–1982* (Cambridge, 1983).

Stevenson, John, *Popular Disturbances in England, 1700–1832* (London, 1992).

Storch, Robert (ed.), *Popular Culture and Custom in Nineteenth Century England* (London, 1982).

Thomas, J. E., *Social Disorder in Britain 1750–1850: The Power of the Gentry, Radicalism and Religion in Wales* (London, 2011).

Thomas, Keith, *Man and the Natural World* (Harmondsworth, 1994).

Thomas, Keith, *Religion and the Decline of Magic* (New York, 1971).

Thomas, Peter D. G., *Politics in Eighteenth-Century Wales* (Cardiff, 1998).

Thomis, Malcolm, and Jennifer Grimmett, *Women in Protest 1800–1850* (London, 1982).

Thompson, Dorothy, *The Chartists* (London, 1984).

Thompson, Dorothy, *Outsiders: Class, Gender and Nation* (London, 1993).

Thompson, E. P., *Customs in Common: Studies in Traditional Popular Culture* (New York, 1993).

Thompson, E. P., *The Making of the English Working Class* (Harmondsworth, 1968).

Tilly, Charles, *Popular Contention in Great Britain 1758–1834* (Cambridge, 1995).

Tilly, Charles, *The Rebellious Century 1830–1930* (London, 1975).

Tobit Evans, Henry, *Rebecca and her Daughters: Being a History of the Agrarian Disturbances in Wales Known as the 'Rebecca Riots'*, ed. G. T. Evans (Cardiff, 1910).

Tosh, John, *Historians on History* (London, 2000).

Tosh, John, *Manliness and Masculinities in Nineteenth-Century Britain* (Harlow, 2005).

Tosh, John, *The Pursuit of History* (London, 1984).

Tudor, Henry, *Political Myth* (London, 1972).

Turner, Victor, *The Forest of Symbols: Aspects of Ndembu Ritual* (Ithaca, 1967).

Turner, Victor, *The Ritual Process: Structure and Anti-Structure* (London, 1969).

Vernon, James, *Politics and the People: A Study in English Political Culture c.1815–1867* (Cambridge, 1993).

Vicinus, Martha (ed.), *Suffer and Be Still: Women in the Victorian Age* (London, 1980).

Wallace, Ryland, *Organise! Organise! Organise! A Study of Reform Agitations in Wales 1840–1886* (Cardiff, 1991).

Welsh, Frank, *The Four Nations: A History of the United Kingdom* (London, 2002).

Wilks, Ivor, *South Wales and the Rising of 1839: Class Struggle as Armed Struggle* (London, 1984).

Williams, David, *John Frost: A Study in Chartism* (Cardiff, 1939).

Williams, David, *The Rebecca Riots: A Study in Agrarian Discontent* (Cardiff, 1955).

Williams, Glanmor, *History in a Modern University* (Swansea, 1959).

Williams, Glyn (ed.), *Crisis of Economy and Ideology: Essays on Welsh Society, 1840–1980* (1983).

Williams, Gwyn A., *The Welsh in Their History* (London, 1982).

Williams, John, *A Digest of Welsh Historical Statistics* (Cardiff, 1985).

Wright, A. R., *British Calendar Customs* (3 vols, London, 1936–40).

Yeo, Eileen Janes (ed.), *Radical Femininity: Women's Self-Representation in the Public Sphere* (Manchester, 1998).

Unpublished Theses

Rhian E. Jones, 'An analysis of the significance of popular ritual, with special reference to the "Scotch Cattle" movement in early nineteenth-century Wales' (M.St. dissertation, Oxford University, 2005).

W. King, 'A statistical study of the rural population of Wales in the nineteenth and twentieth centuries' (Ph.D. thesis, University of Wales, 1929).

Martin Waterhouse, 'On the edge: peripheral communities and marginal anthropology' (Ph.D. thesis, University of Glamorgan, 2002).

Index